Brief Information on
Major Historic Sites under National Protection
in Henan Province

河南文化遗产

全国重点文物保护单位

河南省文物局　编

文物出版社

总体设计：宁成春
责任印制：王少华
责任编辑：李　莉　姚敏苏

图书在版编目（CIP）数据

河南文化遗产．全国重点文物保护单位／河南省文物局编．—北京：文物出版社，2007.11
ISBN 978-7-5010-2174-1
Ⅰ．河… Ⅱ．河… Ⅲ．①文化遗产—简介—河南省②文化遗址—名胜古迹—简介—河南省 Ⅳ．K928.706.1

中国版本图书馆 CIP 数据核字（2007）第 072185 号

河南文化遗产

——全国重点文物保护单位

河南省文物局 编

文物出版社出版发行
（北京市东直门内北小街2号楼 邮编：100007）
http://www.wenwu.com
E-mail:web@wenwu.com

制版　北京文博利奥印刷有限公司
印刷　文物出版社印刷厂
经销　新华书店
开本　889 × 1194毫米　1/16
印张　27.75
版次　2007年11月第1版
印次　2007年11月第1次印刷
书号　ISBN 978-7-5010-2174-1
定价　360.00元

《河南文化遗产——全国重点文物保护单位》顾问与编委会名单

河南省全国重点文物保护单位分布示意图

154. 三苏祠和墓

漯河市 155. 郝家台遗址

临颍 156－157
156. 小商桥
157. 受禅碑与受禅台

郾城 158－159
158. 许慎墓
159. 彼岸寺碑

舞阳 160. 贾湖遗址

南阳市 161－166
161. 张衡墓
162. 张仲景墓及祠
163. 南阳武侯祠
164. 南阳知府衙门
165. 瓦房庄冶铁遗址
166. 鄂城寺

社旗 167. 社旗山陕会馆

内乡 168. 内乡县衙

邓州 169－170
169. 八里岗遗址
170. 福胜寺塔

淅川 171－172
171. 荆紫关古建筑群
172. 仓房香严寺

唐河 173. 泗州寺塔

驻马店市 174. 杨台寺遗址

上蔡 175. 蔡国故城

西平 176－177
176. 酒店冶铁遗址
177. 宝严寺塔

遂平 178. 嵖岈山卫星人民公社旧址

确山 179. 中共中央中原局旧址

泌阳 180. 下河湾冶铁遗址

汝南 181. 悟颖塔

信阳市 182. 城阳城址

新县 183－184
183. 鄂豫皖革命根据地旧址
184. 中国工农红军第二十五军司令部旧址

光山 185. 邓颖超祖居

罗山 186. 红二十五军长征出发地

固始 187－188
187. 番国故城遗址
188. 陈元光祖祠

潢川 189. 黄国故城

注：繁塔、延庆观、辟雍碑、荥阳故城、神垕钧窑址、巩义窑址、韩王陵、上蔡楚国贵族墓地、长城9处全国重点文物保护单位为合并项目。

世界文化遗产——龙门石窟

世界文化遗产——殷墟

目　录

CONTENTS

石窟寺及石刻

古遗址

古墓葬

近现代重要史迹及代表性建筑

序

中华人民共和国国家文物局局长　单霁翔

河南地处中原，是中华民族文明的主要发源地，而且长期是我国政治、经济、文化的中心，有着悠久的历史和灿烂的文化。千百年来，先民们栉风沐雨、辛勤耕耘，在这块古老的土地上，创造了无数的辉煌，留下了许多珍贵的文化遗产。1961年、1982年、1988年、1996年、2001年和2006年，国务院相继公布了六批全国重点文物保护单位共2351处。其中河南省全国重点文物保护单位为189处198项，是全国重点文物保护单位最多的省份之一。

全国重点文物保护单位是从我国目前已发现的四十余万处不可移动文物中精选出来的，具有重要的历史、艺术和科学价值，包括了古遗址、古墓葬、古建筑、石窟寺及石刻、近现代重要史迹及代表性建筑。目前，全国重点文物保护单位基本上已由所在地省、市、自治区人民政府依照《中华人民共和国文物保护法》划定了必要的保护范围，做出了标志说明，建立了记录档案，设置了专门机构或专人负责管理。从整体上看，全国重点文物保护单位均得到了较好的保护。

全国重点文物保护单位在我国社会主义现代化建设中发挥着越来越大的作用。首先，我们每一个中国人都为中华民族拥有光辉灿烂的古代文明感到由衷的自豪，这对于增强整个民族的自信心和凝聚力，激发广大人民群众的爱国主义热情，具有重要的意义。其次，许多全国重点文物保护单位是爱国主义教育基地，生动、直观的文物已成为学校教育园地之外的第二课堂，使广大人民群众深受历史唯物主义和爱国主义教育。第三，随着近些年旅游业的发展，文物扮演着越来越重要的角色。相当一部分全国重点文物保护单位以其独特的魅力，吸引了大批国外客人来华参观，宣传了博大精深的中国传统文化，加深了世界人民对中国的了解，促进了中国人民与世界各国人民的友谊。

河南省是文物大省，全国重点文物保护单位数量多，价值高，反映了中华文明发展的轨迹，折射出中国历史发展的脉络，是5000年中华文明的缩影。在河南省各级党委、政府的重视和支持下，河南省的全国重点文物保护单位不仅得到了妥善保护，而且发挥着愈来愈大的作用。为了实现中共河南省委提出的文化大省向文化强省的跨越，河南省文物局编著了《河南文化遗产——全国重点文物保护单位》一书，书中以翔实的内容，简洁的文字，精美的图片，准确地提供了河南省189处全国重点文物保护单位的基本信息，图文并茂，雅俗共赏，并附有英文提要。我相信，这部书将受到广大专业人员和非专业人员欢迎、喜爱，也会为促进河南省文化遗产保护工作发挥重要的作用。

Foreword

Shan Jixiang

Lying on the Central Plains,Henan, a main cradle of Chinese civilization,has a long,splendid history as the political,economic and cultural center of the country. Generations of our ancestors lived and worked on this land through centuries, leaving behind an abundant cultural legacy. Six lists of total 235 sites and monuments for national-level protection were made public respectively in 1961, 1982, 1988, 1996, 2001 and 2006. Having boasted of 189 on the lists, Henan ranks first among all of China's provinces and autonomous regions.

Ever selected from among more than four hundred thousand immovable remains so far discovered in the country, the sites and monuments listed for national-level protection are of great historical, aesthetic and scientific values. They include ancient sites, tombs, grotto shrines and stone carvings as well as historical spots and representative buildings of modern periods. By now, local governments of different levels have precisely defined these sites and monuments in terms of circumference, having them indicated, documented, and managed by special institutions and staff, according to the Law of the People's Republic of China on Protection of Cultural Relics. Most of them are well preserved.

These survivals of the past have been playing an increasingly important role in the process of China's socialist modernization. Firstly, a wonderful past helps to bring all Chinese together by giving each one a pride in or love for China. Secondly, many of these sites and monuments have served as a base for education on patriotism and historical materialism, that is, another classroom with vivid, touchable teaching aids. Thirdly, they are attracting streams of international tourists and by doing so, publicized China's traditional culture, deepened other peoples' understanding of this people, and improved friendship between this part and the rest parts of the world. A province with the most and best national level protected sites, Henan can be read as an outlined history of Chinese civilization over 5000 years. With support from the provincial and local Party committees and governments, these sites and monuments have received good protection and moreover, exerted more and more influence. To move toward Henan government's strategic goal of a province even more powerful culturally, CPAM of Henan compiles this album under the title of Henan's Cultural Legacy: Sites and Monuments for National-level Protection, with succinct texts and exquisite pictures that provide basic information about each site or monument in a way both professional and general readers can enjoy.

序

中共河南省委常委　宣传部长
河　南　省　副　省　长　孔玉芳

河南位于黄河中下游，自古有中原之称，是我国古代文明的主要发祥地之一，我们的祖先很早就在这块土地上生息繁衍、辛勤劳作，以卓越的智慧创造了光辉灿烂的文化，留下了许多珍贵的文化遗产。

在河南省境内，从纵贯南北的旧石器时代遗存，到遍布各地的新石器时代聚落；从历朝历代的都邑遗址，到各个时期的墓葬；从美轮美奂的石刻艺术，到雕梁画栋的古代建筑……目前，全省已发现各类不可移动文物30000多处，全国重点文物保护单位189处，省级文物保护单位761处，市（县）级文物保护单位5000余处；全国八大古都中河南占有4座，国家历史文化名城8座，中国历史文化名镇（村）3座。这些蔚为壮观的历史文化遗产，是华夏民族优秀文化的物质载体，更是河南辉煌历史的实物见证。

文化遗产凝结历史，连接今天，传承未来。做好文化遗产保护工作意义深远，责任重大。河南省委、省政府对文化遗产保护工作高度重视，采取了一系列切实有效的措施，各地、各有关部门做了大量工作，文化遗产保护工作取得了明显成效：洛阳龙门石窟和安阳殷墟成功列入世界文化遗产名录，郑州嵩山古建筑群和新乡潞简王墓等项目顺利进入我国申报世界文化遗产预备名单，全国重点文物保护单位数量位居全国前列，文物抢救保护工程和文物安全工作得到进一步加强，文化遗产保护工作开始步入规范化和法制化轨道，大遗址保护展示工程全面启动，重大考古发现不断涌现，博物馆数量和陈列展览水平稳步提高，科学研究硕果累累，对外文物交流日趋频繁。所有这些不仅使珍贵的历史文化遗产得到有效保护，提升了河南文化的品位，也大大提高了河南的知名度和影响力。

源远流长、博大精深的文化遗产是我们建设先进文化、构建社会主义和谐社会的宝贵财富，保护好这些文化遗产，弘扬民族优秀文化，为改革开放和现代化建设提供强有力的思想保证、精神动力和智力支持，是历史赋予我们的神圣责任。我们要坚持“保护为主、抢救第一、合理利用、加强管理”的文物工作方针，妥善处理、有效保护和合理利用文化遗产的关系，以创新的精神做好文化遗产保护工作，使其能长久发挥社会效益，世代传承下去。为此，河南省文物局组织编写了《河南文化遗产——全国重点文物保护单位》一书，此书的发行对于推动河南文化遗产宣传、弘扬民族文化、促进对外文化交流等方面必将起到积极作用。希望河南省文物局以此为契机，不断推出更多高品位、高质量的文化精品，为建设文化强省做出新的更大的贡献！

Foreword

Kong Yufang

Lying at the lower reaches of the Yellow River, Henan, known as Central Plains since ancient times, is one of the cradles of Chinese civilization. Our ancestors, having populated the region since immemorial times, created a splendid culture and left abundant precious cultural heritages.

The province is rich in Paleolithic and Neolithic sites, the ruins of ancient capitals, ancient tombs, beautiful stone carvings and ancient architectures. It has more than 30,000 immovable cultural heritages, 189 major historic sites under national protection, 761 under provincial protection, and over 5,000 under municipal or county-level protection. It has four of the eight greatest ancient capitals in the country, eight national famous historical and cultural cities, and three national famous historical and cultural towns/villages. These are material carriers of the Chinese culture, attesting to the glorious history of Henan.

Cultural heritage serves to connect the past, the present and the future. Its protection is therefore a significant and demanding task. Attaching great importance to that, the Party Committee and government of Henan have taken practical and effective measures and local authorities have also made their efforts. Great progress has been made: Longmen Grottoes in Luoyang and Yin Ruins in Anyang were successfully inscribed into World Heritage List; the ancient architectural complex at Song Mountain in Zhengzhou and the tomb of Prince Lujian in Xinxiang have had access to the tentative list for inscribing world heritage; the province has more major historic sites under national protection than most of other provinces; the rescue, protection and security work for cultural relics have been strengthened; the protection of cultural heritage is being standardized and legalized; a project has been launched for the protection and demonstration of large sites; important archeological discoveries followed closely upon one another; there are more museums with better qualifications; research is fruitful; overseas exchanges on cultural relics are becoming more frequent. These not only contribute to the effective protection of culture in Henan, but also make the province better known and more influential in the world.

The cultural heritage is an asset for the building of 'advanced culture' and the'socialist harmonious society'. It is our historical responsibility to protect it, so that we may promote our culture and provide spiritual and intellectual support to the opening-up and modernization drive. We will adhere to the principle of 'protection oriented, rescue first, proper use and management', coordinate the relationship between effective protection and rational use, and be innovative in our work, so that our cultural heritage will endure and have a lasting influence on society. It is for this purpose that the Provincial Cultural Relics Administration compiled this book. We expect its release to be conducive to the publicity of our cultural heritage, the development of the national culture and the promotion of overseas cultural exchanges. We hope that the Administration will take this opportunity to issue more first-class cultural works in order to make greater contributions to a culturally powerful province and the rise of the Central Plains.

前　言

河南省文化厅厅长　郭俊民

我国上古时代分为九州,即冀、豫、雍、扬、兖、徐、梁、青、荆。位于中间的是豫州,与今河南省的位置、范围大致相当,因此河南省简称豫,又称中州。因河南大部分为广袤的平原,又称中原。在中华五千年的文明历史进程中,河南曾多次成为全国政治、经济和文化的中心。

正是中原积淀深厚的文化底蕴,博大精深的文明内涵,才为后人留下了丰富多彩的文化遗产,也为中原文化的解读做了最好的注脚。这些幸存至今的文化遗产,尤其是被国务院公布为全国重点文物保护单位的文化遗产,均记录了先民们的杰出智慧和伟大的创造精神,它们中既有被联合国教科文组织列入世界文化遗产名录的安阳殷墟和洛阳龙门石窟,还有以最早发现地命名的古文化遗址,如新郑裴李岗、渑池仰韶、偃师二里头、郑州二里岗等;既有声名远播的中岳汉三阙、汉魏洛阳故城、隋唐洛阳城,又有近年新发现的被称为"中国的庞贝"的内黄三杨庄汉代庭院及农田遗址;既有享誉世界的北宋东京城遗址,又有规模宏大的北宋皇陵;既有中国现存最早的十二面密檐式砖塔北魏嵩岳寺塔,又有元代天文学家郭守敬创建的里程碑建筑登封观星台等等。这些文化遗产就像镶嵌在中州大地上的一颗颗璀璨明珠,绽放着夺目的光彩。

为了弘扬民族优秀文化,实现河南由文化资源大省向文化强省的跨越,河南省文物管理局组织编写了这部《河南文化遗产——全国重点文物保护单位》。全书分古建筑、石窟寺及石刻、古遗址、古墓葬、近现代重要史迹及代表性建筑五个部分。每个部分均按国务院公布的第一批到第六批全国重点文物保护单位的顺序编写,对河南省189处198项全国重点文物保护单位的名称、时代、位置、概况、价值作了简明扼要的介绍和描述,言简意赅、图文并茂。书中所选400余幅照片,艺术地体现了全国重点文物保护单位绰约的风姿和旖丽的风光,给人以美的享受。每处国保单位还都附有英文提要,这不仅适于国人同时也便于国外读者了解河南的文物遗产,此种形式不失为一次有益的尝试。

文化遗产是一种重要的文化资源,对于社会主义物质文明、政治文明、精神文明建设,对于建设社会主义和谐社会,对于中华民族的伟大复兴,发挥着越来越重要的作用,也越来越引起全社会、全人类的重视和关注。本书将使我们在饱览河南国保单位的同时,进一步了解河南、认识河南、热爱河南,推动河南文物保护事业和文化事业的大发展大繁荣,创造无愧于先人的新业绩,创造河南更加美好的未来。

Preface

Guo Junmin

Head of Henan Provincial Cultural Department

China in ancient times was divided into nine zhous (prefectures), namely Yu, Ji, Yang, Yan, Xu, Liang, Qing and Jing. Yu was located in the middle of them, roughly coinciding with the current location and boundary of Henan Province. For this reason, Henan Province has been called Yu for short, or Zhongzhou (Central Prefecture). As Henan Province is mainly a vast expanse of flatland, it is also called Zhongyuan (Central Plains). In the 5000-year-long evolution of the Chinese civilization, Henan repeatedly became the national political, economic and cultural center. In all, over 200 emperors in over 20 dynasties established their capital in Henan or relocated it to Henan. This gave rise to the stories of usurping the throne or fighting for the throne in the Central Plains, and explained why heroes came to the Central Plains from all directions and why those in control of the Central Plains controlled the whole country. These old and meaningful stories and phrases all illustrated Henan's importance and glory in China's history.

These rich culture and extensive civilization have become colorful cultural heritages to later generations and provided best connotations of the Zhongyuan Culture. These surviving cultural heritages, especially those placed under national protection by the State Council, are all witnesses to the outstanding wisdom and great creativeness of our forefathers. They include both the Yin Ruins in Anyang and the Longmen Grottoes in Luoyang, which have been included by UNESCO into the World Heritage List, and also the ancient cultural sites named after the places where they were discovered, such as the Peili Hill in Xinzheng, the Yangshao Culture in Mianchi, the Erlitou in Yanshi, and the Erli Hill in Zhengzhou. They include both the well-known Three Han Que Gates at Mount Songshan, the ancient cities of the Han and Wei dynasties in Luoyang and the Luoyang City of the Sui and Tang dynasties, and also the ruins of courtyards and farm fields of the Han Dynasty at Sanyang Village in Neihuang, which was discovered in recent years and was cited as China's Pompeii. They include both the world-famous ruins of the east capital and the grand imperial tombs, all of the Northern Song Dynasty. They include both the Mount Songshan temple pagodas of the Northern Wei Dynasty, the oldest of their kind still existing in China, and also the Dengfeng Observatory, a milestone architecture built by astronomer Guo Shoujing of the Yuan Dynasty. All of them are glittering gems of the Central Plains. Guo Yu and Guo Xuan, who resided in the southern kapok province of Guangdong but repeatedly traveled to the Central Plains, once said,"Henan is a picture scroll of history, a picture scroll of religion, a picture scroll of art, a picture scroll of personages, and a picture scroll of folk customs. Don't say this land today is dull. Each inch of this land records the life of history."

In order to carry forward our fine culture and pursue a transition from being a major province with cultural resources to being a strong province in culture, the Henan Provincial Bureau of Cultural Relics Administration compiled a book, entitled the Henan's Cultural Heritages ®C Key Cultural Sites Placed under National Protection. The book comprises five parts: ancient architectures, grotto temples and stone carvings, ancient ruins, ancient tombs, and major contemporary and modern sites and representative architectures. Each part is arranged according to the sequence from the first to the sixth batch of cultural sites promulgated by the State Council. The book contains brief descriptions about the 198 nationally-protected cultural relics at 189 sites, including their names, eras, locations, general information and values. Concise descriptions are matched with fine pictures. The photos, numbering over 400, artistically mirror the elegance and scenery of these protected relics and give people an aesthetic enjoyment. Each cultural relic has a brief summary in English, making it easy for foreign readers to appreciate. This is no doubt a useful attempt.

Cultural heritage is an important cultural resource, which plays growingly important roles in building socialist material civilization, political civilization and spiritual civilization, in building a socialist harmonious society and in pursuing a great rejuvenation of the Chinese nation. Cultural heritage has also attracted growing attention and care from the general public and the whole world. This book will direct us to each of the key nationally-protected cultural sites in Henan and help us to understand and love Henan. Furthermore, it will help develop and flourish Henan's cause of protecting cultural heritage sites and promoting cultural undertakings, help create new achievements comparable with those of our forefathers, and help build a better future for our province.

概　述

河南省文物局局长　陈爱兰

黄河流域是中华民族的文化摇篮，河南则是摇篮里的一颗明珠，这里地处华夏腹地，自古因中天下而立，八方辐辏而史称中原。北依河北、山西，南靠湖北，东与山东、江苏、安徽为邻，西部与陕西接壤，辖辖南北，枢纽东西，地理位置十分重要。境内群山起伏，河流纵横，平原辽阔，深得天时地利之便。北、西、南三面由太行山、伏牛山、桐柏山和大别山环抱，东部为大平原。黄河自陕晋边境折向东流，横亘在河南北中部，在中条山和崤山之间穿过三门峡，向东流入华北平原。淮河发源于桐柏山，蜿蜒于豫南大地，流经皖苏而入海。这里气候温和，物产丰富，交通便利。我们的祖先很早就劳动、生息、繁衍在这方神奇的热土上。由于战争的频仍，王朝的兴衰，人民的迁徙，河南又成为各民族交融汇合的大熔炉。历史的长河奔腾呼啸而去，日月交替，沧桑更迭，物华天宝，人杰地灵，源流有宗，衍变有绪，孕育了中华民族光辉灿烂的古代文化。旧石器时代，南来北往，东播西传，都要经过中原沃野；新石器时代，这里更是华夏文明的源头；夏商周时期，河南已成为三代文明的核心；两汉魏晋，河南仍处于全国的中枢地位；直到北宋定都汴京，还展现了中原最后的辉煌。历史对河南如此厚爱，造就了数以千计彪炳古今的历史文化名人，留下了极为丰富的遗迹和遗物。新中国成立以来，国务院先后公布了六批全国重点文物保护单位共2351处，其中河南省有189处，另有合并项目9处，合计共为198项，位于全国前列。其中古遗址67处，古墓葬19处，古建筑79处，石窟寺及石刻19处，近现代重要史迹及代表性建筑14处，这些都是河南现存文物之精华，奠定了全国文物大省的历史地位。

河南古遗址中，有1处旧石器时代原始洞穴，即荥阳织机洞遗址，洞内有厚20多米的第四纪堆积物，上层为新石器时代堆积，中下层为旧石器时代晚期堆积，还有多处用火痕迹。这里展示了旧石器时代与新石器时代的过渡和交替，对追溯中原远古文化的渊源和研究中原古代环境风貌及其与人类的关系，具有重大学术价值。新石器时代遗址有24处，包括距今9000～7000年的新郑裴李岗遗址和著名的舞阳贾湖遗址。裴李岗遗址内涵丰富，是裴李岗文化的命名地。贾湖遗址则发现一批在龟甲、骨器和石器上的契刻符号；还出土有不少骨笛，经测定已具备七声音阶结构，至今仍可吹奏出优美的旋律；这里还发现有当时的人工栽培稻，显示了中原地区稻作的历史是多么久远。这些令人惊叹的考古发现，对中国古代文明起源产生了非常深远的影响。长葛石固和新郑唐户遗址，也有丰富的裴李岗文化遗存。距今7000～5000年的仰韶文化，是以1921年发掘渑池县仰韶村遗址而命名的，这里是近代考古学的发轫之地，其学术价值和历史影响绝对不可低估。郑州西山遗址是仰韶文化晚期的古城址，距今约5300年左右，在目前已发现的城址中，城址年代又提前了一千年。灵宝北阳平遗址面积约100万平方米，是由30多处遗址组成聚落群的中心聚落。其中的西坡遗址发现有多座面积达200～500平方米的大型单体房屋建筑基址，还发掘出数十座仰韶文化大中小型墓葬，墓内出土多件玉器，这在全国也是十分罕见的。三门峡庙底沟遗址中带有花卉图案的彩陶最为突出，成为仰韶文化庙底沟类型的标志，其影响可达陕晋豫三省甚至更远的地方。庙底沟二期文化印证了仰韶文化向龙山文化的过渡，二者一脉相承，具有重大的学术价值。洛阳王湾遗址有三层文化叠压，下层是仰韶文化，中层是仰韶文化向龙山文化过渡，上层为龙山文化，文化传承没有缺环。郑州八里岗遗址数十人甚至近百人葬于一穴，数十间房连结成长屋，显示出豫西南地区仰韶文化的地方特色。郑州大河村遗址文化层堆积厚达12.5米，在考古地层学和类型学上为中原地区仰韶文化树立了一个典型的分期标尺。其描绘日月星辰的彩陶图案，成为古代天文学研究不可替代的实物资料。驻马店杨台寺遗址是河南南部重要的仰韶文化遗存。距今5000～4000年的河南龙山文化，在中国古代文明起源与早期发展中占有重要地位。永城王油坊遗址代表了龙山文化的一个重要类型，也可能是先商文化的源头之一。柘城李庄遗址九牛大牢祭祀坑的发现，使这里的龙山文化与先商文化有了更紧密的联系。汤阴羑里城龙山文化遗址，文化层堆积很厚，更因其上有周文王被囚演周易的旧址而名满天下。淮阳平粮台遗址、登封王城岗遗址、辉县孟庄遗址、新密古城寨遗址及新砦遗址、漯河郝家台遗址和平顶山蒲城店遗址等，都是河南龙山文化晚期的古城址，距今约4000多年。登封王城岗遗址是禹都阳城所在，这里还发现了青铜容器残片和刻有“共”字的陶片。淮阳平粮台遗址则是传说中的太昊之墟，发现有城门两侧的门卫房、地下排水管道和铸铜的遗存。辉县孟庄遗址还发现了二里头文化和殷商文化的城墙。种种迹象表明，河南龙山文化已经迈入古代文明社会的门槛。而河南龙山文化晚期即公元前2070年前后，则是属于夏代早期，这是国家夏商周断代工程取得的重要成果之一。偃师二里头遗址发现有宫城和多座大型宫殿遗址，以及铸铜、烧陶、制骨等作坊遗址，出土了大批精美的青铜器、玉器等遗物，当为夏代中晚期的王都。近年发现的荥阳大师姑城址，则可能是夏代防御东方的重镇或当时的方国。1955年发现的郑州商城遗址和1983年发现的偃师尸乡沟商城遗址都有三重城垣，均为商代早期的都城遗址。郑州小双桥遗址是略晚于郑州商城的一处重要商代遗址。刚刚列入世界文化遗产名录的安阳殷墟则是闻名中外的商代后期都城，其范围约30平方公里。发现有大批宫殿建筑，铸铜、烧陶、制骨、制玉作坊，多座王陵大墓，出土有为数众多的青铜器、玉器、陶器、石器和极其重要的甲骨文。最近发现的洹北商城，应是盘庚最初迁殷之地。焦作府城商代遗址，可能是商前期雍国的都邑。新郑郑韩故城是郑国和韩国的都城，前后延续500余年之久。城垣、宫殿、作坊、大墓等历历在目。1923年出土的新郑彝器曾轰动国内外。近年发现大量郑国祭祀青铜礼器坑和乐器坑，出土青铜礼乐器348件，还发现有韩国兵器坑，出土各种铜兵器180多件，大多刻有铭文。上蔡蔡国故城和固始番国故城，分别是诸侯国的都邑。信阳城阳故城又称楚王城，楚国兵败东迁时作为临时都城。濮阳戚城则是春秋时期重要的诸侯会盟之地，均有很多考古发现。而商丘宋国故城，淇县卫国故城、潢川黄国故城、辉县共城、偃师滑国故城、叶县叶邑故城、济源轵国故城等，也都是周代的通都大邑，具有重大学术价值。在全国重点文物保护单位合并项目中的长城，在河南境内突出的是豫北的赵长城、中部的魏长城、豫南的楚长城等。东周时期前有春秋五霸，后有战国七雄，遍及华夏的同姓或异姓诸侯国，矛盾尖锐，战争迭起，兄弟阋墙，同室操戈，在中原尤为惨烈。这些长城遗址就成为这段历史重要的实物见证。洛阳汉魏故城、隋唐洛阳城、开封北宋东京城都是显赫一时的帝都，发现有城垣、城门、里坊、街道、宫殿、衙署、寺院、桥梁、古塔等遗存，在中国城市发展史上占有举足轻重的地位，对周边国家的城市布局也产生很大影响。焦作山阳故城、内黄三杨庄遗址，则是汉代城市和农村的典型代表。此外，西平酒店乡和泌阳下河湾战国及汉代冶铁遗址、郑州古荥镇和南阳瓦房庄及鲁山望城岗汉代冶铁遗址、巩义黄冶唐三彩窑址、宝丰清凉寺汝官窑址、修武当阳峪窑址、汝州张公巷窑址、禹州宋代钧台钧窑址和扒村窑址等，都代表了当时世界冶铁生产和烧造瓷器工艺的最高水平。

古代墓葬是反映历代文化面貌的重要载体。三门峡虢国墓地是周代北虢的遗存，北虢在公元前655年为晋所灭，著名的“假虞灭虢”的故事就发生在这里，并给后人留下了“辅车相依，唇亡齿寒”的千古遗训。虢国墓地发掘出国君、国君夫人、太子、大夫、士及庶民的大批墓葬，出土数以万计的珍贵文物，尤以玉器、青铜器和铜芯玉柄铁剑为最，后者把我国铸铁出现的时间提早到西周晚期。平顶山应国墓地，则向世人展示了一个记载不详的西周小国的编年史。永城汉梁王墓群包括14座西汉梁国诸侯王和王后大墓，均为斩山为廓，穿石为藏，开凿在山体内。结构复杂、气势恢宏。数千块上吨重并有刻字的墓道塞石，大幅龙、虎、朱雀、云气的彩色壁画，金缕玉衣和陶俑，多达5吨的青铜钱币窖藏，大型寝园建筑遗址，都在西汉考古中占有一席之地。南阳石桥张衡墓和南阳东关张仲景墓是两位杰出的汉代科学家和医学大师的长眠之地。新密打虎亭汉墓，是汉代画像石墓和壁画墓的又一重大发现。洛阳和孟津的邙山陵墓群，则是东汉、曹魏、西晋及北魏诸多帝王的陵墓，有着重大的历史价值。偃师唐恭陵是武则天长子李弘的陵墓，也是陕西唐陵之外现存最大的一座唐陵。陵台和神道石刻保存完好，其旁哀皇后陵近年抢救性发掘出一批前所未见的精美釉陶。新郑后周皇陵包括太祖郭威的嵩陵、世宗柴荣的庆陵、恭帝柴宗训的顺陵、世宗符皇后的懿陵。薄葬且形制较小、不立石像是后周皇陵的一大特色，陵前只有历代的祭碑。这是中国封建王朝陵寝制度研究不可或缺的实物例证。巩义北宋皇陵是全国著名陵区之一，保存有北宋王朝大部分皇帝、皇后、皇室宗亲贵族和大臣的墓葬。每座帝陵都坐北朝南，由南向北依次为鹊台、乳台、神道石刻、陵园、陵台、下宫等。神道石刻保存较为完整，是一批无与伦比的艺术瑰宝。新乡潞简王墓及王妃墓，是北京十三陵和南京明孝陵之外最为重要的明代王陵之一，规模宏大，神道石刻、陵园建筑、墓碑及五供、地宫等保存完好。明朱元璋九世孙朱载堉，是一位杰出的科学家、数学家、音乐理论家，对世界科学发展做出了伟大的贡献，其墓地位于沁阳丸峰山下，保存完好。

河南省全国重点文物保护单位的古建筑中，阙和塔是具有地方特色和高超历史价值和艺术价值的两大类。著名的登封汉三阙——太室阙、少室阙、启母阙是汉代的庙阙，阙身四周浮雕有人物、历史故事、车马出行、马戏、各种动物等画像，并刻有铭记，是难得的汉代建筑实例。登封嵩岳寺塔，是我国现存最早的砖塔，建于北魏正光年间，已历经近1500个寒暑春秋，登封净藏禅师塔是少见的唐代单层八角形亭阁式仿木结构砖塔；登封永泰寺塔和法王寺塔都是唐代叠涩密檐式砖塔；安阳修定寺唐塔，四壁砌有各种浮雕砖5000多块，内容为仙人、武士、侍女、飞天、伎乐童子、力士、龙、虎、狮、象、花卉等72种图案，有极高的艺术价值。登封少林寺塔林，现存唐、宋、金、元、明、清各代和尚塔243座，可以说是内容丰富的古塔博物馆。汝州法行寺唐塔别具一格。武陟妙乐寺塔是国内少见的五代大型砖塔，为唐塔向宋塔嬗变的一个特例。安阳五代天宁寺塔，介于单层多檐与多层塔之间，上大下小，十分罕见。开封开宝寺塔是典型的宋塔，其外壁用褐黑色琉璃雕砖砌筑，俗称为铁塔，为古都开封一大标志。滑县明福寺宋塔、开封宋代繁塔（天清寺塔）、睢县圣寿寺宋塔、鄢陵乾明寺宋塔、唐河泗洲寺宋塔、尉氏兴国寺宋塔、济源延庆寺宋塔，修武胜果寺宋塔、西平宝严寺宋塔、永城崇法寺宋塔、汝南宋悟颖塔、商水寿圣寺宋塔、邓州福胜寺宋塔、修武百家岩寺金塔、沁阳金代天宁寺三圣塔、三门峡宝轮寺金塔、许昌明代文峰塔等各有千秋。佛教传入中原以来，在河南留下了大量建筑遗存。洛阳白马寺、汝州风穴寺、登封初祖庵及会善寺、济源大明寺、温县慈胜寺、南阳鄂城寺、辉县白云寺、淅川香严寺等，都是历史悠久，内涵丰富的佛教建筑群。沁阳北大寺、朱仙镇清真寺、开封东大寺则为伊斯兰教的建筑精华，说明了历史上文化交流与交融的活跃。济源济渎庙和奉仙观及阳台宫、嵩县两程故里、南阳武侯祠、淮阳太昊陵庙、周口关帝庙、开封延庆观和山陕甘会馆、社旗山陕会馆、洛阳潞泽会馆和关林、卫辉比干庙及望京楼、登封中岳庙、武陟嘉应观、汤阴岳飞庙等都是有名的庙祠馆观建筑。南阳府衙和内乡县衙及叶县县衙是全国保存完好相当少见的古代府县衙门。商丘明归德府城墙、开封清代城墙、鹿邑太清宫唐宋建筑基址、辉县百泉明清园林、淅川荆紫关镇古建筑群、巩义清代康百万庄园等，都是各具特色的古代建筑。临颍宋代小商桥是河南现存的唯一一座早期敞肩圆弧石拱桥，屹立在颍水之上已达千年之久。而登封告成元代观星台的历史、科学价值更是蜚声中外。固始陈元光祖祠，为唐代大将、首任漳州刺史陈元光的祠堂，至今在闽南、台湾、海外侨胞中影响很大。

佛教石窟是河南又一项辉煌的文化遗产。洛阳龙门石窟，开凿于北魏至唐代，是我国三大石窟艺术宝库之一。其丰富的石窟造像，尤其是奉先寺卢舍那大佛，千百年来为世人所倾倒；龙门二十品北魏石刻题记，是古代书法艺术的珍品。龙门石窟已被列入世界文化遗产名录。北魏至宋代开凿的巩义石窟寺，保存有完整的“帝后礼佛图”，场面宏伟壮观、人物刻画细腻传神，为国内现存同类石刻中最精美者。安阳东魏至宋代的灵泉寺石窟，有着全国数量最多的浮雕塔林。义马北魏鸿庆寺石窟、安阳北齐小南海石窟和浚县大丕山摩崖大佛，都是佛教艺术的明珠。临颍三国时期受禅碑(包括“公卿将军上尊号奏”碑和“受禅表”)记述了汉献帝让位及曹丕受禅登基的史实，传为王朗撰文，梁鹄书丹，钟繇镌刻，世称三绝，为书法之经典。偃师西晋辟雍碑，记述晋武帝司马炎及太子司马衷数次视察辟雍，颂扬其敦礼明化、崇尚儒学之圣德。登封大唐嵩阳观纪圣德感应之颂碑，通高9米，造型复杂，气势磅礴，为浑然一体的石质建筑，为国内罕见的巨碑。此外，最新公布的博爱青天河南北朝至唐摩崖石刻，新乡南北朝西明寺造像碑、偃师唐升仙太子碑、登封唐崇唐观造像，鲁山颜真卿撰书的唐代元次山碑，淇县宋至民国的云梦山摩崖石刻，漯河宋彼岸寺碑，登封北齐刘碑寺碑，濮阳元代唐兀公碑等，均有重要的历史和艺术价值。新安千唐志斋石刻，为张钫先生所建15孔砖券窑洞所收藏。包括唐代墓志1185件，其他时期石刻228件，是一座巨大的历史和艺术价值很高的石刻博物馆。

近现代重要史迹及代表性建筑中，新县鄂豫皖革命根据地旧址，地处大别山，主要集中在新县县城，包括中共中央鄂豫皖分局、革命军事委员会、省委、省苏维埃政府、军委航空局等处。中共中央鄂豫皖分局旧址在县城中原路62号，为一座包括五进、七栋旧式楼房大宅院。新县中国工农红军第二十五军司令部旧址，罗山铁铺乡何家冲红军二十五军长征出发地，包括军部旧址、红军医院旧址和集合出发地的大银杏树。这些都反映了土地革命时期共产党人艰苦卓绝的斗争。确山竹沟是中共中央中原局旧址，是刘少奇、彭雪枫、李先念领导中原地区人民进行抗日战争的中心地区，为革命培养了大批干部。八路军洛阳办事处旧址，冀鲁豫边区革命根据地旧址，为抗日战争和中国革命做出了巨大的贡献。光山邓颖超祖居，开封和尉氏刘青霞故居，扶沟吉鸿昌吕潭学校旧址，均为近代史中的一个个亮点。河南留学欧美预备学校旧址，也就是河南大学近现代建筑群，保存完好，记录了近代中国打开国门引进西方文化的史实。郑州二七纪念塔和纪念堂，铭刻了二七大罢工先烈的足迹。嵖岈山卫星人民公社旧址，则反映了一段特殊历史的幻灭，给人以警示。林州红旗渠，展示了中国人民战天斗地大无畏的革命精神。兰考焦裕禄烈士墓，树立了共产党人为人民服务的公仆典范。这些近现代革命斗争的丰碑，如日月经天，江河行地，永垂不朽。

探索遥远的古代文明，是人类一个永恒的主题，走进新世纪的中国人，对回溯过去、建设现在和展望未来有着不可遏制的激情，只有把过去、现在和未来紧密联系在一起，才能够实现“传承文明，开拓创新”。我们要把祖先留下的文化遗产，特别是这一大批全国重点文物保护单位保护好，利用好，使其充分展示我们的民族智慧、民族创造、民族精神和民族文化。

最后我要说明一点，《河南文化遗产——全国重点文物保护单位》，是河南省文物局推出的河南文化遗产系列丛书的第一部，以后其他卷将陆续出版。

Summary

Chen Ailan

The Yellow River Basin is the cradle of the Chinese civilization, and Henan a pearl in that cradle. Situated in the heart of China, it is called in history 'Central Plains'. It borders Hebei and Shanxi in the north, Hubei in the south, Shandong, Jiangsu and Anhui in the east, and Shaanxi in the west, enjoying great geographical importance as a pivot of communications. It has a diversified landscape, with four mountains-Taihang, Funiu, Tongbai and Dabie-in the north, west and south, and vast plains in the east. The Yellow River, turning east at the border between Shaanxi and Shanxi, crosses northern central Henan, running east into North China Plain through Sanmenxia Valley between Zhongtian Mountain and Xiao Mountain. The Huai River, with its source in Tongbai Mountain, meanders across southern Henan, rushing into the ocean through Anhui and Jiangsu. Gentle in climate, rich in resources and convenient in transportation, Henan has been populated since time immemorial.

Henan was made a melting pot of ethnic groups by recurrent wars, the rise and fall of dynasties and the migration of populations. During the process it fostered a brilliant ancient culture. In the Paleolithic Age it was a center to conduct exchanges all over the country; in the Neolithic Age, it was the source of Chinese civilization; in the Xia, Shang and Zhou dynasties, it became the very core of that civilization; in the Han, Wei and Jin dynasties it remained the nucleus of the country; its glory continued till the Northern Song Dynasty, whose capital was in Bianjing (present-day Kaifeng). History's partiality to Henan left it with numerous historical famous persons, sites and heritages.

Since the founding of the People's Republic of China in 1949, the State Council has announced six groups of major historic sites under national protection successively, totaling 2,351. Of them, 198 (including 9 merged sites) are located in Henan, which surpasses any other provinces. They include 67 ancient sites, 19 ancient tombs, 79 ancient architectures, 19 sites of grottoes and stone engraving, and 14 modern sites and symbolic structures. These are the cream of all the cultural heritages in Henan, qualifying the province as a national treasure house of cultural heritage.

One of the sites, Zhiji Cave in Yingyang, dates back to the Paleolithic Age. It contains a 20-meter-thick deposit of Quaternary remains, whose upper layer dates from the Neolithic Age, and middle and bottom layers from the late Paleolithic Age. There are also many traces of the use of fire. These, which reflect the transition from the Paleolithic Age to the Neolithic Age, are important for research into the origin of ancient culture and the relationship between ancient environment and mankind in the Central Plains.

There are another 24 Neolithic sites, including Peiligang Site in Xinzheng, which dates back to 7, 000 to 9,000 years ago, and the well-known Jiahu Site in Wuyang. The former, after which Peiligang Culture was named, is rich in heritages. In Jiahu symbols engraved on tortoise shells, bone wares and stone wares were found, and a number of bone flutes were excavated, which are still capable of the heptatonic scale. Also found were planted rice, which indicate the long history of the growing of rice in the Central Plains. Shigu Site in Changge and Tanghu Site in Xinzheng are also rich in heritages of Peiligang Culture. Archeological discoveries like these have had far-reaching impact on the study of the origin of Chinese civilization.

In 1921 the site of Yangshao Village in Mianchi, dating from 5,000 to 7,000 years ago, was excavated, after which was named Yangshao Culture. As the origin of modern archeology, it is of tremendous academic value and historical importance.

Xishan Site in Zhengzhou, the site of an ancient city dating from the late Yangshao Culture period about 5,300 years ago, is 1,000 years older than the oldest city previously discovered.

Beiyangping Site which covers an area of about 1 million square meters in Lingbao lies at the center of the cluster consisting of more than 30 sites. Among them, foundations of several large single-room houses covering 200 to 500 square meters each were found in Xipo Site. In addition, dozens of Yangshao-culture tombs of various sizes have been discovered, containing many jade wares, a rare finding in the country.

Miaodigou Site at Sanmenxia distinguishes itself by colored pottery with flower designs, which is considered symbolic of the Miaodigou Type of Yangshao Culture, with its influence having covered at least three provinces-Shaanxi, Shanxi, and Henan. Stage-II Miaodigou Culture is of great academic value in that it attests to the transition from Yangshao Culture to Longshan Culture.

Wangwan Site in Luoyang consists of three cultural layers. The bottom layer represents Yangshao Culture, the upper layer Longshan Culture, and the middle layer the transition between the two.

Baligang Site in Dengzhou, where there are tombs that contain dozens or even hundreds of bodies each, and long houses consisting of dozens of rooms, reflect local characteristics of Yangshao Culture in the southwest of Henan.

Dahecun Site in Zhengzhou has a culture deposit as thick as 12.50 meters, setting a stratigraphic and typological standard for the time division of Central-plains Yangshao Culture. Designs on pottery that depict heavenly bodies are irreplaceable material for research into ancient astronomy.

Yangtaisi Site in Zhumadian is an important site of Yangshao Culture in the south of Henan.

Longshan Culture, which came into being in Henan 4,000 to 5,000 years ago, played an important role in the origin and early development of ancient Chinese civilization. Wangyoufang Site in Yongcheng represents an important type of Longshan culture, which might also be one of the origins of pre-Shang culture. The discovery of the pit used for making nine-ox sacrifices at Lizhuang Site in Zhecheng established closer link between Longshan Culture and the pre-Shang culture. The Longshan-Culture site at Youli, Tangyin has a thick cultural deposit, and is well-known for King Wen of Zhou used to be imprisoned there. Sites of late Longshan Culture in Henan include Pingliangtai Site at Huaiyang, Wangchenggang Site at Dengfeng, Mengzhuang Site at Hui County, ancient city site and Xinzhai Site at Xinmi, Haojiatai Site at Luohe and Puchengdian Site at Pingdingshan; they date from about 4,000 years ago.

Wangchenggang Site at Dengfeng was the location of Yudu Yangcheng, where fragments of bronze vessels and porcelain pieces inscribed with characters were discovered.

Pingliangtai Site in Huaiyang is the grave of the legendary figure Tai Hao. Remains of guards' rooms on both sides of the city gate, underground sewage pipelines and cast copper were discovered.

At Mengzhuang Site in Hui County city walls dating from the periods of Erlitou Culture and Yin-Shang Culture were discovered.

A multitude of signs indicate that Longshan Culture had entered into the ancient civilized society. The late Longshan culture, dated back to around 2070 BC, was in the early Xia Dynasty. That discovery was one of the results of the National Project on the chronology of Xia, Shang and Zhou.

Erlitou Site in Yanshi, where remains of palace compounds, several large palaces, and workshops for making bronze, pottery and bone wares, as well as exquisite bronze wares and jade wares were discovered, has been judged to be the national capital in the middle and late Xia Dynasty. The site of Dashigu site, Yingyang discovered a few years ago might be an eastern fort or a fangguo ('local state') in that dynasty.

Two sites of Shang cities, discovered respectively in Zhengzhou in 1955 and in Shixianggou, Yanshi in 1983, both of which have three circles of walls, were both capitals in the early Shang Dynasty. Xiaoshuangqiao Site in Zhengzhou is an important Shang-dynasty site with a history a bit shorter than the Shang city in Zhengzhou. Yin Ruins in Anyang, which has just been inscribed into World Heritage List, was a capital in the late Shang Dynasty. Within the 30 square kilometers that it covers were discovered the remains of palace architectures, workshops for making bronze, pottery, bone wares and jade wares, large tombs of princes; a large number of wares made of bronze, jade, pottery and stone, and oracle bones were unearthed. The recently discovered Shang city in Huanbei has been judged to be the first settlement of Pangeng in Yin. The Shang site in Fucheng, Jiaozuo might be the capital of the Yong State in the pre-Shang period.

The City of Zheng and Han in Xinzheng, which was the capital of the states of Zheng and Han for more than 500 years, retains sites of city walls, palace, workshops and large tombs. In 1923, sacrificial vessels unearthed in Xinzheng astonished the world. Recent years saw the discovery of many Zheng-state pits containing 348 bronze vessels and musical instruments used for offering sacrifices, and the unearthing of 180 bronze weapons of various kinds, most of which bear inscriptions, from Han-state pits. The Cai City in Shangcai and the Fan City in Gushi were capitals of feudal states. The Chengyang City in Xinyang, also named Capital of Chu, served as the temporary capital of Chu when the state moved east as the result of a military defeat. The Qi City in Puyang, an important site for the forging of alliance between feudal states in the Spring and Autumn Period, yielded rich archeological discoveries. Major cities in the Zhou Dynasty including the former city of Song in Shangqiu, city of Wei in Qi County, city of Huang in Huangchuan, city of Gong in Hui County, city of Hua in Yanshi, city of Yeyi in Ye County, and city of Zhi in Jiyuan, are of great academic value.

The merged sites among major historical sites under national protection include ancient Great Walls. In Henan there are the Zhao-section Great Wall in the north, Wei-section Great Wall in the central area, and Chu-section Great Wall in the south. They attest to the frequency, scale and intensity of wars between feudal states in the Eastern Zhou Dynasty.

Luoyang was the capital in the Han, Wei, Sui and Tang dynasties, and Kaifeng was the capital in the Northern Song Dynasty. They played an important role in the development history of Chinese cities, and had great influence on the layout of cities in neighboring countries. Historical remains include city walls, city gates, blocks, streets, palaces, government offices, temples, bridges and towers.

The City of Shanyang in Jiaozuo and Sanyangzhuang Site in Neihuang are respectively typical of urban and rural areas in the Han Dynasty.

The following sites reflect the highest achievement in iron smelting and porcelain making in the world in their respective periods: Jiudian site in Xiping and Xiahewan site in Miyang for iron smelting dating from the Warring States Period and the Han Dynasty, Guyingzhen site in Zhengzhou, Wafangzhuang site in Nanyang and Wangchenggang site in Lushan for iron smelting in the Han Dynasty, Huangye kiln of Tang tri-colored glazed pottery in Gongyi, the government-run Ru Kiln in Baofeng, Dangyangyu kiln in Xiuwu, Zhanggongxiang kiln in Ruzhou, Jun kiln in Yuzhou and the Ba Village kiln.

Ancient tombs are important reflections of ancient culture. The cemetery of Guo at Sanmenxia contains relics of Beiguo, a Zhou-dynasty state which was annexed by Jin in 655 BC was the origin of two Chinese idioms. In the cemetery tombs of the king and his consort, the crown prince, ministers, officials and common people were discovered; thousands of relics were unearthed, the most of which are jade wares, bronze wares, and swords with jade handles. The swords made of bronze inside and iron outside place the time of the invention of iron casting at the late Western Zhou Dynasty, earlier than the previously assumed period.

The cemetery of Ying in Pingdingshan reflects the chronicle of a small Western-Zhou state of which there is no detailed records. The cemetery of Prince Liang in Yongcheng contains 14 large tombs of feudal princes and their consorts in the state of Liang in the Western Han Dynasty. Cut between mountain rocks, they are complicated in structure and awe-inspiring. Relics discovered, such as thousands of inscribed stones filling tomb passages, each weighing about a ton, large colored murals featuring dragons, tigers, rosefinches and clouds, jade clothes sewn with gold threads, pottery figurines, bronze coins that weigh five tons, and large funereal structures, are among the most important of archeological finds dating from the Western Han Dynasty.

In Nanyang there is the tomb of Zhang Heng, a Han-dynasty scientist, and the tomb of Zhang Zhongjing, a Han-dynasty physician.

The tomb at Dahuting, Xinmi is another important discovery of the Han sculptured stone tomb and mural tomb.

In Mang Mountain at Mengjin County in Luoyang, there are mausoleums of emperors of the Eastern Han Dynasty, the Wei Dynasty (founded by Cao Pi), the Western Jin Dynasty and the Northern Wei Dynasty.

Gong Mausoleum in Yanshi is the tomb of Li Hong, the first son of Wu Zetian. It is the largest of all Tang mausoleums outside Shaanxi. The tomb mound and stone carvings along the tomb passage remain integral. The mausoleum of Empress Ai nearby, which was broken into by grave robbers a few years ago, has yielded beautiful glazed pottery, the likes of which had never been seen.

In Xinzheng there are imperial mausoleums of the Later Zhou Dynasty, including Song Mausoleum of Guo Wei, the founder of the dynasty, Qing Mausoleum of Chai Rong (Shizong), Shun Mausoleum of Chai Zongxun (Gongdi) and Yi Mausoleum of Chai Rong's consort Fu. They are characterized by the lack of luxury, modest size, and the absence of stone statues, with nothing but sacrificial steles in front of the tombs. They are indispensable for the study of mausoleums in ancient feudal China.

As one of the most famous cemeteries in the country, the Northern Song Imperial Cemetery in Gongyi contains tombs of the majority of the emperors, empresses, members of the imperial clan, and ministers of the dynasty. Each imperial mausoleum, facing south, consists of the following (from south to north): Que platform, Ru platform, stone carvings along tomb passage, graveyard, tomb mound and 'lower palace'. The well preserved stone carvings are of great artistic value.

The tomb of Prince Lujian and that of his wife in Xinxiang are among the most important tombs of Ming princes, apart from Ming tombs in Beijing and Ming Xiaoling in Nanjing. Both are large, and contain well preserved stone carvings along tomb passages, structures, the gravestones, the five stone sacrificial vessels, and coffin chambers.

At foot of Wanfeng Mountain in Qinyang is the well-preserved tomb of Zhu Zaiyu, ninth-generation grandson of Zhu Yuanzhang (the founder of the Ming Dynasty), a world-class scientist, mathematician and musical theorist.

The following are ancient structures under national protection.

In Dengfeng there are three que (stone towers erected in front of temples)-Taishi Que, Shaoshi Que and Qimu Que, all dating from the Han Dynasty. As rare Han architectural relics, they have pictures carved in relief that feature human figures, historical stories, horse-pulled carriages, circus performances and animals, accompanied by inscriptions.

Also in Dengfeng are four pagodas: 1) the pagoda of Songyue Temple. Built in the reign of Zhengguang in the Northern Wei Dynasty nearly 1,500 years ago, this is the oldest brick pagoda that remains. 2) Jingzang Chanshi Pagoda, a single-story octagonal brick pagoda simulating the wooden-structured pavilion; built in the Tang Dynasty, it is of a type that was rare at that time; 3) the pagoda of Yongtai Temple; 4) the pagoda of Fawang Temple. The last two, built in the Tang Dynasty, are brick towers with dense eaves.

In Anyang is the Tang pagoda of Xiuding Temple, with more than 5,000 engraved bricks featuring 72 patterns in relief, including immortals, warriors, maids, flying Apsaras, boys dancing or playing music, guardians, dragons, tigers, lions, elephants and flowers.

The 'pagoda forest' of Shaoling Temple in Dengfeng, containing 243 Buddhist monk pagodas dating from six dynasties from Tang to Qing, is nothing short of a museum of ancient pagodas.

In Ruzhou there is a specially designed Tang pagoda. In Wuzhi there is the pagoda of Miaole Temple, a large brick pagoda dating from the Five Dynasties, and a special case in the transition from the Tang pagoda to the Song pagoda. The pagoda of Tianning Temple in Anyang, also built in the Five Dynasties, has the exceptional shape of a reversed taper. The pagoda of Kaibao Temple in Kaifang is a typical Song pagoda, with brownish black glazed tiles on the outside. Popularly known as the Iron Pagoda, it is a symbol of Kaifeng as an ancient capital. Other valuable pagodas are: the pagoda of Mingfu Temple in Hua County, the pagoda of Tianqing Temple in Kaifeng, the pagoda of Shengshou Temple in Sui County, the Pagoda of Qianming Temple in Yanling, the pagoda of Sizhou Temple in Tanghe, the pagoda of Xingguo Temple in Weishi, the pagoda of Yanqing Temple in Jiyuan, the pagoda of Shengguo Temple in Xiuwu, the pagoda of Baoyan Temple in Xiping, the pagoda of Chongfa Temple in Yongcheng, Wuying Pagoda in Ru'nan, the pagoda of Shousheng Temple in Shangshui, the pagoda of Fusheng Temple in Dengzhou (all the above were built in the Song Dynasty), Golden Pagoda of Baijiayan Temple in Xiuwu,

Jin-dynasty Sansheng Pagoda of Tianning Temple in Qinyang, Golden Pagoda of Baolun Temple in Sanmenxia, and Ming-dynasty Wenfeng Pagoda in Xuchang.

Baima Temple in Luoyang, Fengxue Temple in Ruzhou, Chuzu Temple and Huishan Temple in Dengfeng, Daming Temple in Jiyuan, Cisheng Temple in Wen County, Echeng Temple in Nanyang, Baiyun Temple in Hui County, and Xiangyan Temple in Xichuan are Buddhist architectural complexes with long history and rich cultural relics. Beida Mosque in Qinyang, Qingzhen Mosque in Zhuxian and Dongda Mosque in Kaifeng are the best of Islamic architecture.

Famous shrines, (Taoist) temples and guild halls are: Jidu Temple, Fengxian Taoist Temple and Yangtai Palace in Jiyuan, former residences of Cheng Yi and Cheng Hao in Song County, Wuhou Shrine in Nanyang, the mausoleum and temple of Taihao in Huaiyang, Guandi Shrine in Zhoukou, Yanqing Taoist Temple and Shanxi-Shaanxi-Gansu Guild Hall in Kaifeng, Shanxi-Shaanxi Guild Hall in Sheqi, Luze Guild Hall and Guanyu Cemetery in Luoyang, Bigan Shrine and Wangjing Tower in Weihui, Zhongyue Temple in Dengfeng, Jiaying Taoist Temple in Wuzhi, and Yuefei Shrine in Tangyin. The government offices in Nanyang, Neixiang and Ye County are among the several well preserved ancient government offices in the country.

The Ming city walls in Shangqiu, the Qing city walls in Kaifeng, the foundations of Tang and Song structures in Taiqing Palace in Luyi, the Ming and Qing gardens at Baiquan in Hui County, the ancient architectural complex at Jingziguan Town in Xichuan, and Kangbaiwan Manor dating from the Qing Dynasty in Gongyi are ancient structures of distinct characteristics.

Xiaoshang Bridge in Linying, built over the Ying River in the Song Dynasty a thousand years ago, is the only early stone arch bridge (with small arches above the main arch) that remains in Henan. The observatory in Gaocheng, Dengfeng, built in the Yuan Dynasty, is well known at home and abroad for its history and scientific value. The ancestral temple of Cheng Yuanguang (a Tang general, the first governor of Zhangzhou) in Gushi is still influential among people from Taiwan or the south of Fujian and overseas Chinese.

The following are grottoes and stone carvings.

Longmen Grottoes in Luoyang is one of the three 'artistic treasure houses' in China, known for its abundance of Buddhist statues, particularly the statue of Buddha Losana at Fengxian Temple. The twenty inscriptions engraved on stones dating from the Northern Wei Dynasty mark the summit of ancient calligraphy. The grottoes have been inscribed in the World Heritage List.

The cave temple at Gongyi, built from the Northern Wei Dynasty until the Song Dynasty, keeps a complete stone engraving depicting the emperor and empress worshipping Buddha. Magnificent, elaborate and vivid, it is the most beautiful of its kind in China. The grottoes of Lingquan Temple in Anyang, which date from the Eastern Wei Dynasty to the Song Dynasty, have the largest number of pagodas decorated with relief sculptures in the country.

The Northern-Wei grottoes of Hongqing Temple in Yima, Northern-Qi Xiaonanhai Grottoes in Anyang and the great Buddha image carved on a cliff at Dapi Mountain in Jun County are pearls of Buddhist art.

In Linying there is a stele that records Cao Pi's accession to the throne abdicated by Emperor Xiandi of Han. The texts, said to have been composed by Wang Lang, written by Liang Hu, and engraved by Zhong You (the three were masters in their respective fields) are classics of calligraphy.

The Western-Jin Piyong Stele in Yanshi records the inspections to Piyong by Emperor Sima Yan (Wudi) of Jin and Crown Prince Sima Zhong, eulogizing their promotion of rites, education and Confucianism. The 9-meter-high Tang stele of Songyang Temple in Dengfeng is rare in size and complicated in structure, its five parts blending into a magnificent whole.

Other steles of high historical and artistic value are: the recently publicized cliff engravings made from the Southern and Northern Dynasties to the Tang Dynasty along Qingtian River in Bo'ai, the stele with Buddhist statues at Ximing Temple made in the Southern and Northern Dynasties in Xinxiang, the Tang 'Immortal Crown Prince' stele in Yanshi, the Tang Taoist statues of Chongtang Temple, the Tang Yuancishan Stele whose text was composed and written by Yan Zhenqin (famous Tang calligrapher) in Lushan, cliff engravings made from the Song Dynasty to the Republican Period at Yunmeng Mountain in Qi County, the Song stele of Bi'an Temple in Luohe, the Northern-Qi stele of Liubei Temple in Dengfeng, and the Yuan Tangwugong stele in Puyang. The stone inscriptions of Qiantangzhi Studio in Xin°Øan were collected in the 15 brick-arched loess caves built by Zhang Fang, including a collection of 1, 185 epitaphs made in the Tang Dynasty and 228 stone carvings dating from other periods. It is a museum of stone engravings with high historical and artistic value.

The following are historical sites and structures dating from the modern times.

In the Dabie Mountains are former sites of the revolutionary base of Hubei, Henan and Anhui, most of which are located in the town of Xin County. They include the Hubei-Henan-Anhui branch of the Central Committee of the Communist Party of China (CPC), Revolutionary Military Commission, Provincial Party Committee, Provincial Soviet Government, and Aviation Bureau of the Military Commission.

The former site of the Hubei-Henan-Anhui branch of the Central Committee of CPC, the address of which is No. 62, Zhongyuan Road, County Town, is a large compound with seven old-fashioned buildings in five rows. In Xin County there is also the former site of the headquarters of the 25th Army of the Chinese Red Army; at Hejiachong, Tiepu Township, Luoshan County is the 25th Army's starting point to the Long March, consisting of the former sites of the headquarters and an army hospital, and a tall gingko tree where the troops assembled and set off. All these attest to the Communists' hard struggles in the revolutionary period.

In Zhugou Town, Queshan County there is the former site of Central Plains Bureau of the CPC, where such communist leaders as Liu Shaoqi, Peng Xuefeng and Li Xiannian led people of the Central Plains during the fight against Japanese invaders, and a large number of revolutionary cadres were trained. The former site of the 8th Army's office in Luoyang and the former site of the revolutionary base of the border areas between Hebei, Shangdong and Henan witnessed tremendous contributions made by communists to fighting against the Japanese invaders and the Chinese Revolution.

The ancestral home of Deng Yingchao in Guangshan, the former residence of Liu Qingxia in Weishi County, Kaifeng, and the former site of Lütan School (Ji Hongchang School) in Fugou were important in modern history.

The site of Henan Preparatory School for Studying in Europe and America, is the modern building complex in Henan University, contains well-preserved buildings. In Zhengzhou there is a monument to the February 7th Strike and a memorial hall for the event.

The site of Weixing People's Commune is located at Chaya Mountain. In Linzhou is the Red Flag Canal reflects the Chinese people's revolutionary courage to combat nature. In Lankao is the tomb of Jiao Yulu, a communist official who died of overwork. These are immortal monuments to revolutionary struggles in modern times.

The exploration of ancient civilization is an eternal undertaking of mankind. In the new century, the Chinese has a passion for reviewing the past, building the present and looking to the future. 'The passing on of civilization and innovation' cannot be realized unless the past, present and future are welded together. Our cultural heritage, especially the major historic site under national protection, will be well protected and appropriately used as reflections of the wisdom, creativity, spirit and culture of the nation. Therefore, Henan's economic prosperity and modernization will not eclipse its ancient glory.

Major Historic Sites under National Protection in Henan is the first volume of the series on cultural heritages in Henan published by the Provincial Cultural Relics Administration. More volumes are forthcoming.

古建筑
Ancient Architecture

河南文化遗产

全国重点文物保护单位

Brief Information on Major Historic Sites under National Protection in Henan Province

古建筑

Ancient Architecture

太室阙

第一批全国重点文物保护单位

东汉

Taishi Que Tower

太室阙是汉代太室山庙的神道阙，与少室山庙前的少室阙、启母庙前的启母阙并称为“中岳汉三阙”，位于登封市城东4公里的中岳庙门前500米处。

太室阙东汉元初五年（118年）四月由“阳城—长江左冯诩万年吕常始造”，为二重子母阙形式，分东西两阙，阙门间距6.75米，两阙结构完全相同。由阙基、阙身、阙顶三部分组成。母阙和子阙的阙身联为一体，正阙在内，子阙在外，正阙高，子阙低。东阙的母阙高3.92米、子阙高2.61米。西阙的母阙高3.96米、子阙高2.65米，系用两层长方形石板垒砌，平铺在坚实的红土之上。最上层石块凿成斗形，上宽下窄，左、右、下部边沿刻卷草纹，上部则刻水纹。阙顶用三块巨石雕成四阿顶，高0.35米、残长2.3米、残宽1.42米。正脊用一块整石雕成，安置在阙顶正中，脊两端向上翘起，前后两面雕成扣合的筒瓦，两头正面各雕六个瓦当。正脊之下雕出垂脊和瓦垄，四角垂脊为叠瓦脊，南北两面各雕五条，瓦垄间距约18厘米。檐部雕瓦当、板瓦和椽头。南北两面各雕六

太室阙石刻画像朱雀图拓片

太室双阙

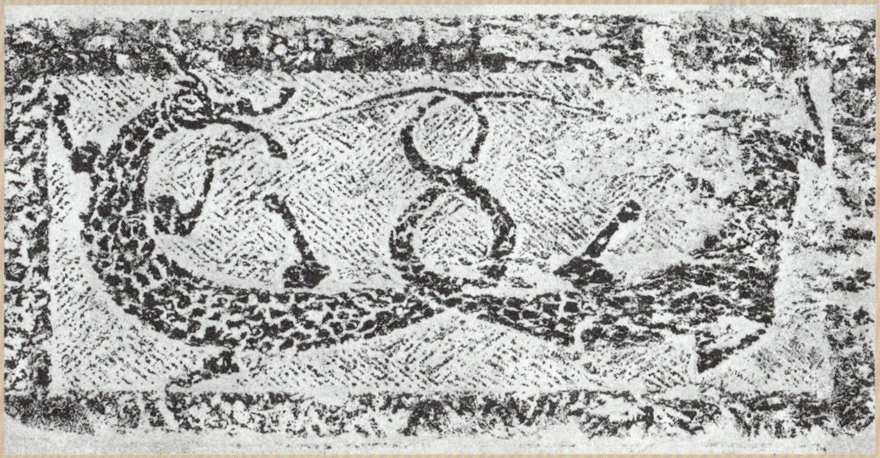

太室阙石刻画像交龙图拓片

个椽头，间距21厘米，东西两面较窄，仅刻四椽。子阙的阙顶结构与母阙顶基本相同。因一面紧靠在正阙上，所以只做成三面坡顶的四阿形式。阙身四面雕刻百戏、狩猎、神话故事、斗鸡、马戏、奇禽怪兽以及贵族生活等画像。最典型的是西阙南面三层“车骑出行图”，一马驾轺车，饰伞形华盖，华盖下坐二人，前为驭手，后一人头戴进贤冠，拱手端坐，车后一人头戴平帻，身着斜襟长服骑马随行。

阙上雕有两方阙铭，能辨识者仅六十六字，内容是对岳神灵异功德无量的颂辞，后附有官职姓名。每段之前均以圆圈做标志，在汉代石刻文字中较为罕见。

This is located south of Zhongyue Temple, Chengguan Town, Dengfeng City. Built in the 5th year of Yuanchu period (118 AD) in the Eastern Han Dynasty, it is a pair of stone towers erected beside the passageway in front of the Temple of Taishi Mountain. Each consisting of 8 layers, they are adorned with over 50 relief images of human figures, carriages and horses.

少室阙

第一批全国重点文物保护单位

东汉 **Shaoshi Que Tower**

少室阙，中岳汉三阙之一，位于登封市城西5公里的十里铺村西。该阙是少室山庙的神道阙，坐南向北。

据《汉书·地理志》记载，少室山庙始建于汉武帝时，安帝时又在庙前建阙。少室山庙，又称少室祠、少姨庙，明代初期坍毁。阙后有一东西长60余米、南北宽40余米的平台，地上散存着绳纹砖、筒瓦、板瓦等汉代建筑构件，当为少室山庙旧址。

据叶井叔《嵩阳石刻记》推知，少室阙的建造年代当与启母阙同时，均为颍川太守朱宠营建于汉安帝延光二年（123年）前后。少室阙二重子母阙，东西阙间距7.6米。结构相同，东阙通

少室东阙

少室阙石刻画像月宫图和阙铭拓片

高3.37米，子阙高2.71米，西阙通高3.75米。其造型和结构与太室阙相同。阙的底部用两层长方形石板平铺于坚实的黄土上，阙身用长方形石块垂直垒砌，共十层，高2.99米，最上层石块制作成方斗形，承托阙顶。阙顶用三块青石雕作四阿式，屋面雕出瓦垄，垂脊，四边雕柿蒂纹瓦当和板瓦，檐部雕椽。正脊单独用一块长条石雕成瓦条脊，中间低，两端高。子阙一侧与正阙相连，其他垒砌方法、造型与正阙相同。在西阙北面第三层中部有“少室神道之阙”题铭。南面刻有篆书铭文，约有五十五行，行四字。由于风化，前三十六行已漫漶不清，仅存十九行。阙身除刻题铭，还浮雕狐逐兔、赛马、蹴鞠、兽斗、斗鸡、马戏、玄鸟生高、四灵、羽人、双龙穿璧、车马出行、铺首衔环及山水等画像七十余幅。画像中有不少柏树，当与汉人柏能驱鬼辟邪的习俗有关。

This is located at Xingjiapu Village at the foot of Shaoshi Mountain, Chengguan Town, the City of Dengfeng. Built between the 5th year of Yuanchu period and the 2nd year of Yanguang period (118 ~ 123 AD) in the Eastern Han Dynasty, it is a pair of stone towers erected beside the passageway in front of the Temple of the Shaoshi Mountain. The tops of the carvings are in the hip-roof style, and their sides are adorned with relief images of carriages and horses.

启母阙

第一批全国重点文物保护单位

东汉

Qimu Que Tower

启母西阙

启母阙，又名开母阙，中岳汉三阙之一，位于登封市区西北2公里的万岁峰下。它原是启母庙前的神道阙，阙北190米处有启母石，为一椭圆形巨石，高约10米，周长43.1米，重约5300多吨。石的北部有明隆庆三年（1569年）蒋机立石碑一通，记述了夏启之母化为巨石的神话传说。据《登封县志》记载，启母阙为东汉安帝延光二年（123年）颍川太守朱宠创建。

启母阙为一对二重子母阙，阙门间距6.80米，西阙的母阙（即正阙）高3.17米；东阙的母阙高3.18米。东西阙结构基本相同。

西阙阙基为两层长方形石板，下层石板大而薄，长3.07米、宽1.62米、厚9厘米。阙身长方形石块垂直垒砌在阙基上，共七层，每层用石二至三块，总高2.75米。最上层的石块雕作斗形，上宽下窄，其上承托阙顶。阙顶雕作四阿式，因残毁过甚仅存东侧部分，且阙顶正脊无存。阙顶雕瓦垄、垂脊，四周雕柿蒂纹瓦当和板瓦。下部刻仿木椽子，基本仿木结构建筑。阙的北面有两方阙铭，一方为“启母阙铭”，一方是“堂溪典祟高庙请雨铭”。启母阙铭为篆书，内容分两部分，前十二行约八十字，记述了鲧围堵治水失败而丧生，大禹疏通河道排泄洪水获得成功。赞颂大禹为征服洪水三过家门而不入的精神。后二十四行约二百八十八字，叙述了汉朝圣德广布，为此立阙刻铭，传之千秋万代。堂溪典崇高庙请雨铭系东汉颍川郡主簿堂溪协于熹平四年（175年）所撰书。字体为隶书，计十八行，每行五字，因剥蚀较甚仅存十一行五十五字。内容是中郎将堂溪典于熹平四年来崇高庙请雨的过程。阙身镌刻有人物画像、骑马出行、斗鸡、驯象、吐火、幻术、倒立、进谒、饮宴、羲和御日、启母化石、夏禹化熊、郭巨埋儿、月宫、交龙穿环、犬逐兔、果下马、蹴鞠、鹤衔鱼、虎扑鹿、孔甲畜龙等七十余幅图像。

启母西阙阙铭拓片

启母阙石刻画像狩猎图拓片

This is located at the foot of Wansui Peak, Chengguan Town, the City of Dengfeng. Built in the 2nd year of Yanguang period (123 AD) in the Eastern Han Dynasty, it is a pair of stone towers erected beside the passageway in front of Qimu Temple. Each consisting of 8 layers, they are adorned on their sides with over 60 relief images of human figures, horses and carriages.

嵩岳寺塔

第一批全国重点文物保护单位

北魏

The pagoda in Songyue Temple

嵩岳寺塔

嵩岳寺塔是北魏古刹嵩岳寺的重要组成部分，位于登封市区西北6公里的嵩山南麓。

嵩岳寺始建于北魏宣武帝永平二年（509年），原是宣武帝的离宫，后改建为寺院。孝明帝正光元年（520年）改名为“闲居寺”，大加增建，殿宇达千余间，僧众七百余人，正光四年（523年）建造佛塔。隋文帝仁寿二年（602年）改名为嵩岳寺。唐代以后寺废塔存。现塔后大雄殿及两侧的伽蓝殿、白衣殿均为清代所建。

嵩岳寺塔塔刹

嵩岳寺塔的形制为密檐式砖塔，是我国现存最早的砖塔。塔的外观呈抛物线形，平面为十二边形，是古塔中的孤例。塔总高约37米、底层外径10.6米、内径5米余、壁体厚2.5米，由基台、塔身、十五叠涩砖檐和宝刹组成。密檐之间的矮壁上砌出各式门窗四百九十二个。密檐自下而上逐层内收，塔顶为砖质宝刹。基台平面为十二边形，高86厘米。塔身以腰檐将其分为上下两部分，下部高3.59米，上下垂直，四面辟拱券式塔门通向塔心室。券门采用两伏两券砌筑法，门上有尖拱形门楣和卷云形楣角，门楣顶部置三瓣莲花组成饰物。塔身外壁正八面各砌出一座单层方形塔龛，龛下部为长方形须弥座，门内有砖雕护法狮子。上部即十五层叠涩密檐，各层叠涩檐之间的壁高自下而上稍有递减，檐宽逐层收分，使塔的外轮廓呈现出抛物线形。叠涩檐之间塔壁上均辟有一门二窗。塔刹通高4.74米，自下而上由基座、覆莲、须弥座、仰莲、相轮及宝珠组成，皆用青灰条砖砍制后平顺垒砌成型。

1985年在对嵩岳寺塔地宫和天宫的清理中，发现地宫北壁有唐开元二十一年（733年）墨书题记一方，唐代文物七十余件，最有价值的是一尊用红砂岩雕造的佛像，高11厘米，背面刻有“大魏正光四年”造像记，为此塔的始建年代找到了依据。

This is located at Datasi Village north of Dengfeng City. Built in the years of Zhengguang period (520 ~ 525) in the Northern Wei Dynasty, the pagoda is about 37.045 meters high, with a dodecagon cross-section and close eaves. It consists of four parts-the base, the body, the eaves and the top.

祐国寺塔

北宋

The pagoda of Youguo Temple

祐国寺塔

祐国寺塔位于开封市区东北隅的铁塔公园内。是我国最大的琉璃塔。因塔身为褐色琉璃砖砌筑，呈铁褐色，故又称铁塔。

据塔上第三层“治平四年”和塔顶“熙宁”题记，可以推知该塔落成时间应在宋神宗熙宁年间（1068～1077年），初名灵感塔。明代由开宝寺易名为祐国寺，塔随寺名改为祐国寺塔。

祐国寺塔为八角形仿楼阁式建筑，高十三层，由塔基、塔身、塔刹三部分组成。明清时期黄河几度淹没开封，塔基被埋于地下，目前地面以上部分高55.08米。塔身外壁除圭形门和八面转角所立的倚柱，其他采用模制花砖。用平丁砖做框，顺立砖为心，预制卯口，比连组合成镶嵌式壁面结构。模制花砖上的图案丰富多彩，内容有佛龛、菩萨、飞天、立僧、供养人、伎乐人与胡人；有宝相花、海石榴、莲花、牡丹和芍药花；有狮子、云龙、降龙、双龙、麒麟；有璎珞和流苏等。塔身各层檐部以重抄计心五铺作斗栱承托。从一层到十三层斗栱规格相同。各层面阔的尺度，随着檐部与平座斗栱数目的多少而变化。檐口以龙纹瓦当和莲瓣形重唇板瓦作装饰，瓦的后部则做成平砖。塔檐转角处撩檐枋相交呈八字形，檐角安置蝉形老角梁，梁的两侧用砖砌成升头木，使翼角挑起。老角梁之上用两块牛腿形的砖制作成子角梁，前端安置麒麟套兽。塔顶为八角攒尖式，八角垂脊的顶端合拢托起一个莲花座，座上安置铜质宝珠形塔刹。塔身底层东南西北各面辟有圭形门，唯有北门是真门可入塔内。门内设置砖砌梯道，绕塔心柱盘旋登一百六十八级台阶至顶层。该塔共有十三个真门，每层一个，所开方向不同。有人将这些门误认为“盲窗”，其实均起到采光、通风和眺望的作用。

祐国寺塔塔身自下而上逐层收分，轮廓流畅，秀丽挺拔；塔外壁的琉璃砖壁面更是集北宋琉璃工艺之大成。此塔是宋代建筑与艺术的完美结合。

祐国寺塔塔檐

祐国寺塔琉璃砖雕狮子

The pagoda is located in the northeast corner of the urban area of Kaifeng City. It was built in the 1st year of Huangyou period (1049 AD) in the Northern Song Dynasty. It is popularly known as 'the iron pagoda' because it is coated in dark brown glazed tiles. Built of glazed brick pagota in the pavilion style, it has 13 stories and a hexagon cross-section.

白马寺

第一批全国重点文物保护单位

金至清 White Horse Temple

白马寺，位于洛阳市老城东12公里处，是佛教传入中国后所营建的第一座寺院，被佛教界尊称为“中国佛教祖庭”。白马寺初创于东汉明帝永平十一年（公元68年）。《事物纪原》记载：“汉明帝时，自西域以白马驮经来，初至鸿胪寺，遂取寺名置白马寺，即僧寺之始也。”今存建筑与布局，基本是明、清时期的规模。

白马寺坐北朝南，呈长方形，面积34000平方米，建筑百余间。中轴线上有山门、天王殿、大佛殿、大雄殿、接引殿和清凉台等。附属建筑分布于两侧，左右对称，有门堂、云水堂、祖堂、客堂、禅掌及方丈院等。山门为牌楼式石砌三洞券门，歇山式灰瓦顶。正门上方镶嵌“白马寺”石匾，为明嘉靖二十五年（1546年）冬司礼监印太监黄锦所题写。第二进天王殿原是北魏时期白马寺的山门，元代在其内塑造四大天王像，明代在寺前又建山门。该殿面阔五间，进深三间，歇山式建筑，正脊上透雕二龙戏珠。第三进大佛殿为明代建筑，面阔五间，进深四间，歇山顶。殿后壁和两山墙均以楔形汉代砖石叠砌，颇为罕见。殿内正面塑释迦牟尼立像。第四进大雄殿面阔五间，进深四间，悬山式。殿前有宽敞的月台。殿内供奉释迦牟尼像。第五进接引殿，面阔14、进深10.7米，悬山式建筑，重建于清光绪九年（1883年），殿内主尊为阿弥陀佛，两旁为观世音和大势至菩萨。清凉台与接引殿相连，是一座高台建筑。永平年间蔡音等从印度取经归来，佛经和

白马寺山门

齐云塔

白马寺千佛殿

白马寺千佛殿元代罗汉

佛像即放置在清凉台上；印度高僧摄摩腾和竺法兰在此翻译佛经，故又名清源台。台长42.8、宽32.4、高6米。上有门楼、放生池、毗卢阁、摄摩腾殿、竺法兰殿以及廊房，构成幽静的小庭院，院内有两株明代所植柏树，古柏上有凌霄环绕，营造出古朴典雅的氛围。毗卢阁面阔五间，进深三间，重檐歇山式，四角置有铁马。

在白马寺山门内东西柏树林中，有两座用青石包镶的圆冢墓，东为“汉启道圆通摩腾大师墓”，西为“汉开教总持竺法兰大师墓”，二位高僧共同译出了最早的汉文佛经《四十二章经》。

位于白马寺山门外东南200余米的齐云塔，本名“释迦舍利塔”，亦称“金方塔”，为金大定十五年（1175年）在五代木塔原址上重建的四方形叠涩密檐式砖塔，共十三层，通高约25米，底部为方形须弥座式，边长7.8米。塔身略呈抛物线状，第一层塔檐下面，用小砖饰砌仿木结构的普拍枋和一斗三升斗栱。顶置宝瓶式塔刹。

寺内现存历代碑石约四十方，其中宋代四方，金代一方，元代三方，明代八方，清代二十方。

The temple is located at Baimasi Village, 12 km east of the old city of Luoyang. Founded in the 11th year of Yongping period (68 AD) in the Eastern Han Dynasty, it was the first officially built Buddhist temple after the introduction of Buddhism into China. Remaining buildings, built from the Jin Dynasty to the Qing Dynasty, cover a total floor space of 34,000 sq. m.

观星台

第一批全国重点文物保护单位

元

Observatory

观星台

观星台，是元代天文学家郭守敬主持建造的观测星象的建筑，是我国现存时代早、保护好的天文台，位于登封市东南15公里的告成镇周公庙内。周公庙现存有大门、周公测景台、拜殿、观星台等建筑。

观星台为砖石结构，由覆斗状台体和台体北侧的石圭两部分组成。台高9.46米，连同台顶上增建的小室，通高12.62米。台体平面近正方形，台基底边长16米余，向上有明显收分。台顶每边8米余。台体东西两边设有对称踏道，可由此盘旋登至台顶。台上是观星和测景的工作台面。台顶北部的小室据记载始建于明嘉靖七年（1528年），上距元初建观星台时已有二百余年，小室应为安装仪器之处。台体北壁正中

周公测景台

有一凹槽，凹槽南壁上下垂直，东西两壁有明显收分，凹槽与台下的石圭是一组测量日影长度的元代圭表装置，因为它比以往的八尺之表高出五倍，故称为“高表”。石圭在台体以北下部，南端伸入北壁的凹槽内，与直壁相距36厘米。自南至北由三十六方青石接连铺设的石圭长31.196、宽0.53、南高0.53、北高0.62米，圭面水平误差甚微。上刻两条平行双股流水渠，深2、宽2.5厘米，两槽相距15厘米。渠南端有方形注水池，北端有长条状泄水池，池两端有泄水孔。这种水渠为测水平之用。

观星台在全世界，也属于最早的天文建筑之一。

Located in Gaocheng Town, Dengfeng City, this is an ancient observatory, the building of which was presided over by Guo Shoujing, a Yuan-dynasty astronomer. It consists of a platform in the shape of an overturned dipper and a stone sundial on its north side. It is the oldest observatory that remains in China.

修定寺塔

唐

The stupa of Xiuding Temple

修定寺塔，位于安阳县城西北35公里的清凉山东南麓修定寺旧址上。

修定寺塔为一座单层方形佛塔，由塔顶、塔身、台基三部分组成，通高约20米。此塔是我国稀有的利用雕砖饰面的砖塔，具有很高的历史价值与艺术价值。塔身四壁用模制的各种形状的雕砖嵌砌而成，共用雕砖三千七百七十五块。其中四壁雕砖以菱形为主，图案内容有道人、武士、菩萨、飞天、童子、舞乐及狮、龙、象、马等形象和以莲花为主的各种花卉等，浮雕面积为300平方米。每一壁面的浮雕都设计成一幅华丽的幔帐构图，帐头上雕彩铃、华缨、彩带等装饰图案。南壁中部设拱券式塔门，高330厘米、

修定寺塔

修定寺塔塔门浮雕

宽195厘米、进深55厘米，全部用青石雕刻而成。门额与门楣为整石雕成，石面雕三世佛造像龛，两侧雕阿难、迦叶、胁侍菩萨和天王像。雕刻手法和造像形式均具有唐代特点。

据《大唐邺县修定寺传记》碑载，修定寺为僧人张猛创建于北魏太和十八年（494年），初名天城寺。北齐时期改名为合水寺，北周时武帝灭法，寺院被毁，隋代佛法重兴，营建此处伽蓝改称修定禅寺。唐代贞观年间修定寺得到全面修复，清代末期尚存三进院落，建筑由南向北依次为天王殿、浮雕砖塔、大佛殿、二佛殿和建于最高处的铁瓦殿。后殿宇渐毁，唯塔独存。

Located south of Qingliang Temple, Anyang County, the stupa was built from the years of Jianzhong to the years of Zhenyuan period (780 ~ 804 AD) in the Tang Dynasty. It is in a square shape, with single eaves, and measures 9.30 meters high.

修定寺塔塔壁浮雕

社旗山陕会馆

清

Shanxi-Shaanxi Guild Hall in Sheqi

社旗山陕会馆位于社旗县县城中心。

会馆始建于清乾隆二十一年(1756年)，光绪十八年(1892年)竣工，是山西、陕西两省富商巨贾集资兴建的同乡会所在地。据记载，修建会馆曾“运巨材于楚北，访名匠于天下”，花费白银达八万八千七百八十八两。

山陕会馆坐北朝南，南北长152.5米、东西宽62米，面积9455平方米，分三进院落，中轴线上有琉璃照壁、木旗杆、铁旗杆、石狮、悬鉴楼、石牌坊、拜殿、大殿、春秋楼，两侧有东西辕门、钟鼓楼、厢房、腰楼、药王殿、马王殿、配殿、马厩、道房院等。木旗杆和春秋楼于清末焚毁，其他建筑保存完好。

会馆前院南端的琉璃照壁，高10.3米、宽10.6米，下为石筑须弥座，上覆绿琉璃瓦硬山顶，壁身用百块琉璃方砖砌成，设计精巧，色泽绚丽。悬鉴楼亦

社旗山陕会馆全景

社旗山陕会馆大拜殿

社旗山陕会馆木雕

名戏楼，兴建于清嘉庆元年（1796年），道光元年（1821年）竣工。历时二十五年。楼高22米、面阔11.88米、进深13.48米，为三重檐歇山式，绿琉璃瓦顶。檐下置重昂五踩斗栱。第二层结构南简北繁，北部为面阔三间的戏台，檐下悬挂“悬鉴楼”匾额。拜殿与大殿以天沟相连为一体，是会馆的中心正殿，清同治八年（1869年）始建，光绪十八年（1892年）竣工。拜殿为单檐绿琉璃瓦歇山式卷棚顶，高15.1米，面阔三

社旗山陕会馆石牌坊

间15.39米、进深9.6米。殿前左右侧有八字石墙，高2米、宽0.9米，上雕歇山式屋顶，下砌须弥座。中间为透雕图案，左壁为“十八学士登瀛洲”，右壁为“渔樵耕读”及山水、人物和鸟兽等。

社旗山陕会馆建筑布局紧凑，质量高超，是同时代建筑的经典作品之一。

社旗山陕会馆石雕

Located north of Ciqi Stree, Sheqi County, the guild hall was built in the 21st year of Emperor Qianlong's reign (1755) in the Qing Dynasty with donations made by the commerce chambers of Shanxi Province and Shaanxi Province. It covers 5,400 sq. m. Sitting on the central axis, from south to north, are the following structures: a screen wall of colored glaze, Xuanjian Tower, a stone archway, Dabai Hall and Chunqiu Tower.

风穴寺及塔林

第三批全国重点文物保护单位

唐至清

Fengxue Temple and its pagoda forest

风穴寺全景

风穴寺及塔林位于汝州市东北9公里群山环抱之中。因山有穴，每每将风，穴辄先鸣，既而风作，岩木震撼，得名风穴寺。风穴寺又名千峰寺、白云寺和香积寺。现存唐至清代建筑百余间，主体建筑有天王殿、中佛殿、毗卢殿、方丈院、七祖塔、望州亭、观音阁、钟楼、藏经阁、地藏殿等。

中佛殿，坐落在高1米的砖砌台基上，面阔三间，进深三间，单檐歇山式。据《风穴七祖千峰百云禅院记》碑记载，始建于五代后汉时期，但从平面布局、斗栱造型、梁架结构、用材大小及艺术风格分析，当属金代建筑。毗卢殿，面阔五间，进深三间，单檐悬山式，为寺内最大的一座木构建筑。据碑文载，始建于五代后汉乾祐二年（949年）以前，元末毁于兵燹。明成化十一年（1475年）重修，工未讫主持圆证卒，故暂停工，直到正德二年（1507年）才竣工。清康熙、道光年间曾作整修。殿前建月台，台四隅置石兽。殿内中部有横占三间的神坛，坛上原塑毗卢佛像，已不存。后将明代永乐七年（1409年）周王所赠白玉石佛像安置坛上。钟楼始建于北宋宣和七年（1125年），楼内悬挂重达800公斤的铜钟。据明万历十二年《重修钟楼记》碑文载，“盖寺钟之设久已，犹随唐宋以千峰白云名寺传者”。由此可知在宋代因钟建楼，后楼废而钟存，明代再修楼而悬钟如初。

七祖塔，位于毗卢殿右前方，相传为佛教禅宗七祖贞禅师而建，故又名贞禅师塔。建于唐开元二十六年（738年），系方形九层密檐式砖塔，高22米，每层四角置风铎，第一层设塔心室。

寺院周围分布有唐、元、明、清和近代砖塔一百四十六座。

Located in the Fengxue Mountain north of Liugou Village, Ruzhou City, these date back to the period from the Tang Dynasty to the Qing Dynasty (618 ~ 1911 AD). Along the central axis are the following buildings: the main gate, Tianwang Hall, Zhongfo Hall, Pilu Hall, abbot's courtyard, caves and Wangzhou Temple. Outside the temple there are an upper pagoda forest and a lower one, which contain 73 tomb-pagodas of monks who lived in the Ming and Qing dynasties.

风穴寺塔林

024

净藏禅师塔

第三批全国重点文物保护单位

唐

Master Jingzang's Pagoda

净藏禅师塔

净藏禅师塔位于登封市西北6公里的会善寺西侧。系唐代会善寺高僧净藏禅师的墓塔，塔身背面镶嵌着《嵩山会善寺故大德净藏禅师塔铭并序》青石塔铭一方，由此可知唐天宝五年（746年）净藏禅师圆寂，其弟子为恩师建此塔。

塔由地宫、基座、塔身和塔顶四部分组成，高10.35米，坐北面南。地宫平面为方形，内存放净藏禅师骨灰罐，室内有彩色壁画。塔身平面为八角形，每角砌出倚柱，倚柱突出墙外三个面，柱下未施柱础，柱头作覆盆式。柱上部用阑额连接两柱，额枋下有门额、立颊、子梃等，柱的中部有连接两柱的腰串，柱根由地相连，腰串与地之间有障水板，构成了塔身每面的基本框架。塔身南面为拱券式塔门，门作单券无栿式。八角形塔心室。东西两面各作一合仿木实门，门中央雕一把大锁。其余四面各砌出直棂窗。塔顶由叠涩砖檐、花纹雕砖及石雕宝刹组成。

净藏禅师塔为我国现存唯一一座唐代八角形仿木结构砖塔，是研究唐代建筑和佛塔的重要实物资料。

净藏禅师塔直棂窗

净藏禅师塔塔刹

Located west of Huishan Temple in Chengguan Town, Dengfeng City, the pagoda was built in the 5th year of Tianbao period (746 AD) in the Tang Dynasty. Built of bricks in the wooden pavilion style, it has a single story and an octagon cross-section. Its north side carries a slab of stone inscribed with an account of the master's life.

初祖庵及少林寺塔林

唐至清

Chuzu Temple and the pagoda forest of Shaolin Temple

初祖庵位于登封市少林寺西北2公里的五乳峰下。是为纪念达摩而修建的寺院。占地3000多平方米，由山门、大殿、千佛阁及方亭组成。

初祖庵大殿建于北宋宣和七年（1125年），单檐歇山式，面阔、进深各三间。殿顶采用绿琉璃瓦剪边做法，檐部使用重唇板瓦。檐下置三铺作单抄单下昂斗栱根，补间铺作用真昂。明间安装板门两扇，两次间辟直棂方窗。大殿用石柱十六根，金柱四根。石柱、佛龛须弥座和墙下肩部分，浮雕游龙、翔凤、武士、佛像、飞天、莲花化生、凤戏牡丹、麒麟等图案，是北宋石雕艺术的杰作。大殿较多地保留了宋代创建时的原貌，是研究《营造法式》匠作制度的宝贵资料。庵内存宋、元、明、清、民国石刻五十品。

少林寺塔林位于少林寺西

初祖庵大殿

300米处，是少林寺历代僧人的墓地，占地19000平方米。塔林中现有唐、宋、金、元、明、清代砖石墓塔二百二十八座，其中唐塔两座，宋塔三座，金塔十六座，元塔五十一座，明塔一百四十六座，清塔十座。塔的造型多样，形制不一，有方形、长方形、圆形、六角形、八角形、亭阁式、经幢式、碑体式、堵婆式、密檐式、喇嘛式、楼阁式等等。少林寺塔林是国内最大的塔林。

少林寺塔林远眺

少林寺塔林近景

Located at the foot of Wuru Peak, Shaoshi Mountain, Dengfeng City, Chuzu Temple was built in the Song Dynasty (960 ~ 1277 AD). Remaining buildings are: main gate, main hall, two pavilions and Thousand-Buddha Pavilion.

Located 300 meters southwest of Shaolin Temple, the pagoda forest is the cemetery of monks who lived in the period from the Tang Dynasty to the Qing Dynasty (618 ~ 1911 AD). It contains 243 tomb-pagodas.

少林寺塔林近景

济渎庙

第四批全国重点文物保护单位

宋至清

Jidu Temple

济渎庙清源洞府门

济渎庙位于济源市西北2公里的庙街村，是历代帝王为祭祀济渎水神而建的庙宇。济渎庙始建于隋开皇二年（582年），唐贞元十二年（796年）又在济渎池后创建北海庙。据《济源县志》载，因济渎池有海眼潜通北海，故建庙附祭北海神于此。历代帝王每年要派遣朝廷大臣到此举行御祭，投金龙玉简于济渎池。

济渎庙总面积86255平方米，现存建筑分为四组，前为济渎庙，后为北海祠，西为天庆宫，东为御香院。整体采取纵轴线布局，平面呈“甲”字形，南北长510米、东西宽215米，最窄处30米，中轴线上依次为清源洞府门（左右置掖门）、清源门、源德门、源德殿及辅道遗址、寝宫、临渊门、龙亭、济渎池、灵渊阁；天庆宫内有玉皇殿、小碑林、长生阁、西道房；御香院内有御香殿、接官楼、东西厢房等。庙内共有宋、元、明、清各时代建筑二十三座。

济渎庙的山门——清源洞府门建于明代初年，系三间四柱挑山造木牌楼，斗栱九踩重翘重昂重栱计心造，为河南明代木牌楼之冠。寝宫系河南最古老的木结构建筑之一，建于北宋开宝六年(973年)，面阔五间，进深三间，单檐歇山式，殿顶平缓，出檐深远，斗栱梁架结构用材硕大，有着明显的宋初建筑风格。临渊门重建于元大德二年(1298年)，是豫北地区保存比较完好的元代建筑之一。

济渎庙内古柏参天，碑碣林立。庙内尚存唐、宋、元、明、清各代碑碣四十余通，书法有真、草、隶、篆等书体，弥足珍贵。玉皇殿前的桧柏高20余米，树围6米许，传为汉柏。五代后汉皇帝封其为“将军柏”。

济渎庙龙池

济渎庙寝宫转角铺作

济渎庙寝宫

Located on Miao Street, Chengguan Town, Jiyuan City, the south-facing temple dates back to the period from the Song Dynasty to the Qing Dynasty (960 ~ 1911 AD). Remaining buildings are: Qingyuan Dongfu Gate, Qingyuan Gate, Yuande Gate, a shrine, Linyuan Gate, and Dragon Pavilion. The shrine was built in the Song Dynasty. The temple contains over 30 stone tablets made during the period from the Tang Dynasty to the Qing Dynasty.

南阳武侯祠

第四批全国重点文物保护单位

元至清

Wuhou Shrine in Nanyang

南阳武侯祠，又名诸葛庐，位于南阳市南郊卧龙岗上。

南阳武侯祠坐西向东（偏南），现存殿堂廊庑一百六十五间，总面积12万平方米。主要建筑有牌坊、仙人桥、山门、大拜殿、茅庐、小虹桥、宁远楼等，依次排列在中轴线上。两侧为诸葛井、碑廊、古柏亭、野云庵、老龙洞、半月台、躬耕亭等。武侯祠北路为三顾祠，南路二进四合院为卧龙道院。与卧龙岗十景共同构成一组雄伟壮观的古代建筑群。祠内碑碣四百余通，匾联七十余幅。

据《明嘉靖南阳府志校注》记载，南阳武侯祠始建于魏晋时期，此后又经历代修葺。唐刘禹锡《陋室铭》中“南阳诸葛庐，西蜀子云亭”之句，表明诸葛庐在

南阳武侯祠三顾堂

南阳武侯祠草庐

唐代已名冠于世。宋元时期武侯祠屡遭兵燹，今日基本保存了明清时代的布局，其木构建筑多为明宣德以后重建或增建的。南阳武侯祠的文化内涵丰富，建筑组合多变，群体布局和谐，是一座颇富园林风趣的祠庙建筑，也是一座集名人名胜为一体的历史文化宝库。

南阳武侯祠望月楼

Located at Wolonggang in the western suburbs of Nanyang City, the shrine was built in the Ming Dynasty (1368 ~ 1644 AD) and covers 120,000 sq. m. It contains over 400 stone tablets and over 70 plaques and couplets made in various dynasties.

归德府城墙

明

The city wall of Guide Prefecture

归德府城墙位于商丘市睢阳区，是我国目前保存最好的古城墙之一。

明弘治十五年（1502年），原宋城毁于水，正德六年（1511年）知州杨太又在城北筑城，今南门即原城北门故址。同年知州周冕继修竣工。正德八年（1513年），知州刘信建东、西、南、北四座瓮城门楼。嘉靖二十四年（1545年），归德州升为归德府，此城即为归德府城。嘉靖三十四年（1555年）知府王有为建西门和北门内楼两座。同时增建四个角楼，敌台十三个，警铺三十二个。嘉靖三十七年（1558年），巡抚都御史章焕又檄知府陈学夔包砖门四座。知府王范和指挥梅闵先后在南门的东西两侧各建一水门。明朝末年城楼毁于战火。康熙二十六年（1687年）知县周宗义重修，复建城门楼。至今除城

归德府城墙俯瞰

归德府东城墙

门楼之外，其他城墙、城湖、土城墙、城内道路格局等，都保存完好。

该城外圆内方。土城墙为圆形，周长8公里，宽30米、高1.5米。砖城墙平面近似长方形，东西城墙各长1210.1米、南城墙长950.6米、北城墙长993.14米，周长4355米。城墙用黄土分层夯筑而起，每层厚30～50厘米，内外用青砖包砌，收分比较明显。高6.6米、底宽10米、顶宽7米，城上有三千六百个垛口，四角设有四个凸出墙外的角楼，楼已毁仅存角台。城周有九个方形马面，凸出墙外6.7米，东西南北各设砖券城门。城内面积1.13平方公里，共有九十三条街道，每条街道长200米，纵横交错。城外有城湖，水域面积近4平方公里。

Located in Suiyang District, Shangqiu City, the city wall was built in the 6th year of Zhengde (1511 AD) in the Ming Dynasty, with a circumference of 4,355.21 meters, 3,600 battlements, 4 turrets, 9 horse-face embattlements and 4 arched gates. Above the city gate is a two-story tower with a hip and gable roof. Beyond the wall is a moat and a protective dyke.

太昊陵庙

明、清

The temple of Taihao Mausoleum

太昊陵庙位于淮阳县城北1.5公里的蔡河之阳。是“三皇之首”太昊伏羲氏的陵庙。太昊陵庙是我国帝王陵庙中大型宫殿式建筑之一，更是华夏民族谒祖朝圣之地。

据《陈州府志》记载：此地春秋时已有陵墓，汉以前有祠，唐太宗李世民颁诏“禁民刍牧”；宋太祖赵匡胤诏立陵庙；明太祖朱元璋自制祝文，亲临致祭；至清末，历代皇帝遣官祭奠。

太昊陵庙坐北朝南，占地八百七十五亩。现存建筑为明正统十三年（1448年）的规模。陵庙的午朝门之内称外城，先天门以内谓内城，太极门及城垣形成紫禁城。庙院南北长750米、东西宽700米。陵庙内现存殿堂建筑一百七十八间，中轴建筑依次为渡善桥、午朝门、先天门、太极门、钟鼓楼、统天殿、显仁殿、寝殿、太始门、八卦坛、墓冢、蓍草园等。统天殿是陵庙中最主要的建筑之一，单檐歇山顶，面阔五间，进深三间，黄琉璃瓦覆顶，殿内正中神龛内塑伏羲像。显仁殿是陵庙内最高大的建筑，重檐歇山顶，通高16.4米，面阔七间，进深五间，坐落在2米高

太昊陵庙统天殿

太昊陵庙三才门

太昊陵庙午朝门

的直壁式台基上。八卦坛相传是伏羲画卦的地方。墓冢高26米、周长150米，上圆下方，寓意天圆地方。

太昊陵庙建筑群规模宏伟。在中轴线两侧，还有历代修建的岳飞观、老君观、火神台、三清观、祖师观、更衣亭等建筑。

Located in the northern suburbs of Huaiyang County, the temple was built in the Ming Dynasty (1368 ~ 1644 AD), extending over 700 meters from north to south and 500 meters from east to west. Remaining buildings are the outer city, the inner city, and the palace city.

比干庙

第四批全国重点文物保护单位

明、清

Bigan Temple

比干庙位于卫辉市西北7.5公里的比干庙村。

据《尚书·武成》和清乾隆时《汲县志》等史书记载，比干墓为周武王所封，北魏孝文帝因墓立庙。孝文帝以及唐太宗、宋仁宗、元仁宗等都曾凭吊比干，并下诏对比干庙进行大规模的维修。

现存比干庙为明清时期重建。建筑坐北朝南，前为庙，后为墓，占地面积44000平方米。中轴线上依次排列有照壁、山门、二门、三门、享殿、日月坊、墓冢等。山门檐下悬挂“殷太师比干庙”匾额。二门为木牌坊形式，檐下置重翘重昂斗栱，门额上悬“谏臣极则”匾额，门两侧为碑廊，内有海内外林氏宗亲祭祖碑五十余通。三门面阔三间，灰瓦顶硬山式建筑，门前立石狮一对。享殿由卷棚和大殿组成，面阔五间，进深三间，歇山顶式，檐下施斗栱。两侧有配殿和厢房，皆硬山式建筑。殿后为日月石坊和墓冢，墓冢直径50米、高6米，下部用青石垒砌，并镶嵌有历代文人学士颂扬比

比干庙照壁及山门

比干庙二门

干的诗词碑刻数十方。墓冢周围植有数百株翠柏，形成古柏森森的墓园。

比干庙内现存有唐、宋、元、明、清各代碑刻六十四通，其中魏孝文帝《吊比干文》（宋代重刻）、唐太宗《祭比干文》、元代《皇元敕修忠烈公比干庙碑铭》和清乾隆皇帝《御制诗》碑最负盛名；特别是明嘉靖年间立《重修比干祠碑记》，详细记述了林姓渊源，有很高的史料价值。

Located at Biganmiao Village, Weihui City, the temple was founded by Emperor Xiaowen in the 18th year of Taihe (494 AD) in the Northern Wei Dynasty. The currently standing buildings, built in the 7th year of Hongzhi (1494 AD) in the Ming Dynasty, cover 44,000 sq. m. It contains a tomb that is 20 meters high, with a circumference of 50 meters, and surrounded by a granite wall.

开封城墙

清

The city wall of Kaifeng

开封城墙位于七朝故都开封市。

根据1991年的勘测，开封城墙现存高度5～8米、顶宽5米、底宽7米、周长14.4公里。八十一座马面，四座角台。城墙青砖规格为45 × 23 × 12厘米，重20公斤，与文献基本相符。

有关开封城墙的记载始于唐代。唐德宗建中二年（781年）宣武军节度使李勉重修汴州城，周围二十里一百五十步。此后五代梁、晋、汉、周和北宋相继建都开封，对开封城墙都有不同程度的修葺。特别是北宋时期，在汴州城的基础上又进行了大规模的扩建，使开封城成为外城、里城、宫城三重结构的大都城。之后，黄河泛滥淹没了宋城。元世祖至元二十七年（1290年）重修汴梁城。明洪

开封城汴梁门

开封东城墙马面

开封城大梁门

武元年（1368年）重修开封府城。周围二十里一百九十步，高三丈五尺，广二丈二尺，护城河深一丈，阔五丈，建有五座城门，角楼四座，敌台八十四座，警铺八十三座。崇祯十五年（1642年）河决灌城，使开封城墙残破不堪。清康熙、乾隆、道光年间曾多次修补，“各门营建如旧制”。1928年在南门东侧另开一门，直对北门，即成今日开封城墙的状况。

Located in the urban area of Kaifeng City, the wall was built in the Qing Dynasty (1644 ~ 1911 AD). It is 7.60 meters high, with a circumference of 14.15 km, retaining 81 horse-face embattlements and 4 turrets.

周口关帝庙

清

Guandi Temple in Zhoukou

周口关帝庙全景

周口关帝庙位于周口市富强街西段。该庙创建于清康熙三十二年（1693年），咸丰二年（1852年）落成。

关帝庙坐北面南，原为旅居周口的山西、陕西商贾联谊之所。经雍正、乾隆、嘉庆、道光年间多次增修，现存楼阁殿廊一百零二间，占地约17600平方米。整个庙宇为三进院落，布局严谨，巍峨壮观，木雕、石雕及彩绘精美绚丽，有较高的艺术价值。

关帝庙自南而北依次有照壁、山门、铁旗杆、石牌坊、碑亭、享堂、大殿、舞楼、拜殿、春秋阁等建筑。两侧有钟鼓楼、河伯殿、炎帝殿、药王殿、灶君殿、财神殿、酒仙殿、老君殿、马王殿、瘟神殿、东西看楼、廊房、马房等建筑。整个庙院为城堡式建筑群，城墙底部用红石砌出下肩，上部用大砖砌就，墙头砌成垛口，院墙宽1米、高6米。每座建筑上都有华丽的木雕、石雕及彩绘，刻画出形态各异的花鸟神兽和传说故事，如“关云长义释曹操"、"竹林七贤"、"福禄寿喜"、"鲤鱼跳龙门"、"狮子滚绣球"、"四季花鸟"等等。造型别致的铁旗杆也是一景，铁旗杆是清嘉庆二年（1797年）陕西同州大荔、朝邑、澄城县天平会众商敬献，下部为正六棱柱青石底座，高1米、边长0.7米。石座上为高0.9米、上边长0.41米、底边长0.57米的束腰六棱台铸铁座，石雕底座和铸铁座上雕铸有人物、花卉、龙凤及"八吉祥"图案，上置直径24厘米的铸铁旗杆，高22米。杆分三节，杆身饰有形态生动的两条行龙，以及两个官寿如意斗，顶端铸有日、月和"大义"、"参天"四个字，斗的四角悬有风铎。

Located on Fuqiang Street, Zhoukou City, the temple started to be built in the 32nd year of Emperor Kangxi' s reign (1693 AD) in the Qing Dynasty and covers 16,500 sq. m. Remaining buildings are: Main Gate, Xiang Hall, Main hall, Theatre, Worship Hall, and Chunqiu Tower. It contains over 2,000 wooden carvings, stone carvings and brick carvings.

周口关帝庙石牌坊

内乡县衙

第四批全国重点文物保护单位

清

County government office at Neixiang

内乡县衙全景

内乡县衙位于内乡县城东大街。

县衙坐北朝南，南北长230米，东西宽80米，总面积近20000平方米，原有房屋二百余间，现存一百一十七间。中轴线上建筑有宣化坊、大门、大堂、二堂、三堂、后花园等，两侧相应有吏、户、礼、兵、刑、工六科房，花厅、账房、库房、狱房等。是我国现存较完整的县衙建筑群。

据清康熙年间《内乡县志·公署》记载："县治居城之中，元大德八年（1304年）县尹潘逵始建厅堂廨舍。……成化十五年（1479年）知县沃频见厅廨卽颓，基址狭窄，于是开拓鼎建，规模宽广。"后历经数次修葺，现存建筑为清光绪年间知县张炳焘主持营建。

内乡县衙建筑群的整体格局、形制、规模是按堪舆学的八卦方位及其含义进行设计的，反映了封建时期官署衙门左尊右卑、左文右武和前衙后邸的建筑规制。它是研究封建社会县级政府职官和机构设置、职权、典章制度、衙署形制的重要建筑。

内乡县衙二堂

内乡县衙菊潭坊

内乡县衙仪门

Located on the Eastern Avenue of the town of Neixiang County, the south-facing government office was built in the Qing Dynasty (1644 ~ 1911 AD) and covers over 20,000 sq. m. On the central axis are a screen wall, Xuanhua Archway, the main gate, the main hall, the second hall and the third hall. These are flanked by over 260 houses.

宝轮寺塔

金

The pagoda of Baolun Temple

宝轮寺塔位于三门峡市陕州故城东南隅宝轮寺旧址上。宝轮寺塔原名为宝轮寺三圣舍利宝塔，俗称“蛤蟆塔”，因在其周围拍掌或击石，回音似蛤蟆鸣叫而得名，是目前我国现存古代四大回音建筑之一。

宝轮寺塔坐北向南，为方形十三级叠涩密檐式砖塔。平面近似正方形，高度为27.2米，系用长36厘米、宽17厘米、厚5.5厘米青灰砖三顺一丁垒砌而成，整个塔身自下而上逐层收分，每层高度均匀递减，外轮廓呈抛物线形，各层檐上均无平座。自第一层塔身以上，每层辟圆券真门或设佛龛、窗洞等。每层檐部均由塔壁上砌出拔檐砖一层，其上砌棱角相错的菱角砖二层，再上砌出五层或七层、八层、九层叠涩砖，檐之上部砌反叠涩砖五层。塔心室结构奇巧，第二至第六层塔心室为正方形，室顶均用叠涩砖和菱角砖砌成四角攒尖形藻井，塔心室壁上设有脚蹬，可蹬至塔顶。每层外檐四角用木质角梁，梁头呈三角形，梁头下装有风铎。塔刹基座为石质莲花形，其上置五重相轮和宝瓶。

根据清光绪十七年（1891年）《陕州直隶州志》载：“寺建于唐代，塔建于金大定年间。”“宝轮寺，州东南隅。唐僧道秀建，金僧智秀复置砖塔。”在塔的第二层嵌一长方形石刻塔铭，上刻“三圣舍利宝塔”和“金大定十六年四月五日起塔，十七年五月八日竣工”等字样。据此可知，塔建成于金大定十七年（1177年），至今已有八百多年的历史。

宝轮寺塔局部

Located west of Sanliqiao Village, Sanmenxiao City, the pagoda was built in the 17th year of Dading (1177 AD) in the Jin Dynasty. Built of bricks, it measures 27.20 meters high, with 13 stories and densely set eaves.

宝轮寺塔

山陕甘会馆

第五批全国重点文物保护单位

清

Shanxi-Shaanxi-Gansu Guild Hall

山陕甘会馆位于开封市龙亭区徐府街北侧。会馆建于清乾隆年间，是由山西、陕西、甘肃三省商人集资兴建的同乡会馆。会馆的大部分建筑早已移作他用，现仅存中轴线建筑和唱堂会的东西跨院。建筑坐北朝南，南北长88.44米、东西宽42米，面积3714.48平方米。会馆采取四合院的建筑布局，最南端为邻街照壁，向北依次有戏楼、牌楼、拜殿；两侧的建筑有左右掖门、垂花门、钟楼、鼓楼、厢房、东西跨院等。

照壁高8.6米、长16.5米、厚0.65米，正背两面有砖雕人物、花果、山水、鸟兽等精美图案，背面当中镶嵌二龙戏珠石雕图案。牌楼为三间六柱五楼式，主楼高耸，次楼略低，正脊浮雕琉璃牡丹，中置方亭，两侧为狮子拥莲台、大象托宝瓶，鸱尾剑把上东书“日”，西写“月”；楼之正中南悬“大义参天”，北挂“流芳千古”匾额，次楼垫板上绘有八幅表现忠义仁勇

山陕甘会馆木牌楼

山陕甘会馆大殿

的故事图画，是河南现存清代牌楼中的珍品。大殿是会馆的主要建筑，由歇山、硬山、卷棚三座不同形式的殿顶毗连而成，面积540平方米，内外檐梁枋等部件均以木雕装饰，外部隔扇门上雕牡丹、莲花、水仙、石榴、梅花等四季花卉，台基置汉白玉栏杆，三面环护，把大殿烘托得更加宏伟壮观。

会馆的砖雕、石雕、木雕艺术成就最高，每座建筑的构件上，遍布雕饰，内容丰富，题材广泛，山水树木、花鸟虫鱼、珍禽异兽、亭台楼阁、人物故事、民间传说无不入画。雕刻技法分别采用了圆雕、半圆雕、高浮雕、多层次浮雕、悬雕等手法。雕刻细腻流畅，技艺娴熟高超，是研究美术史、民俗史的重要实物资料。

山陕甘会馆木雕

Located on the middle part of Xufu Street, Kaifeng City, the south-facing guild hall was built in the Qing Dynasty and covers a floor space of 3,870.29 sq. m. Main structures are: a big screen hall, a theatre, a bell-drum tower, a colored archway, a main hall, wing chambers and flanking courtyards.

康百万庄园

清

Kangbaiwan Grange

康百万庄园位于巩义市西北2公里的康店镇康店村（包括康北、康南）。是康氏家族的宅院。康氏创业于明，渐兴于清初，乾隆时进入全盛期，咸丰以后逐步没落，民国中期衰败。

康百万庄园是中原地区封建官僚地主的大型居住区，背依邙岭，门临洛水，依山就势，居高临下，临街建楼房，靠崖筑窑洞，四周修寨堡，濒河设码头，集农、官、商风格为一体，布局严谨，等级森严。庄园主要分布为十大部分：寨上住宅区、寨下住宅区、南大院（含书院等）、祠堂区、栈房区、作坊区、龙窝沟区、金谷寨、饲养区和花园区，辅以碑楼、牌坊、庙宇、碑林等。有三十三个庭院、五十三座楼房、九十七间平舍、七十三孔窑洞，总计五百七

康百万庄园全景

十一间，建筑面积64300平方米。

康百万庄园砖雕门楼

寨上住宅区南北长83米、东西宽73米。筑于邙山半腰，为寨堡式建筑群。由30余米长的寨门洞进入寨上，门洞及寨堡四周皆以青石、青砖垒砌。寨墙高12～15米，墙筑有城垛。上宅区由两个建筑群体组成，东西路以北有五个院落，皆坐北向南；路南有两个院落，皆坐西面东。北五院，又称“芝兰茂”或“功德窑”院。前窄后宽，前后院以月亮门隔开。前后院西崖共建六孔砖券窑，窑门额均雕刻不同纹饰的门罩（仿古建筑的倒挂楣）。前院一窑为磨房窑，二窑为厨房窑，三窑为库房窑。后院四窑为账房窑，五窑为功德窑，六窑为医诊窑。窑洞均为两层，青砖券砌，内

康百万庄园院落

康百万庄园正房

设木棚，中设木雕落地罩，里间设置木梯。尤其是第五窑，不仅窑中的木罩雕刻精细，人物花鸟鱼虫生动多变，而且外间的两壁上镶嵌着当时名流的书法，真、草、隶、篆各有千秋，亦称“石屏窑”。

庄园中各个庭院建筑形制基本属于封闭型两进式四合院，但又具有园林、官府的一些特点，院落之间既各成体系，又互相联系；前院采用古代园林传统的障景法设计，以假山、曲廊、透明墙和葡萄、石榴、竹子等增加层次，达到移步换景的艺术效果，侧门通各院；后院则用衬景法，以小衬大，以幽深衬开阔，通过狭窄的过道进入庭院，豁然开朗，欲扬先抑，是18、19世纪华北黄土高原封建堡垒式建筑的代表。

Located at Kangnan Village, Gongyi City, the grange was built in the late Ming Dynasty and early Qing Dynasty. Covering about 64,300 sq. m, it consists of 33 courtyards, which are divided into six parts-living quarters, workshops, warehouses, livestock quarters, Jin'gu Village and a shrine.

天宁寺三圣塔

第五批全国重点文物保护单位

金

Sansheng Pagoda of Tianning Temple

天宁寺三圣塔

天宁寺三圣塔创建于金大定十一年（1171年），坐落在沁阳市城内东南隅。

天宁寺始建于隋，原名长寿寺，唐代改名为大云寺，并在寺后建木楼阁，金大定年间更名为天宁寺，并在唐代木楼阁处修塔。寺院早废，唯塔独存。

三圣塔平面为方形，塔门南向，由基座、塔身、塔刹三部分组成。是一座叠涩密檐式十三级砖塔，总高32.76米。石造回廊式基座边长12.24米、高5.6米。基座南面开一券门，门楣上方有青石题额“中天一柱”，为清怀庆府知府张曾羽题。基座以上内收呈须弥座，再上即为塔身。塔外形仿唐，内部结构又似宋代做法，每层平面为正方形，四壁等分，无分毫之差。在所有的金代砖塔中，唯此塔保留有回廊。第一层塔身四面设门，施隐窗，在普拍枋以上设置砖砌一斗三升斗栱承托撩檐枋，枋上为出檐的叠涩砖。转角之上以圆雕力士承托塔之四角。各层檐角均设木制角梁，上悬风铎。各级塔体与每层出檐自下而上高度递减，宽度亦逐级收敛，使整体外轮廓呈抛物线形。塔刹由相轮、宝瓶、宝珠构成，十三天相轮内部中空为天宫，下部相轮四向开方口。宝瓶、宝珠为生铁铸造，分块箍合，由中心柱将塔刹上下连为一体。

三圣塔使用了砖、木、石、铁等材料，石造基座，塔身和地宫为砖木结合。无论是塔身的条砖、气窗风洞的栱砖，还是密檐上的菱角砖、三角砖、楔形砖、画像砖等均为模制，按照设计烧制而成，未用刀砍和锯割，故有“三圣塔地接天，建塔不用刀砍砖”之说。空腹铁质宝瓶实为天宫，这在古塔中独有。唐大足元年（701年）刻立的“大云寺皇帝圣祚之碑”，详细记载了河内郡王武懿宗奉诏改寺名的原因，有较高的史料价值。塔内还保存有金代建塔题记“舜都栖岩寺髑髅和尚铭”和六处一佛二菩萨石刻造像。

Located on Dengta Street, Qinyang City, this brick pagoda started to be built in the 11th year of Dading (1171 AD) in the Jin Dynasty. Measuring 29.35 meters high, it has a square cross-section, 13 stories and close eaves.

妙乐寺塔

第五批全国重点文物保护单位

五代

The pagoda of Miaole Temple

妙乐寺塔

妙乐寺塔位于武陟县城西南7.5公里古怀城遗址上。

塔始建于唐，后周显德二年（955年）重修。该塔原名真身舍利塔。据后周重建碑载：为瘗藏佛祖舍利灵骨，建宝塔一十九所，妙乐寺塔其一也，序列第十五。

妙乐寺塔为十三级密檐叠涩式方形砖塔，内部中空，底面边长9米、通高34.19米。塔门拱券形，南向。塔身自下而上每层高度均匀递减，塔檐逐渐内收，外轮廓呈优美的抛物线形。各层造型基本一致，唯有第二层檐部用砖砌出，再用泥抹就山花蕉叶三十一朵；第九层南面辟门，门侧置一碑，记述清代献佛之事。塔身四角有陶质模印力士八尊，经考证为清代之造像。塔体四面辟有数目不等的佛龛，内供佛像。该塔建筑风格颇具唐风，其檐部曲线及山花蕉叶的做法，在唐以后的砖塔中较为罕见，故此塔为唐塔向宋塔嬗递的特例。塔刹为铜制鎏金，高6.74米，由须弥座、七级相轮、宝华盖、水烟、仰月、三重宝珠、刹尖组成。须弥座平面呈正方形，由下枭、束腰、上枭及山花蕉叶组装而成。须弥座外表铸成火焰形透空花纹，座本身不承重，中心耸立的刹柱承担了整个刹身的重量。刹柱为木制，外套铸铁管，管头相接处制成坡口，互相扣合，防雨水流入。刹柱上四根铁链，系于塔顶四角，由四尊鎏金铜狮镇压。塔刹所有构件都是一次浇铸成型，没有焊口和铆钉，实为全国古塔中之珍品。

塔前有后周、宋、元、明、清碑刻二十余通，塔东北方有宋太平兴国六年（981年）刻立的石经幢，高约7米，由十三节组成，幢体刻“武陟县祉邑降魔大隋求经幢”。另据《资治通鉴》载，重修妙乐寺塔时正是后周限制佛教发展、大拆佛寺之时，因“敕额”而得以重修。故该塔对研究佛教史有着独特的价值。

Located at Zhang Village, Wuzhi County, this brick pagoda was built in the 3rd year of Guangshun (953 AD) in the Later Zhou Dynasty during the Five Dynasties period. Measuring 30 meters high, it has a square cross-section, 13 stories and close eaves.

嘉应观

第五批全国重点文物保护单位

清 Jiaying Taoist Temple

嘉应观位于武陟县城东南13公里的杨庄村南，为宫、庙、衙三体合一的清代建筑群。

嘉应观始建于清雍正元年（1723年）。康熙六十年（1721年）黄河四次决口于武陟，时雍亲王胤禛督办河工。胤禛登基后，立“御坝”碑于大坝上，敕建“淮黄诸河龙王庙”祭祀河神，封赏治河功臣。

嘉应观占地一百四十亩，建筑五十座，分南北两大院。北院中部为祭祀河神、巡河行宫建筑群。中轴线依次有山门、御碑亭、严殿、大王殿、恭仪亭、禹王阁；两侧对称有掖门、御马亭、钟楼、鼓楼、更衣殿、龙王殿、风神殿、雨神殿。东西跨院为河台、道台衙署。南院原有戏楼、牌坊，观西原有陈公祠，后塌毁。

山门面阔三间，进深二间，单檐歇山顶，孔雀蓝琉璃瓦覆顶。檐下施五踩斗栱，里外檐有精致的彩绘图案。明间为青石拱券门，券石上浮雕龙、云、水图案，上方有雍正帝亲书“敕建嘉应观”石刻匾额。两次间辟石雕月亮形假窗。山门两侧设置硬山式掖门。门外列石狮一对。御碑亭平面为六角形，立于六角形须

嘉应观山门

嘉应观御碑亭

弥座台基之上。台基高0.82米，南北设五级垂带式踏垛。碑亭设六柱，辟六门，檐下置五踩重昂斗栱。上檐为圆伞形结构，下檐为六角形，均以黄琉璃瓦覆盖。亭内立御制大铜牌，高4.3米、宽0.95米、厚0.24米，碑首浮雕三条龙环绕着“御制”二字，碑身四边沿雕有二十四条龙和回纹花边。碑座为一铜制蛟龙，身长1.15、高0.6米。碑文为雍正帝亲自撰文并书丹，内容叙述了他关心黄河水患，修筑堤防，修庙祭祀河神，以靖国安民为念。对研究当时治水安澜有重要的史料价值。在铸造上，采用了铁胎铜面、铜铁合一的铸造工艺，这种特殊铸造工艺，在我国冶炼史和铸造史上应是一个奇迹。碑周雕龙，底座为蛟，工艺精湛，为全国罕见。

大王殿为重檐歇山回廊式建筑。面阔七间，进深四间，殿顶覆以孔雀蓝琉璃瓦。檐部用五踩重昂斗栱，彩绘明丽。殿内天花藻井彩绘六十五幅龙凤图。殿内正中挂“钦赐润毓”金牌，经考证“润毓”是雍正帝赐予在武陟堵口的都御史牛钮的封号，牛钮是雍正帝叔父，曾是嘉应观首任主持。

嘉应观雍正铁胎铜面御碑细部

Located at Yangzhuang, Wuzhi County, the temple started to be built in the 2nd year of Emperor Yongzheng' s reign (1724 AD) in the Qing Dynasty. It covers 21,000 sq. m. The stele pavilion on the central axis houses a 4.3-meter-high iron stele coated with copper, which was made by imperial order in 1724.

小商桥

第五批全国重点文物保护单位

宋

Xiaoshang Bridge

小商桥位于临颍县皇帝庙乡商桥村，南北跨于小商河（古颍河）上。

小商桥始建于隋开皇四年（584年），宋代大修，元大德年间重修，明正德年间整修，清康熙十四年（1675年）再度整修。桥主体结构为北宋早期风格。结构古朴，使用并列砌筑法，主拱与两侧小拱横券均用二十道拱石并列砌筑而成，拱券纵向使用腰铁加固。桥全长21.3米、宽6.45米，主拱券净跨度12.14米、矢高3.06米，矢跨之比近于1：4。小拱净跨度2.83米、矢高1.02米。桥拱、桥基、雁翅均用红砂岩砌成。东西券脸雕刻有动物花卉图案，主拱四角雕有金刚力士，力士作半蹲状，双手按膝，用肩膀扛起大桥。桥面用青石铺砌，共有青石望柱二十八根，柱头雕刻狮子、莲花、仙桃等；栏板二十六块，雕刻着记载当时各界捐款修桥事宜的题记和水、鱼、龟、牡丹、莲花、窗棂等图案，刻工精细，造型生动。

小商桥现存构件多为宋、金遗物，券面及栏板、望柱等部分，均为宋代以来的精美石刻艺术品。

小商桥望柱柱头

小商桥

Located at Shangqiao Village, Linying County, the bridge was first built in the 4th year of Kaihuang (584 AD) in the Sui Dynasty, and rebuilt in the Song and Yuan dynasties. Its main structure is in the early Northern-Song-dynasty style. It is 21.30 meters long, 6.45 meters wide and 6.50 meters high, and paved with granite.

南阳知府衙门

第五批全国重点文物保护单位

清

The office of the prefect of Nanyang

南阳知府衙门位于南阳市民主街（原察院街）100号。

南阳知府衙门始建于元至元八年（1271年），坐北面南，南北长240米、东西宽150米，规模宏大，占地36000平方米。衙署建筑自南向北依次有照壁及两侧的召父坊、杜母坊、豫南首郡坊、大门和两侧的榜房、仪门、戒石坊、大堂、六部房、寅恭门、二堂、东西廊房、招稿房、书简房、内宅门、三堂、架阁库、府花园等。东侧建筑有申明亭、宾兴馆、衙神庙、萧曹庙、龙神庙、税课司、经历司、军厅、粮厅、军粮二募外藩以及东花厅（包括桃李馆、桂香室、虚日轩等）；西侧建筑有旌善亭、财神庙、监仓和狱神庙、照磨所、理刑厅以及西花厅（包括师竹轩、对月轩、爱莲堂、槐荫

南阳知府衙门仪门

南阳知府衙门大堂

静舍等）。此外还有东西官邸、吏宅、军械库、马号和各色仓库等。

府衙现存明、清建筑一百四十余间。基本保留了明代建筑规制和清代建筑风格。其建筑特点一是主要建筑均使用斗栱，二是建筑形式为硬山式，三是大堂为使用功能所需要减掉了前排金柱，扩大了内部的空间，增强了大堂的威严气势。

Located west of Minzhu Street, Nanyang City, the office was first built in the 8th year of Zhiyuan (1271 AD) in the Yuan Dynasty, and renovated and expanded in the 5th year of Zhengtong (1440 AD). It covers 36,000 sq. m., retaining over 90 houses and the ancient integral layout.

潞泽会馆

第五批全国重点文物保护单位

清

Luze Guild Hall

潞泽会馆位于洛阳市九都东路北侧，濒临洛河。

潞泽会馆始建于清乾隆九年（1744年）。系山西潞安府（今长治市）、泽州府（今晋城市）两地商人集资所建，主要用于同乡商人传递信息和物资集散。整个建筑群层次分明，结构严谨，中轴线上建筑主要有舞楼、大殿、后殿，两侧建筑有钟、鼓楼，东、西穿房，东、西廊房，东、西配殿，西跨院等，占地面积15750平方米。舞楼既是戏台又是会馆的大门，面阔五间，进深三间，把前台的歇山式和后台的硬山式组合在一起，形成重檐歇山式。前后檐有十二根檐柱，柱顶石为成对的金睛兽、狮子、麒麟托着莲花瓣，之上为6米高的檐柱。檐下置五踩斗栱，雀替、小额枋、大额枋，平板枋上有八仙过海、龙穿牡丹等四层透雕图案。里外檐均饰彩绘。明间金柱上挂对联一副：“人为鉴即古为鉴且往观之，鼓尽神兼舞尽神必有以也。”舞楼东西各开一门，通过穿房与钟

潞泽会馆

潞泽会馆大殿

鼓楼连为一体。舞楼戏台宽敞可演各种文武戏，是河南最大的戏楼之一。

大殿为重檐歇山式建筑，绿琉璃瓦覆顶，面阔五间，进深五间，呈正方形，面积为594.55平方米。殿前有月台，面积129.79平方米，地面皆用青砖铺地，青石镶边，台前、左、右设置七级垂带式踏垛。大殿回廊计三十二根檐柱，柱高4.1米，径0.41米。金柱四根，全用通柱，柱高8.5米，直径0.42米，柱顶石有三层磉墩组合而成，上刻鸟、花、鹿、狮等。大殿采用减柱造，减去两根前金柱，加大使用面积。大梁长11.7米、直径0.54米、净跨度为11.54米。大梁上的二龙戏珠彩绘采用沥粉贴金工艺，在中原地区比较罕见。

潞泽会馆大殿内景

Located on Xin Street, Chanhe District, Luoyang City, the guild hall started to be built in the 9th year of Emperor Qianlong's reign (1744 AD) in the Qing Dynasty, with the donations made by merchants from Luding Prefecture (present-day Changzhi) and Zezhou Prefecture (present-day Jincheng County) in Shanxi Province. It covers 15, 750 sq. m. Main buildings on the central axis are: Wu Tower, Main hall and Back Hall.

大明寺

第五批全国重点文物保护单位

元至清

Daming Temple

大明寺位于济源市轵城镇。

大明寺原为西汉初诸侯轵王祖庙，北宋时改为寺院，元至元十四年（1277年）重建，后代屡有增建和重建，现存元、明、清各代建筑十三座四十一间。

大明寺坐北朝南，总体平面呈长方形，南北长149米、东西宽137米，总面积20000多平方米。依中轴线而建，左右对称，依次分别为山门、金刚殿、阎君殿、配殿、中佛殿、伽蓝殿、僧房、后佛殿。

山门，面阔三间，进深六架椽，前后设廊，系明代单檐硬山式木构建筑。中佛殿为寺内主体建筑，重建于元至元年间，面阔三间，进深三间，单檐歇山式。前后檐柱有明显的柱生起和柱侧脚，柱头有卷杀。平面布局为室内单槽，减柱造。梁架、斗栱，柱枋等仍为元代构件，甚至柱侧脚、柱生起也保持着元代建筑风格。此殿为河南省建筑结构纯度较高的四座元代单体建筑之一，具有很高的历史、科学和艺术价值。伽蓝殿，面阔三间，进深四架椽，单檐悬山式木结构建筑。檐下施单昂三踩斗栱，明间两朵，次间一朵。

大明寺中佛殿

大明寺山门

内部梁架为彻上明造，施五架梁。此殿为明成化六年（470年）所建的大式木构建筑。后佛殿，面阔三间，进深三间，单檐悬山式木结构建筑。前檐柱为小八角形石柱，柱头有卷杀。内部梁架为彻上明造，结构为七架梁，脊檩和攀间置隔架科斗栱。前檐斗栱为五踩双下昂计心造，昂嘴刻成三幅云或龙首状。后檐斗栱为三踩单下昂。殿内彩绘保存较好，色泽鲜艳，颇具地方特色，是研究清代中原地区彩绘艺术的实物资料。特别是斗栱上使用替木，是清代地方建筑手法袭古的实证。

此外，寺内还有元《大明寺恩公勤德之碑》、明《重修大明寺前殿之记》、石狮等附属文物二十余件（通），以及树冠高大的千年梭罗树，弥足珍贵。

Located at Zhicheng Village, Jiyuan City, the temple was founded in the Northern Song Dynasty (960 ~ 1127 AD). Remaining buildings are Middle Buddha Hall and Back Buddha Hall, the former dating from the Yuan Dynasty.

奉仙观

金至清

Fengxian Taoist Temple

奉仙观，位于济源市北海区荆梁北街。因观中主殿三清大殿用荆木作梁，故又称“荆梁观”。

奉仙观于唐垂拱元年（685年）创建，为历代道士修真之所，唐代道家二鲁真人（鲁希言、鲁和光）、宋代贺兰栖真曾先后修道于此。后代屡有增建和重建，现存金、明、清各代建筑山门、玉皇殿、三清大殿、厢房等十座三十间。建筑坐北朝南，总体为长方形，长90.5米、宽45.5米。

山门，面阔三间，进深二间，系清代单檐悬山式建筑。明间置实榻门，次间装八边形斜方格窗，梁架采用中柱式，前后为对称的双步梁和单步梁。门两边为悬山式垂花门。玉皇殿，面阔三间，进深四架椽，系明代单檐悬山式木构建筑。其主体建筑三清大殿重建于金大定二十四年（1184年），面阔五间，进深七架椽，单檐悬山造。建筑平面布局为减柱造，仅施两根后金柱。是

奉仙观三清大殿

奉仙观玉皇殿

中国减柱造建筑的最典型作品。檐柱为硕大的小八角形石柱，覆盆式柱头。阑额断面狭而高，不出头，额枋上未施普拍枋。前檐下置五铺作单抄单下昂，补间铺作在花头子上使用真昂。后檐设四铺作单抄。梁架采用荆木、柿木做梁，桑木、枣木为柱的做法，甚是奇特。整体木结构保留着标准的金代建筑手法。观内还存有唐《太上老君石像碑》和北宋《章圣皇帝御制诗碑记》等珍贵碑刻。

Located on Jingliang Avenue, Jiyuan City, the temple was founded in the 1st year of Chuigong (685 AD) in the Tang Dynasty. Remaining buildings are: Main Gate, Yuhuang Hall and Sanqing Hall, the last one dating from the Jin Dynasty.

荆紫关古建筑群

第五批全国重点文物保护单位

清

Ancient architectural complex in Jingziguan

荆紫关古建筑群位于淅川县境内的丹江上游，鄂、豫、陕三省的交界处。

荆紫关自古以来就是险关隘口，更因丹江航运的发展，逐渐成为北通古都长安、南达江汉平原的重要码头，所以历代在这里都有建制。秦汉时称“草桥关”，南宋时因荆紫关多荆花、荆籽，由此改称为“荆籽关”，清朝时改“籽”为“紫”，取“紫气东来”之意，遂改为荆紫关。明成化十年（1474年）在此设置巡检司、营千总镇守，清时在荆紫关设置副将、都司等军事长官，作为一个特殊地域而综合管理。清嘉庆七年（1802年）在荆紫关设协镇都督府（府台衙门），清道光十二年（1832年）设分防县丞。明清时荆紫关达到了空前的繁荣，在长期大量收购、贩运、销售货物过程中，逐渐形成了三大公司、八大帮会、十三大骡马店、二十四大商行，许多有成就的客商因各自商业竞争和周转货物的需要在荆紫关建立了宫房和会馆，较大的有平浪宫、禹王宫、

荆紫关古街道

荆紫关禹王宫

万寿宫、山陕会馆、清真寺等，形成了南北长约2.5公里的古街道。现存二千二百多间房舍和七百多间店铺均为明清建筑。临街门面房，木板嵌面，昼启夜闭，每个店铺里面多是一进院落，两侧有对称的厢房。院院相连，门面房顶都有两米长的封火墙相隔，屋脊上多有花鸟人物作为装饰。历史上的荆紫关是一座昼启夜闭的商业镇，关门位于街道的最南端，1914年重建。

平浪宫始建于明崇祯年间（1628～1644年），坐东面西，有戏楼、门楼、钟鼓楼、前殿、过厅、后殿、厢房等三十五间。万

荆紫关关门

荆紫关平浪宫

寿宫位于南街，坐东面西，是浙江商人集资兴建的，占地八亩，现存宫房三栋二十间。禹王宫位于中街，坐东面西，临街而建，为湖南、广东商人共同筹建。现有宫房三栋九间，即正房、前殿、后殿、厢房等，占地十八亩。协镇都督府（府台衙门）位于古镇南1000米处，有东西城楼、城门、大堂、审衙、厢房等，占地十余亩，现仅存大门、审衙、厢房，占地六亩。法海禅寺在镇北6公里处，唐高宗仪凤二年（677年）西峰禅师所建，占地百余亩，明代重修。现有前殿、中殿、后殿、厢房、藏经楼、文殊殿、普贤殿等建筑。此外，还有关门、马饮桥、青石桥、城隍庙等古建筑。

Located in Jingziguan Town, Xichuan County, at the juncture of three provinces-Hubei, Henan and Shaanxi, the complex dates from the Qing Dynasty (1644 ~ 1911 AD). The town was an important port in the upper reaches of Dan River. In the Qing Dynasty it boasted a 5-meter-wide commercial street extending 2.5 km from north to south. There remain over 2,200 houses and over 700 shops dating from the Ming and Qing dynasties.

慈胜寺

第五批全国重点文物保护单位

元

Cisheng Temple

慈胜寺位于温县番田镇大吴村。

慈胜寺始建于唐代贞观年间，历经唐、宋，毁于兵燹。元代至元年间（1335～1340年）在原基础上重建。全寺共四进院落，五座殿宇，依次为山门、天王殿、大雄殿、毗庐殿、延寿殿，两旁有配殿、厢房，共一百余间，占地近百亩。现仅存山门、天王殿、大雄殿三座建筑，虽经历代维修，仍保持元代结构和建筑手法。

慈胜寺坐北面南，现占地7200平方米，分东院和西院两部分。东院存放散存石刻，西院有三座殿宇，四周环以苍松翠柏。山门面阔三间，进深四架椽，单檐悬山顶，灰筒板瓦覆盖。明间置两扇实榻大门，门前设垂带式踏垛四级。天王殿，面阔三间，进深四架椽，单檐歇山顶，绿琉璃瓦覆盖。檐部用重唇板瓦，檐下用四铺作单下昂，昂下刻出假华头子，补间铺作明次间各一朵，栌斗做成瓜棱形。檐柱径与高的比例为一比七。柱侧脚和生起比

慈胜寺大雄宝殿

慈胜寺天王殿

较明显，柱头有卷杀。殿内东西山墙原有精美的彩色壁画，现仅存西墙的四大天王像，画面通高3.7米、宽5.2米，整幅面积约19平方米。绘画线条粗犷，手法纯熟，有唐、宋遗风，是研究元代绘画艺术的宝贵资料。大雄殿面阔三间，进深六架椽，单檐歇山顶，斗栱结构为五铺作，单抄单下昂，重栱计心造。四翼角向上反翘，造型宏伟，气势壮观，为中原地区元代建筑之典范。殿内尚存元代壁画3平方米，内容为花卉、楼阁等，绘画笔繁色丽，细腻工整。正门上方悬挂“风”字形匾额，制作于元至元五年（1339年），上书“大雄之殿”四字，素有“银钩铁划”之誉。

寺内保存有后晋天福二年（937年）雕凿的《佛顶尊胜陀罗尼经》石经幢，高5.4米，用十七块石材雕刻而成，分上中下三部共十五层。上部七层雕火焰宝珠、仰莲、城堡、宝盖等。中部一层高1.32米，为八棱形石经幢，上刻《佛顶尊胜陀罗尼经序》全文，字迹清晰，书写工整。下部七层雕莲座、束腰须弥座和造像龛，雕刻精湛，造型生动，为五代经幢之珍品。寺内存有元代、明代大铁钟两口及历代石刻五十余通（块）。

Located on North Street, Dawu Village, Wen County, the temple was first built in the Tang Dynasty, and was renovated many times later. Remaining building are: Main Gate, Tianwang Hall and Sakyamuni Hall, which retain Yuan-dynasty architectural structures and techniques.

汤阴岳飞庙

第五批全国重点文物保护单位

明

Yuefei Temple in Tangyin

汤阴岳飞庙

汤阴岳飞庙位于汤阴县城内。今址为明景泰元年（1450年）重建，清代续修，现存大部为明代建筑。

岳飞庙坐北面南，南北长109米、东西宽57.8米，占地面积6300平方米，建筑面积2100平方米。主要建筑有精忠坊、山门、御碑亭、正殿、岳母刺字祠、孝娥祠、岳云祠、四子祠、三代祠、东西厢房等。

精忠坊是岳飞庙的大门，为三间六柱品字形木结构牌楼，上悬明孝宗手书“宋岳忠武王庙”匾额。两侧八字墙上用青石镌出“忠”、“孝”两个大字，字高1.8米，遒劲端庄，格外醒目。山门古朴典雅，檐下悬匾联，上书“精忠报国”、“浩然正气”、“庙食千秋”，明柱上嵌楹联：“存巍然正气，壮故乡山河”。

寺内仪门前两道碑垣，将前

汤阴岳飞庙大殿

院分为三部分，中间为甬道，东西各一小院，院中各有一亭，东曰“肃瞻”，西名“觐光”。在林立的碑刻中，有明清帝王的谒庙诗篇，有各代重修扩建古庙胜迹的纪实，更多的是历代文人贤达颂扬英雄的诗词歌赋。碑碣共有三百余通，笔体有真、草、隶、篆等，其中较为著名的有明代关中布政使吴钟英手书“文官不爱钱，武官不惜死，不患天下不太平”，并附曰“瞻拜者省之”。明代中宣大夫、太常少卿兼翰林院侍读学士董其昌手书《重修宋岳忠武王庙碑记》，概述了的岳飞的丰功伟绩。岳飞亲笔《满江红》和前、后《出师表》更是书法史的重要资料。

大殿面阔五间，进深三间，单檐硬山顶，高10米。殿内外悬挂有包括明太祖、孝宗，清乾隆、光绪、慈禧等帝王将相亲书匾额三十八幅，著名的有“乃武乃文”、“故乡俎豆”、“忠灵未泯”、“百战神威”、“乾坤正气”等匾额。殿内岳飞塑像居中端坐，帅盔金甲，气宇轩昂。岳飞塑像后背上方悬挂贴金巨匾“还我河山”。寝殿面阔五间，进深一间，硬山式建筑。檐下悬“精忠贯日”匾。寝殿左右为岳云、岳雷、岳霖、岳震、岳霆及孝娥祠、三代祠。

汤阴岳飞庙大殿内景

The temple is located on Yuemiao Street in the southwest corner of the town of Tangyin. The time when it was first built is unknown. It was rebuilt in the 1st year of Jingtai (1540 AD) in the Ming Dynasty in memory of Yuefei (1103 ~ 1142 AD), a famous Song-dynasty military commander who fought against Jin invaders. It covers a floor space of about 4,300 sq. m.

安阳天宁寺塔

第五批全国重点文物保护单位

五代至清

The pagoda of Tianning Temple in Anyang

安阳天宁寺塔

安阳天宁寺塔位于安阳市大寺前街，古天宁寺院内。

塔始建于五代后周广顺二年（952年），宋、元、明、清历代均有修葺。为砖木结构密檐式塔，塔体平面为八角形，南向，通高38.65米，共分五层，由塔基、塔身、塔刹三部分组成。塔身自下而上逐层外扩，塔檐也随塔身逐层外展，形成上大下小伞状的优美外观，这种造型在全国是独一无二的，是研究古代建筑以及建筑力学、美学的重要资料。

塔基分为两层，下层为青砖八角形须弥座，上层为七层砖雕莲瓣组成的莲花宝座。须弥座与莲花座之间有一周缠枝西番莲花带，由南边蹬十八级台阶进入塔门。塔身第一层高10.5米，四正面为拱券门，南门为实用门，门额上刻“文峰耸秀”四个大字。其余三门皆为装饰性假门，假门为砖质隔扇门，隔心雕有盘龙、璎珞等图案。四隅为方形直棂假窗，窗框上有砖雕缠枝花卉。八根倚柱为砖砌圆形龙柱，柱上浮雕腾龙和卷云。八面门窗之上部各有一幅高浮雕图案，内容是释迦牟尼降生、修行、说法、涅槃、侍佛和南海观音等佛传故事，形

安阳天宁寺塔浮雕

象生动古朴、端庄丰满，具有晚唐造像遗风。外檐由砖雕斗栱承托出檐，斗栱为五铺作单栱出双抄，补间铺作一、四两层出45度斜栱，三、五两层出30度斜栱。塔体内部结构为八角形筒状塔心室，亦分五层，每层顶部用砖雕斗栱承托，再由青砖叠涩成平座，中间用“井”字形木架组成上下相通的方形孔洞。每层内壁凿有佛龛，内供佛像。各层均有四个通风拱券门洞，层层错置。梯级为壁内折上式，经过旋转梯级可达塔顶平台。塔刹为一高10.8米的喇嘛式塔，八角须弥座刹基，覆钵式刹身，刹顶为铜质十三天。塔刹周围有一平台，登临可饱览安阳古城风光。塔旁有天宁寺照壁、歇山顶大殿和弥陀龛等。

Located in Tianning Temple on Dasiqian Street, Anyang City, the pagoda was built in the 2nd year of Guangshun (952 AD) in the Later Zhou Dynasty. With a total height of 38.65 meters, this five-story octagon pagoda was built of bricks in the pavilion style.

明福寺塔

宋

The pagoda of Mingfu Temple

明福寺塔位于滑县老城明福寺旧址上。

明福寺塔为七级楼阁式砖塔，通高43米，底面直径11米，平面呈八角形，坐北面南，整座塔由塔基、塔身、塔刹三部分组成。塔基用青石砌筑，高2.4米，南面有石台阶和平台。塔身及塔刹由七十余种不同规格的灰砖砌成。第一层高6.1米，南面辟拱券门，自普拍枋以下依次隐刻有素面横披、折叠帷幔幕纹，纹样细腻，线条顺畅。塔身通体嵌砌方砖，砖面作圆龛，龛内雕刻佛像。转角处有八根倚柱，柱身以仰俯莲瓣分成竹节状，为其他砖塔所罕见。檐下置五铺作双抄偷心造斗栱承托出檐，每面补间铺作四朵。铺作之上刻仰莲一周，再上为砖制椽子、飞椽、望板、瓦件，滴水造型为重唇板瓦。二至七层做法相似，四正面辟门，五层与七层四隅面分别施直棂假窗。檐下置普拍枋，其上做规整的五铺作双抄斗栱承托出檐枋、椽子、飞椽。第七层叠涩砖承托出檐，平座遍用栌斗支撑，顶层角梁悬挂八个风铎。塔身每层各角均以仰覆莲浮雕砖组成精美的竹节状倚柱，檐部的重唇板瓦和素面瓦当等为典型的宋代早期风格；外壁镶嵌的五十多种佛像砖(共一千二百三十四块)，人物造型具有唐代遗风。

塔内结构与外檐分层相同，原有木质楼板现已不存，形成八角筒状的空腹结构。梯道砌筑在塔壁内，盘旋而上可至塔顶。顶置桃形塔刹。

明福寺塔

明福寺塔砖雕佛像

Located in Guan Town, Hua County, the pagoda was first built in the Tang Dynasty, and was rebuilt in the 11th year of Hongzhi (1498 AD) in the Ming Dynasty. With a total height of 43 meters, this seven-story octagon pagoda was built of bricks in the pavilion style.

会善寺

第五批全国重点文物保护单位

元至清

Huishan Temple

会善寺位于登封市西北6公里太室山南麓积翠峰下。

北魏孝文帝时在此处建离宫，后改作精舍，隋开皇年间定名会善寺，唐代极盛。著名天文学家僧一行出家此寺，并与元同法师共创琉璃戒坛。

寺院现分西院和东院两部分。西院为常住院，以山门、月台、大雄殿等古建筑构成一条南北中轴线，两侧为配房建筑，对称分布。东院为斋堂院。

会善寺大殿为元代建筑，面阔五间，进深三间，单檐歇山顶，面积280.77平方米。砖木结构，檐下斗栱粗大朴实，昂嘴仿宋批竹昂的做法。昂的后尾很大，是卡接的假昂尾，没有宋代昂的实用价值高。角梁的后尾嵌入殿角的垂柱上面，不与相邻斗栱后尾互相交叉，梁架带有宋代月梁形的做法，但表皮比较粗糙，像剥去树皮经过彩绘加工而使用的原木，梁柱均有同样特点。

会善寺大雄宝殿

会善寺山门

会善寺有四座清代砖塔及大量石刻，特别是寺东南500米处的一座琉璃塔和两座楼阁式砖塔。琉璃塔建于清乾隆六十一年（1722年），由黄、绿、白和天蓝四种颜色的琉璃砖组成，呈六角五层密檐式，塔身与第一层塔檐衔接处饰五踩斗栱一周，塔身雕绘各种仙草花卉、牧牛、狮子等图案。楼阁式砖塔在琉璃塔北50米处的柏树林中，左为“林上大尊塔”，右为“丛首杰尊塔”，两塔相距4米，均建于清雍正八年（1730年）。塔为六角三层楼阁式，塔身雕有仿木门窗、花草图案，造型别致。寺内散存的东魏、北齐时期石刻造像，唐、明、清代碑碣以及明代铁钟等，亦有较高的艺术价值和历史价值。

会善寺大雄宝殿前廊结构和前檐平栱

Located at the foot of Jicui Peak on the southern side of Songshan Mountain, north of Dengfeng City, the temple dates back to the period from the Yuan Dynasty to the Qing Dynasty (1271 ~ 1911 AD). Main remaining buildings are: Main Gate, Sakyamuni Hall, and the side gates flanking the main gate. The hall was built in the Yuan Dynasty.

永泰寺塔

第五批全国重点文物保护单位

唐

The pagoda of Yongtai Temple

永泰寺塔位于登封市区西北11公里的永泰寺村。

永泰寺塔为唐代密檐式砖塔，平面呈正方形，底面边长5.05米、通高24米。塔身南面辟券门，塔身之上为十一层密檐，各檐外轮廓的连线呈明显的抛物线形。塔室内部为方形空筒。塔的最上部是由仰莲、五重相轮等组成的宝刹。塔体外敷白灰皮保护，造型柔和秀丽。均庵主塔位于唐塔西南部，始建于金大安元年（1209年），为四角二级砖塔，高3米余，塔后壁镶嵌有《嵩山永禅寺均庵主塔记》塔铭，记载了金大安、明昌年间的一些史实。肃然无为普同之塔位于唐塔东北约150米处的阜丘上，始建于明崇祯十一年（1638年），是一座喇嘛式砖塔，高约6.18米。基座是六角形台墩，塔身似瓶形，正面是一合石雕实榻门，门上方镶嵌塔铭。塔刹由五层相轮、石柱、覆莲、仰莲和火焰宝珠组成。

永泰寺塔

永泰寺始建于北魏孝明帝正光二年（521年），因南朝梁武帝萧衍之女明练公主和北魏宣武帝元恪永泰公主在此出家，而始称明练寺。唐神龙二年（706年）更名永泰寺。是我国佛教禅宗派的第一座尼僧寺院，在宗教史方面占有重要地位。永泰寺塔与均庵主塔、肃然无为普同之塔及碑刻都是永泰寺的附属建筑。

Located at Yongtaisi Village, Dengfeng City, the pagoda was built in the Tang Dynasty (618 ~ 907 AD). It is a single-story brick pagoda, measuring 24 meters high, with close eaves and a square cross-section.

080

法王寺塔

第五批全国重点文物保护单位

唐

The pagoda of Fawang Temple

法王寺塔

法王寺塔位于登封市北5公里太室山南麓玉柱峰下的山坡台地上。

法王寺塔群南距法王寺院约210米，包括唐塔四座、元塔一座、清塔一座。其中法王寺大塔为密檐式砖塔，高约35米，高大雄伟，秀丽挺拔，为河南省三十多座唐塔中最高大的寺塔，也是全国著名的唐塔之一。

法王寺大塔周围有五座唐至清代砖塔。另一座唐塔为单层方形亭阁式砖塔，塔高约12米、边长4.4米，占地17.6平方米，塔身南面辟一拱券门，塔心室为方形。叠涩檐之上是砖砌仰莲塔刹，之上托云盘，石雕仰俯莲相扣，再上为宝珠，造型相当华丽。2000年4月对其地宫进行了发掘，发现地宫由宫道、隧道、宫室三部分组成。宫室为方形、直壁、四角攒尖顶式结构。宫室内出土珍贵文物二十余件。其中白釉细颈瓶、双系罐、黑釉瓷壶等，经鉴定为晚唐时期河北邢窑系产品。宫室砖砌地面，北半部有一坐坛，坛上为一趺坐真身坐像，虽然残损严重，但这是河南省发现的唯一一尊真身坐化像。对于考古学和宗教学研究都具有较高的价值。元、清两座砖塔，均用灰砖白灰砌筑而成。元塔“月庵海公圆净之塔”，元延三年（1316年）建，为密檐式六角七级仿木结构砖塔，是河南省现存元塔中保存最完整、雕刻最华丽的一座。

法王寺二号塔地宫出土鎏金铜熏炉

法王寺二号塔地宫出土石迦陵频伽盒

Located at the southern foot of Taishi Mountain in Songshan Mountain, Dengfeng City, the temple was built in the 14th year of Yongping (71 AD) in the Eastern Han Dynasty. It contains four Tang-dynasty pagodas, one Yuan-dynasty pagoda and one Qing-dynasty pagoda. The pagoda of the Fawang Temple is the most famous of them. Built of bricks, this 35-meter-high pagoda is hollow with close eaves.

中岳庙

第五批全国重点文物保护单位

清

Zhongyue Temple

中岳庙位于登封市区东3公里中岳庙村。

中岳庙原名太室祠，始建于秦（公元前221～前207年），是历代帝王或大臣封禅或祭祀中岳山神的场所。现存建筑为明代和清顺治十年至乾隆五十一年（1653～1786年）按照官式建筑作法重修而成的。在我国“五岳”神庙中，中岳庙规模最大，中岳大殿是规格最高、面积最大的殿宇。

庙院南北长650米、东西宽166米，占地面积107900平方米，中轴建筑有中华门、遥参亭、天中阁、配天作镇坊、崇圣门、化三门、峻极门、嵩高峻极坊、中岳大殿、寝殿和御书楼，共七进十一层院落。依山而建，错落有致。中轴线东西侧有六座宫院，西侧自南而北为太尉宫、火神宫、祖师宫，东侧自南而北为行宫（遗址）、神州宫、小楼宫，现存古建筑五百一十四间。中岳庙是按照《清工部工程做法则例》在原有基础上重建或重修的官式建筑群。

中岳庙山门

中岳庙大殿

天中阁，原名“黄中楼”，是中岳庙原来的山门，明嘉靖四十一年（1562年）改建为天中阁，清代重修。高约7米，重檐歇山式。

中岳大殿，亦名“峻极殿”，明末火焚，清顺治十年（1653年）重建，乾隆年间多次重修，并饰彩绘。此殿面阔九间，进深五间，占地1205.12平方米，重檐庑殿式，黄琉璃瓦覆顶，上下檐分别施七踩斗栱和五踩斗栱，整个大殿外檐用斗二百攒，雄伟壮观，殿前筑一高约3米的石砌大月台，周围装有石雕栏杆。

寝殿，建于明成化庚子年（1480年），清乾隆元年（1736年）重修，面阔七间，进深三间，单檐歇山式，黄琉璃瓦覆顶，殿内镶满天花板，明间藻井画龙，次间画凤，为清代中期彩画。

庙内有汉代石翁仲、《中岳嵩高灵庙碑》和宋代四大铁人等。翁仲刻立于东汉安帝元初五年（118年）。《中岳嵩高灵庙碑》位于东岳台和南岳台之间的方亭内，刻立于北魏太安二年（456年），碑高2.8米、宽0.99米，额下有一直径约0.1米的透空圆洞，仿汉碑古制。碑文记载着中岳庙的变迁。宋代铁人立于古神库四角，宋英宗治平元年（1064年）铸造，高约3米，武士装束，气宇威严，握拳振臂，怒目挺胸，统称“守库铁人”。

中岳庙碑刻

中岳庙寝殿

中岳庙内宋代铁人

Located at the southern foot of Taishi Mountain, 4 km east of Dengfeng City, the temple dates from the Ming-and-Qing-dynasty period(1368 ~ 1911 AD), originally called Taizong Shrine. It covers over 100,000 sq. m., with a 650-meter-long central axis and 11 rows of courtyards.

百泉

第五批全国重点文物保护单位

明、清

Baiquan Spring

百泉，位于辉县市西北2.5公里百泉镇村。

百泉由苏门山和百泉湖构成，南北长约1100米、东西宽约640米。苏门山属太行山余脉，海拔184米，因其两峰对峙，山形似门，故名“苏门山”。山南麓是卫水源头——百泉湖，因其泉眼众多而得名。苏门山、百泉湖山水相映，久已闻名，《诗经》中就有歌颂百泉的诗句。《荀子·儒效》篇中有“武王伐纣，朝食于戚，暮宿于百泉”的记载。隋代为祭祀卫水之神而在百泉湖北岸建卫源庙，中轴线上有山门、拜亭、清辉殿、寝殿，两旁有钟鼓二楼、厢房。清辉殿面阔七间，进深三间，重檐歇山式，绿色琉璃瓦覆顶，尚存唐宋遗构，具有重要的历史与科学价值。

苏门山西侧的天爷庙，由七座明代无梁殿组成，为河南仅存的明代无梁殿建筑群。湖中清晖阁为面阔五间的重檐高阁。经历代增修添建，到清代乾隆年间，百泉已形成园中套园的大型园林式建筑，成为我国北方重要的古典园林之一。

百泉全景

百泉卫源庙

Located at Baiquan Village in the northwestern suburbs of Huixian County, the site dates from the Ming and Qing dynasties (1368 ~ 1911 AD). Dug in the Shang Dynasty, Baiquan Spring is the source of Wei River. Buildings appeared in the Sui Dynasty, and in the Tang Dynasty steles were made and erected. The buildings were later frequently expanded or rebuilt, and in the Qing Dynasty they had attained the present-day scale. The most important among them are: Weiyuan Temple, Qinghui Tower, Shaofuzi Shrine, Temple of Confucius and a gallery housing steles dating from different dynasties.

百泉啸台

法行寺塔

第六批全国重点文物保护单位

唐至宋

The pagoda of Faxing Temple

法行寺塔位于汝州市塔寺街原法行寺院内。法行寺原名法华寺，建于北魏，史书载“宝志，齐梁高僧，世称宝公或志公。金城朱氏子，先在汝州，曾传法华经。名其寺曰法华寺”。现仅存法行寺塔。

法行寺塔为九级密檐式砖塔，通高21.12米。由塔基、塔身、塔刹三部分组成。塔基座高0.68米。塔身一层为方形，南面辟圆券门，内设方形塔心室，室顶用叠涩砖砌成四角攒尖形藻井，塔身的壁面砖，虽经多次抽换，但外形仍保留了唐代风格，残留有三层叠涩密檐；二至九层为八角叠涩密檐；第五层至第九层，每层檐之八角用木质角梁，梁头下悬椭圆形风铎；第六层北面、第七层南面均有一方形佛龛。塔刹通高2.57米，基座为砖砌方形，高1米，塔刹为三节铜质宝葫芦形。从建筑特征看，塔身第一层为唐代特有的方塔建筑风格。在宋、金时期，法行寺塔由于地震或雷击造成上层倒塌，宋人将二至七层建为八边形密檐式，八至九层系清初重修时的形式。法行寺塔集中了唐宋金三个时期建筑的形式、建筑工艺，为研究这一时期的建筑学、力学以及工艺技术提供了实物依据。

Located at the site of Faxing Temple on Tasi Street in the urban area of Ruzhou City, the pagoda dates from the Tang and Song dynasties (618 ~ 1279 AD). Built of bricks, it has nine stories and close eaves. The first story is square in cross-section, while the second through ninth floors are octagon. The total height is about 30 meters.

法行寺塔

三苏祠和墓

宋至清

The shrine and cemetery of Su Shi, Su Zhe and Su Xun

三苏墓神道

三苏祠和墓位于郏县茨芭乡小峨眉山下，是北宋大文学家苏轼、苏辙的墓冢和其父苏洵的衣冠冢。始建于宋崇宁元年（1102年），历代曾多次修建。现存的三苏祠和墓，由墓院、广庆寺、三苏祠三部分组成。

墓院坐北朝南，占地面积约14800平方米。院内有神道石刻、明代红石牌坊、斋房、飨堂、碑林、祭坛、石供桌、三苏墓冢及宋、明、清古柏等。

广庆寺、三苏祠同在一条中轴线上，位于墓院西南300米处，坐北面南。现存有主院的南天门、天王殿、大雄宝殿和东西厢房及东跨院的过厅、官厅等建筑。

寺北与三苏祠相接，存有祠堂和东西耳房各一间。祠内暖阁保存着珍贵的元代三苏泥塑像，苏洵居中而坐，苏轼、苏辙分坐于左右两侧，三人均身着朝服。祠堂前立金、元、明、清石碑数通，另外，还有保存完好的石刻《三苏先生佳城图》碑。

三苏祠和墓的建筑风格独特，结构严谨。现保存的石刻、塑像等是研究三苏文化的珍贵史料。

三苏祠石碑坊

三苏祠

三苏祠大门

三苏墓

阎庄圣寿寺塔佛像砖

They are located at Sufensi Village, Jia County. The cemetery contains the tomb of Su Shi and Su Zhe respectively as well as the cenotaph of Su Xun, their father. All of them were great writers in the Northern Song Dynasty. The cemetery was first built in the 1st year of Chongning (1102) in the Song Dynasty and renovated many times afterwards. The shrine and the cemetery, plus a temple named Guangqing, cover a total area of 30,281 sq. m.

阎庄圣寿寺塔

第六批全国重点文物保护单位

宋

The pagoda of Shengshou Temple at Yanzhuang

阎庄圣寿寺塔

阎庄圣寿寺塔位于商丘市睢县城西南22.5公里的阎庄。建筑在高出地面3米余的圣寿寺遗址上，寺院已毁圮，仅存圣寿寺塔，从塔的建筑结构和造型特点上看，应为宋塔。

圣寿寺塔为九级密檐式砖塔，平面呈六边形，塔高19.25米。由塔基、塔身、塔刹三部分组成。塔身一层南面辟拱形券门，内为六角形塔心室，室内上部用叠涩砖收砌成六角形攒尖藻井。塔身南面第六、八层辟有圭形小门。一层檐下施一斗三升斗栱，上承三层叠涩砖层托飞椽和檐椽，檐上部用反叠涩砖层，四至九层仅有正反叠涩砖层作檐。塔通体共砌有佛像砖281块，分布在各层，佛砖共有六种类型，均为坐像，少数有背光，佛砖为0.345×0.345米，有释迦牟尼像和罗汉像。塔刹由覆钵、宝珠组成。

圣寿寺塔经历了近千年风雨剥蚀以及数次强烈地震和人为侵害，仍巍然屹立，对研究宋代砖塔的结构和建筑技术提供了珍贵的实物数据。塔身镶砌的佛像砖对研究我国宋代佛教文化艺术具有重要意义。

Located northeast of Yanzhuang Village, Sui County, the pagoda dates from the Song Dynasty (960 ~ 1127 AD). Built of bricks, it has nine stories and close eaves, with a hexagon cross-section and a height of 22 meters.

阎庄圣寿寺塔塔身局部

乾明寺塔

宋

The pagoda of Qianming Temple

乾明寺塔位于许昌市鄢陵县城西北隅龙形岗上。寺院始建于唐长庆四年（824年），民国十七年（1928年）寺废而塔独存。据明《鄢陵县创建乾明寺浮图围廊碑文》载：乾明寺塔始建于隋仁寿四年（604年）。但从塔的建筑形制和结构来看，应为北宋中晚期建筑。

该塔为十三层楼阁式砖塔，平面呈六边形，高38米。由塔基、塔身、塔刹三部分组成。塔基为青砖垒砌，青石阶条压边。塔身南面辟圆拱券门，中为塔心室，北面圆拱券门内筑台阶可盘旋登至塔顶，二层南面亦辟圆拱券门，三至八层和十二层辟壶门。塔身外檐部均施仿木砖雕斗栱，七层以上为四铺作单抄砖雕斗栱，斗栱置普拍枋上，各翼角青石套兽下悬风铃。每层六角均施倚柱。塔刹为明代重建，三层仰莲基座，其上置钵，再上置覆斗，斗上仰莲承铜宝瓶。

乾明寺塔保留有北宋时期的建筑做法，是研究宋塔砖木建筑结构的重要历史佐证。

乾明寺塔

乾明寺塔基座局部

Located in the town of Yanling County, the pagoda was first built in the 4th year of Renshou (604 AD) in the Sui Dynasty, and rebuilt in the Northern Song Dynasty (960 ~ 1127 AD). Built of bricks in the pavilion style, it has 13 stories, a hexagon cross-section and a height of about 38 meters.

泗洲寺塔

第六批全国重点文物保护单位

宋至明

The pagoda of Sizhou Temple

泗洲寺塔位于唐河县城东北部，原菩提寺内。又称“泗水塔”，建于宋绍圣二年（1095年），明万历七年（1579年）重修顶部。

泗洲寺塔为十一级楼阁式砖塔，平面呈八边形，高约51米。由塔基、塔身、塔刹三部分组成。塔基座为砖砌，高1.44米。第一层塔壁有南北二门，南门通塔心室，塔心室为方形，有砖砌阑额及普拍枋，上用五铺作出双抄计心斗栱，第二跳不施令栱，上部用砖叠涩构成方形藻井，顶部以木板封堵。北门有踏道由塔壁内盘旋向上可达九层塔心室，二层至九层均在不同方向开门。塔身各层檐下施斗栱，为五铺作双抄计造斗栱，第二跳直接承托撩檐枋，上承砖雕椽、飞，转角铺作斗栱，上有角梁及石质夔龙首，口内衔环系铁钟。檐上部用四铺作单抄偷心造斗栱，跳头不施另栱，散斗直接承托檐枋，上用砖砌出平座。塔顶为八角攒尖式，覆以灰板瓦、绿琉璃筒瓦。塔刹由绿琉璃仰、覆莲刹座及圆形绿琉璃覆钵宝瓶组成。塔身二层外壁及踏道、塔心室内镶有砖雕、石刻题记、佛像二百余件。

泗洲寺塔内施形制各异的内槽斗栱之栌斗下有皿板遗制等特点，为建筑史研究提供了珍贵的实物资料。

泗洲寺塔局部

泗洲寺塔叠涩式藻井

Located in Chengguan Town, Tanghe County, the pagoda was first built in the 2nd year of Shaosheng (1095 AD) in the Northern Song Dynasty and renovated many times in the Ming and Qing dynasties. Built of bricks in the pavilion style, it has 11 stories, an octagon cross-section, and a height of 49.75 meters.

泗洲寺塔

尉氏兴国寺塔

第六批全国重点文物保护单位

宋至明

The pagoda of Xingguo Temple in Weishi

兴国寺塔位于尉氏县城人民路南侧、建设路西侧。建于北宋太平兴国年间（976～984年），原属兴国寺舍利塔，后寺废而塔存。

兴国寺塔为八级（地面以上）楼阁式砖塔，平面呈正六边形，通高29.15米（地面至塔尖）。因几度被水淹漫，基座及一层被黄土掩埋，现仅见塔身及塔刹两部分。塔身每层高度由下而上逐层递减，平座面阔也渐次收敛。一层塔身西面辟拱券门，设有踏步沿塔心柱可盘旋登至塔顶，除第七层外，每层都置有小门，可供游人登临瞭望；门有拱形、叠涩形，也有半掩状假门和假窗。檐下施五踩双抄计心造砖雕斗栱，令拱之间相互连接，斗栱承托出檐，上覆砖雕筒瓦，檐上部亦施五铺作双抄计心造砖雕斗栱，出平座。塔顶为六角攒尖顶，上置铜宝瓶塔刹。塔体内外壁共有佛龛四百一十个（外壁二百八十八个），每层均有镶嵌，是研究宋代宗教文化和雕塑艺术难得的珍品。

兴国寺塔身佛像砖

兴国寺塔

Located at Dongguan in the town of Weishi County, the pagoda was built in the Northern Song Dynasty (960 ~ 1127 AD). Built of bricks in the pavilion style, it has 8 stories, a hexagon cross-section, and a height of 30 meters.

两程故里

宋至明

Cheng Hao and Cheng Yi's hometown

两程故里位于洛阳市嵩县城东南田湖镇程村。是一组清代建筑群，系北宋著名哲学家、思想家、教育家、宋明理学奠基人程颢、程颐故居。始建于宋崇宁二年（1103年），二程殁，后人即其地立祠。元仁宗皇庆二年（1313年）在此地建宗文阁与国子监，以宋儒程颢、程颐等十人，从祀孔庭。明景泰六年（1455年），皇帝下诏名为"两程故里"，并敕建祠庙。其后经重修扩建，全祠面积达4392平方米；明天顺六年（1462年）四月，敕建"两程故里"石坊一座，位于程村东1公里的官道上，上书有"圣旨"，下书"两程故里"。明弘治十三年（1500年）诏旨重修二程故里，始具规模。

两程故里，整体为五进院，坐北朝南，总面积4592平方米，建筑依次为棂星门、东西坊门、影壁；二进有诚敬门，东"春风亭"，西"立雪阁"，东前"敬斋室"，西前"宰杀所"；三进有"道学堂"大殿与东西两厢房；四进中为礼门，两侧有"留门"各一，中后为启贤

两程故里全景

两程故里棂星门

两程故里诚敬门

两程故里道学堂

堂，两侧设讲堂；五进为著述楼及东西讲堂。祠东毗邻“玩易所”。

两程故里自北宋创建，由于两程历代褒崇，立祠享祀，着为令典，对“两程祠”均有重修与扩建。祠内碑碣林立，现存宋、元、明、清、民国石碑碣五十一通（块），明代石盆两个，石狮子六对，二程全书印版三十四块，古柏树八棵。

Located at Cheng Village, Yichuan County, the house dates back to the period from the Song Dynasty to the Qing Dynasty (960 ~ 1911 AD). It was the hometown of Cheng Hao and Cheng Yi, two famous neo-Confucian scholars in the Northern Song Dynasty. It consists of a five-row-courtyard, and covers 4,392 sq. m.

商水寿圣寺塔

宋至明

The pagoda of Shousheng Temple in Shangshui County

商水寿圣寺塔位于周口市商水县郝岗乡北常社店村。始建于北宋明道二年（1033年），明嘉靖二十八年（1549年）整修。

商水寿圣寺塔为九级楼阁式砖塔，平面呈六边形，塔高41.5米。塔身一层南面辟塔门，门楣上刻“明道二年癸酉岁三月一日丙寅时戊寅日葬舍利院主僧□□建□□功德塔”题记。塔心室内砌有盘旋的塔道可登至顶。塔内一至七层设穹隆顶塔心室，七层以上为竖井式塔心室，东西两侧设脚窝可登顶；塔刹为铸铁宝葫芦形，有“嘉靖二十八年（1549年）”铸造铭文。1998年维修塔时，从塔刹宝顶封盖的天宫中，清理出铅佛像、铜佛像、白釉瓷盘、瓷碗、经卷等。

商水寿圣寺塔有明确建塔题记。塔的建筑式样和风格独特，为研究宋代砖塔建筑提供了实物例证。

Located northwest of Changshe Village, Shangshui County, the pagoda was first built in the Northern Song Dynasty (960 ~ 1127 AD) and rebuilt in the 1st year of Zhengtong (1436 AD) in the Ming Dynasty. Built of bricks in the pavilion style, it has 9 stories, a hexagon cross-section, and a total height of 41.50 meters.

商水寿圣寺塔

鄂城寺

宋至清

Echeng Temple

鄂城寺位于南阳市北25公里的石桥镇。由于石桥镇之西侧即是汉代西鄂县城址，寺及塔因西鄂故城而被称为“鄂城寺”、“鄂城寺塔”。据寺内碑刻与文献的记载，鄂城寺塔始建于隋代，俗称“隋塔”，宋代重建。

鄂城寺塔为七级楼阁式砖塔，平面呈六边形，通高18.88米。一层塔西辟券门，通塔心室，塔心室为六边形，高3.5米，由砖层层叠涩而成穹隆顶，顶部盖石板。塔身檐下均施五铺作双抄偷心造斗栱，第二跳跳头直接承托砖砌撩檐枋，上承砖雕椽、飞，檐上部为砖砌反叠涩屋面。二层塔身每面均镶嵌八块砖雕佛像，佛像砖均记载了雕像的名称、捐赠人等内容。塔刹佚失。鄂城寺塔的建筑形式及结构、遗物都保留了宋代的特征，是研究宋代砖结构建筑的重要实例，具有重要的价值。

鄂城寺现存建筑有山门、前殿、中殿各三间，两侧有东、西配殿各三间，均为清代硬山式建筑。另存有宋代元符二年（1099年）所制石狮两尊。

鄂城寺大殿

鄂城寺塔

Located in Shiqiao Town, Nanyang City, the pagoda was first built in the 13th year of Daye (617) in the Sui Dynasty, and rebuilt in the 2nd year of Yuanfu (1099 AD) in the Northern Song Dynasty. Built of bricks in the pavilion style, it has a hexagon cross-section and a height of 18.88 meters.

柴庄延庆寺塔

宋

The pagoda of Yanqing Temple at Chaizhuang

柴庄延庆寺塔位于济源市天坛区柴庄村。又名龙潭寺塔，延庆寺创建于唐垂拱三年（687年），北宋景祐元年（1034年）建塔。

延庆寺塔为七层密檐式砖塔，平面呈六边形，塔高28.16米。塔南一层辟塔门，可通塔心室，塔腹中空呈筒状；塔身内外雕有佛龛一千余个，故又名千佛舍利塔；塔身镶嵌四块宋景祐元年至五年（1034～1038年）塔铭，其中宋景祐三年（1036年）的为“济源县龙潭延庆禅院新修舍利塔记”。寺内还存有北宋墓塔一座、延庆寺山门和四令堂等附属建筑和唐至清十余件碑碣石刻等。欧阳修《卖油翁》、司马光《四令堂记》皆源于寺藏石刻。

柴庄延庆寺塔基座低矮，内部中空呈筒状，外部轮廓略呈抛物线形，承袭了我国早期佛塔的营造风格，具有很重要的研究价值。

Located east of Chaizhuang Village, Jiyuan City, the pagoda was built in the 1st year of Jingyou (1034 AD) in the Northern Song Dynasty. Built of bricks, it has seven stories, cclose eaves, a hexagon cross-section, and a height of 28.16 meters.

柴庄延庆寺塔

柴庄延庆寺塔局部

胜果寺塔

第六批全国重点文物保护单位

宋

The pagoda of Shengguo Temple

胜果寺塔

胜果寺塔细部

胜果寺塔位于焦作市修武县城老城大街西段南侧。胜果寺始建于唐代，宋绍圣三年（1096年）胜果寺重修时，增建此塔，寺院早废，唯塔独存。

胜果寺塔为九级楼阁式砖塔，平面呈八角形，塔基淤埋地下，现有地坪至塔刹高27.26米。塔门东向，甬道后接塔心室，塔心室为六角形，上部砖砌普拍枋，施五铺作双抄偷心造斗栱，斗栱上砌叠涩六角形，顶部用平砖封顶。西壁为登塔踏道。塔身一至六层每层檐下施五铺作双抄偷心造砖雕斗栱，七、八层为四铺作单杪偷心造砖雕斗栱，第九层檐下砌“丁”砖代替斗栱，为明代修复的遗物。每层檐下砌檐椽和飞椽，其上为三层叠涩砖层；檐上部砌反叠涩砖层；各角置木质角梁，悬挂风铎。塔刹由刹座、刹身、刹顶三部分组成，高2.05米。刹座为八角覆莲，莲瓣上叠涩两层并铸八卦图案，其上为八棱斜面，铸云龙、菊花、牡丹等花卉图案；刹身为三个束腰，两个宝葫芦，上部束腰铸有铭文“万历四十五年四月初十日造”；刹顶为铁质宝葫芦状。

胜果寺塔结构独特，塔身呈八角形，塔心室为六角形，为研究宋代砖塔结构、宗教艺术和建筑史提供了重要实物数据。

Located on Songta Street in the town of Xiuwu County, the pagoda was first built in the 3rd year of Shaosheng (1096 AD) in the Northern Song Dynasty, and was rebuilt in the 45th year of Wanli (1671 AD) in the Ming Dynasty. Built of bricks in the pavilion style, it has 9 stories, an octagon cross-section, and a height of 27.26 meters.

宝严寺塔

第六批全国重点文物保护单位

宋

The pagoda of Baoyan Temple

宝严寺塔

宝严寺塔位于驻马店市西平县城东关原宝严寺外。宝严寺始建于唐代，明洪武十五年（1382年）重建，万历二十六年（1598年）知县张应化修葺，寺外有塔，据塔顶发现铜钱铭文、游人题记及塔的造型特征来看，塔的建造年代应在北宋晚期。

宝严寺塔为七级楼阁式砖塔，平面呈六角形，通高28.8米。由塔基、塔身、塔刹三部分组成。砖砌塔基；塔身一层西面辟拱券门进入塔心室，塔心室为方形，四角攒尖顶，壁面砌佛像、海石榴花等雕砖，塔门道北壁辟踏道可登至二层塔心室，塔心室为四角攒尖顶，由东门南壁有踏步可登至三层塔心室，第三至七层塔心室为六角形，各层均辟小室，顺竖井梯道可登至上层。塔身檐下均施五铺作双抄偷心造砖雕斗栱，上承砖雕椽、飞、反叠涩檐，再上施四铺作砖雕斗栱，上出平座。七层塔檐下施四铺作，上用反叠涩内收为六角攒尖顶，再上为铸铁塔刹。塔刹高2.16米，六角形刹座，仰覆莲上置两层相轮。塔壁镶嵌有飞天、飞兽花砖及修塔纪年砖等。

宝严寺塔具有典型的宋代建筑风格，塔的一、二层塔心室为四边形，三至七层塔心室为六边形，结构独特，是研究宋塔建筑风格和佛教文化的实物资料。

宝严寺塔斗栱

Located at Dongguan in the town of Xiping County, the pagoda dates from the Northern Song Dynasty (960 ~ 1127 AD). Built of bricks in the pavilion style, it has 7 stories, a hexagon cross-section, and a height of 28.80 meters.

崇法寺塔

第六批全国重点文物保护单位

宋

The pagoda of Chongfa Temple

崇法寺塔

崇法寺塔位于商丘市永城县城崇法寺旧址上。北宋绍圣元年（1094年）始建，绍圣五年（1098年）落成。

该塔为九级楼阁式砖塔，平面呈八角形，通高34.6米。塔身自下而上逐层叠涩内收，由塔基、塔身、塔刹三部分组成。塔基用青砖筑砌，上端内置木箍一周；塔基下有长方形覆斗顶地宫，现存须弥座式供台及盛装舍利石匣。塔身一层东、南、西三面辟圭形门，门内小室互不相通，均为四角攒尖藻井；北门梯道可盘旋登塔。二至九层均正向四面辟圭形门。一层转角处为梅花形倚柱，柱下用砖雕莲花覆盆式柱础。一至五层塔檐下用交错叠压的莲花瓣砖出檐，上覆砖雕筒瓦屋面，再上施五铺作双抄计心造斗栱承拖平座。泥道拱处为佛像雕砖。六至九层檐上施四铺作单抄计心造斗栱承拖平座。刹由覆钵、七重相轮、宝盖及宝瓶组成。塔身内外共镶嵌砖、石雕塔铭六块，记载了修塔时间及施主姓名等。塔内壁共镶嵌黄、绿釉模制佛像砖三百二十三块，造像均为一佛二弟子。

崇法寺塔在踏步面、伏地梁、角梁等地采用石料代替其他宋塔中木构件的手法。塔内结构将穿心式、回廊式、方形壁内折上式和八角形壁内折上式糅合在一个塔内，设计别具匠心，建筑材料及建筑工艺精良，混合型结构富于变化，是宋塔中的一个特殊范例，有很高的历史、艺术和科学价值。

崇法寺塔琉璃砖雕

Located in the martyr's cemetery in the northeast of Yongcheng City, the pagoda was built in the 2nd year of Shaosheng (1095) in the Song Dynasty. Built of bricks in the pavilion style, it has 9 stories, an octagon cross-section, and a height of 34.60 meters.

郏县文庙

第六批全国重点文物保护单位

金至清

Confucian Temple in Jia County

郏县文庙位于平顶山市郏县城关镇南街中段。始建于五代后周显德元年（954年），金泰和六年（1206年）重建，明、清时期屡有修建。

文庙坐北朝南，占地面积约9000平方米。整体布局由中、东、西三路建筑组成。中路依次建有化龙坊、贤关门、圣域门、泮池、棂星门、戟门、大成殿、明伦堂、尊经阁和假山花园及后大门；东路南北依次有节孝总坊、节孝祠、崇圣祠和古代儒学署；西路有忠义祠、土地祠等；东南有文

郏县文庙大成殿

郏县文庙大成殿龙柱

奎楼院一处，内有照壁、文奎楼和角门等古建筑。主体建筑大成殿，殿面阔五间、进深三间，歇山式琉璃瓦顶建筑，檐下置斗栱；额枋、斗栱均有雕刻；前檐四根檐柱，通体透雕盘龙，柱头雕虎首，柱础六面浮雕。

大成殿可谓“无木不雕”。其木雕和彩绘是极为罕见的艺术精品，具有浓郁的中原地区特征。

Located on South Street in Chengguan Town, Jia County, the temple was first built in the 6th year of Taihe (1206 AD) in the Jin Dynasty, and was renovated for many times in the Ming Dynasty. Facing south, it retains 71 houses, covering an area of over 9,000 sq. m. and a floor space of 10,000 sq. m.

百家岩寺塔

第六批全国重点文物保护单位

金

The pagoda of Baijiayan Temple

百家岩寺塔位于焦作市修武县方庄镇桑湾村北。北齐时，高僧稠禅法师在天门瀑布东侧结茅而居，修建百家岩寺。民国初年，百家岩寺遭火焚，唯塔独存。塔始建于唐垂拱二年（686年），因获嘉县张氏女殉身投崖而死，其母朱四娘建五级浮屠于此，故又名孝女塔，现存建筑为金代重建。

百家岩寺塔为九级楼阁式砖塔，平面呈八角形，塔高26.15米。一层塔身东壁辟半圆拱券门通塔心室，塔心室呈方形，竖井式，通高约7.30米。在高约5.24米处砖砌阑额、普拍枋，上施四铺作单抄计心造斗栱，斗栱之上用扇形雕砖和叠涩砖砌成八角形藻井，藻井上有木质八角形天花。塔心室正中地面下有地宫，用三层砖封口，地宫平面呈正方形，深约2.30米，分上下两层，上大下小。二层塔身以上的各层东、西、南、北四面辟圭形假门；塔身每层檐下施五铺作双抄计心造斗栱，45度异形华栱承托椽、飞，上覆筒板瓦屋面。九层佛龛上叠涩承托塔刹，现塔刹已佚失仅剩覆莲刹座。

百家岩寺塔是目前河南省保存的唯一的一座大型楼阁式金塔，塔内部结构风格及斗之耳、平、欹比例关系等均具有明显的承宋（塔）启元（塔）特征，是研究宋、金、元塔嬗递关系的珍贵资料，又是研究金代建筑艺术和中国古代建筑技术史的珍贵资料。

百家岩寺塔

Located north of Sangwan Village, Xiuwu County, the pagoda was first built in the 2nd year of Chuigong (686 AD) in the reign of Empress Wu Zetian in the Tang Dynasty, but the current standing one dates from the Jin Dynasty. Built of bricks in the pavilion style, it has 9 stories, an octagon cross-section and a height of over 20 meters.

沁阳北大寺

明至清

Beida Temple in Qinyang

沁阳北大寺位于焦作市沁阳市老城区西北部。创建于元至正年间（1341～1368年），明嘉靖四十年（1561年）重修，清代增建后成现规模。北大寺自创建后一直为当地回族居民礼拜活动的场所。

沁阳北大寺由男寺和女寺两部分组成。其中以男寺为主，占地面积约3100平方米。北大寺坐西面东，三进院落，建筑呈中轴线左右对称布局，主体建筑位于中轴线上，附属建筑分落左右。现存建筑为厦殿、过庭、四讲堂、客厅、前后拜殿、窑殿及两侧沐浴室、居室仓储等。

厦殿即大门，单檐歇山式孔雀蓝琉璃瓦顶建筑，面阔三间，进深两间，设门两道，前檐下置栅栏门，中间置棋盘门。檐下置透雕花鸟斗栱，殿内四角檩下置隔架斗栱。殿前南北两角外出琉璃瓦顶八字墙。

过庭为悬山式卷棚黄绿琉璃瓦覆顶建筑，面阔三间，进深一间，七架梁。前后檐下施三踩单昂斗栱，拱眼壁墨绘山水、花鸟图案。过庭四隅为四讲堂，均为卷棚式单檐硬山灰筒板瓦顶建筑，面阔三间，进深一间，檐下置斗栱。过庭之后为礼拜殿，由客厅、前后拜殿及窑殿组成，由天沟将四座建筑前后勾连搭在一起。客厅为卷棚歇山式绿琉璃瓦

沁阳北大寺

沁阳北大寺过厅

顶建筑，面阔三间，进深一间，六架梁，明间檐下悬挂《明太祖高皇帝御制至圣百字》匾额一块；前殿为单檐歇山绿琉璃瓦顶，后殿为单檐悬山绿琉璃瓦顶，均为七架梁，檐下置五踩重昂斗栱，三个大斗并座，梁架间置三幅云隔架科斗栱。前后拜殿空间宽敞，是该寺中建筑体积最大，年代最早的一座建筑。窑殿面阔三间，进深一间，殿顶为亭塔式与楼阁式相结合，明间殿顶为单檐十字脊歇山顶，两次间为单檐十字脊三面歇山顶，均为三彩琉璃瓦覆顶，殿内为砖砌穹隆顶，明间高，两次间略低，明间后壁正中龛内供奉伊斯兰教的“克尔拜”真主之神位。

女寺位于男寺西北，始建于清道光年间，坐西面东，四合院布局，现存拜殿、东上房、沐浴室及仓储、伙房等建筑。

沁阳北大寺是我国中原地区现存建筑时代最早，规模最大，保存最完整的伊斯兰教建筑群。殿顶将亭塔式与楼阁式巧妙结合，在建筑装饰上多采用莲花图案的作法，都具有鲜明的伊斯兰建筑风格。殿内木作梁架通体彩绘，雕梁画栋，沥粉贴金，堪称我国伊斯兰古建筑的精品之作，融合了中国传统建筑与伊斯兰建筑风格为一体，对研究伊斯兰教在中原地区传播及其伊斯兰建筑风格有着重要的价值。

沁阳北大寺礼拜堂局部

The temple is located in the middle of Zizhi Street in the urban area of Qinyang City. The time when it was founded is unknown. It was rebuilt in the 8th year of Wanli (1580 AD) in the Ming Dynasty. Facing east, it consists of a male section and a female section, with the former as the main part. It retains over 80 buildings, including towers, halls and auxiliary houses, covering about 3,100 sq. m.

叶县县衙

明至清

The government office of Ye County

叶县县衙位于平顶山市叶县东大街。始建于明洪武二年(1369年)，清咸丰八年（1858年）及同治年间（1865～1869年）重修。

叶县县衙坐北向南，占地面积16848平方米，建筑呈中轴线左右对称分布。中轴线现存有大门、监狱、仪门、大堂、二堂、三堂等建筑。大门面阔、进深各三间，东西监狱各二间，外两侧置八字墙，门前置石狮一对。大门内依次为仪门、大堂、二堂、三堂。仪门东西两侧分别为萧曹庙和土地祠；大堂前有抱厦，抱厦面阔三间，进深一间；大堂面阔五间、进深三间。大堂前东侧科房为吏、户、礼及库房，西侧科房为兵、刑、工及承发房等，均

叶县县衙正门

叶县县衙大堂内景

是衙门的职能部门。二堂面阔五间，进深二间，内有幕厅和招书房，是知县和幕僚商议公务和招书师爷办公的场所。二堂前有东西厢房各三间，东厢为会文馆，西厢为会武馆，用以接待外来文武官员。三堂面阔五间、进深三间，是知县办公、审理涉密案件的场所；两侧为东西花厅是其幕僚、师爷办公用房。中轴线东侧建筑依次有狱房、厨院、宅院、东花厅、后花园、东群房，西侧有西群房、虚受堂、思补斋，思补斋两侧分别为南、北群房和南、北书房；其后为大仙祠等建筑。县衙的后花园内有花、草、水、鱼、凉亭、假山，及清代石榴、千年桂花等珍花异木。

叶县县衙三堂

Located on East Avenue, Ye County, the office was first built in the 2nd year of Hongwu (1369 AD) in the Ming Dynasty and rebuilt in the Qing Dynasty. Remaining buildings include a main gate, a doorman's house, the main hall, the second hall, and east and west halls, which cover a floor space of 2,555 sq. m.

洛阳周公庙

第六批全国重点文物保护单位

明至清

Duke Zhou Temple in Luoyang

洛阳周公庙位于洛阳市定鼎南路中段东侧。是为纪念西周时期著名的政治家、思想家、军事家、儒家思想的奠基人周公姬旦而建造的祠庙。周公庙《隋书》、《资治通鉴》等文献均有记载，始建于隋末唐初，为隋将王世充草创。唐太宗贞观年间（627～649年）和唐玄宗开元年间重修，后废弃。明嘉靖四年（1525年）又在旧址重建，明清时期曾多次修葺与扩建，形成如今的规模。

周公庙占地面积4906平方米，现存为明清时期的建筑。建筑为三进院落，沿中轴线依次为南大门、定鼎堂、礼乐堂（会忠祠）、三殿及东西厢房。南大门面阔三间，进深一间，明间为歇山式灰筒瓦顶，两次间为悬山式灰筒瓦顶，檐下施五踩单拱单昂斗栱，三门均为圆拱券实榻门。定鼎堂为单檐歇山式绿琉璃瓦剪边

洛阳周公庙全景

洛阳周公庙山门

灰筒瓦顶建筑，面阔五间，进深三间，檐下施五踩重昂斗栱，抬梁式木构架，七架梁。礼乐堂与三殿均为硬山式灰筒瓦顶建筑，面阔五间，进深二间，木构架为五架梁对前后廊。东西厢房为硬山式建筑，面阔五间，进深一间，木构架为五架梁对前出廊。此外周公庙现存“元圣殿”遗址、明代石质龟趺座三个、清代石狮一对、抱鼓石一对、明代泥塑伯禽像一尊。

周公庙从建筑形制看，整个建筑以定鼎堂为核心，反映出了“居中为尊”的传统理念，布局严谨，合理紧凑，造型古朴庄严，高大庄重，工艺精湛堪称古建精品之作。

洛阳周公庙定鼎堂内明代塑像

Located on the east side of South Dingding Road in the old city of Luoyang, the temple was first built in the Sui Dynasty (581 ~ 618 AD). The main building that remains is the five-bay-wide Dingding Hall, with a hip and gable roof covered by glazed tiles. It dates from the Ming and Qing dynasties.

关林

第六批全国重点文物保护单位

明至清

Guanyu's Cemetery

关林位于洛阳市南郊关林镇关林南路东端。据关林明万历二十四年《重修关王冢庙记》碑文记载："洛阳县南门外离城十里，有关王大冢，内葬灵首，汉时有庙，及今年久毁坏。"明万历二十年(1592年)重建，清代增建，现存建筑主要为明代。关林是明清时期皇帝遣官致祭、地方官吏和百姓朝拜关公的场所。

关林为河南现存规模最大的古建群之一，坐北朝南，东西最宽300米，南北最长500米。四进院落，中轴线主要建筑从南至北有舞楼、大门、仪门、钟鼓楼、拜殿及大殿、二殿、寝殿、石坊、碑亭、关冢等。

舞楼为祭祀关羽时献戏的舞台，清代乾隆五十六年（1791年）由山陕商人施银添建，坐南朝北，平面呈"凸"字形，前后台明间、两次间为重檐歇山绿琉璃筒瓦顶，面阔五间，后台两梢间为硬山式绿琉璃筒瓦顶，面阔三

关林石牌坊

关林钟楼

间，进深均为三间；抬梁式构架，前后台明间木构架连在一起，下层南部五架梁与北部三架梁相连接承托上层五架梁，檐下施五踩双下昂斗栱。

大门硬山式绿色琉璃筒瓦顶建筑，面阔五间三门道，分心通柱前后对双步梁结构，仪门为硬山式绿琉璃瓦顶建筑，面阔五间三实榻门，仪门前立铁狮子一对，系明万历二十五年（1597年）铸造。建于明代的钟、鼓楼位于大殿东西两侧，均为十字脊歇山重檐楼阁式建筑，檐下施五踩斗栱，钟楼上悬挂万历壬寅年（万历三十年，1602年）所铸铜钟一口。

拜殿及大殿是百官僚属谒拜关羽的场所。为前卷棚式后单檐庑殿式绿色琉璃筒瓦覆顶勾连搭建筑。为抬梁式木构架，拜殿面阔五间，进深一间，六架梁，大殿面阔七间，进深三间，五架梁前后对双步梁。大殿檐下施七踩三下昂斗栱，梁架间施隔架科斗栱。

二殿是关林建造年代最早的一座殿宇，单檐庑殿式绿色琉璃筒瓦顶建筑，面阔五间，进深二间。七架梁前对双步梁，檐下施五踩双下昂斗栱，梁架间施隔架科斗栱。圣母殿和五虎殿位于二殿东西两侧，均为硬山式建筑，面阔三间，进深两间，五架梁前后对单步廊。

寝殿，为清代建筑，单檐硬山式琉璃筒瓦顶建筑，面阔五间，进深三间，五架梁前后对单步廊。檐下施五踩双下昂斗栱。

石坊为明代万历甲辰年(1604年)立。四柱三间柱出头式石坊，上刻“汉寿亭侯墓”五字，为明代太监胡滨所书，石坊上有明清题联六幅。石坊北为清代碑亭，内立关林庙碑。

碑亭后为关冢，冢高10余米，直径52米。冢正面南墙上有康熙四十六年（1707年）修筑石墓门，额题“钟灵处”，门两侧行书对联：“神游上宛乘仙鹤，骨在天中隐睡龙”。

关林是林、庙合一的典型特例，前为庙，后为林，既分又合，浑然一体，从前到后层层递进，整组建筑以大殿为核心，反映封建社会“居中为尊”、“建中立极”的传统观念，主要殿宇采用官式建筑和中原地方建筑手法相结合的营造规制。现存明、清修庙碑刻百余通。关林院内有古柏近800株，最大树龄已近700年，在修建庙宇的同时广植侧柏，使庙堂兼具园林特色，墓冢和殿宇掩映其中，庙借柏之翠，柏助庙之幽。

关林舞楼

Located at Guanlin Village, Guanlin Town, the City of Luoyang, the cemetery was founded in the 24th year of Wanli (1596 AD) in the Ming Dynasty, and was expanded for many times in the Qing Dynasty. It is the place where the head of Guanyu, a general of Shu in the Three Kingdoms period, was buried. Remaining buildings include a Wu Tower, a main gate, a secondary gate, a bell-drum tower, a worship hall, a stone archway, and the tomb.

白云寺

第六批全国重点文物保护单位

明至清

Baiyun Temple

白云寺位于新乡市辉县市薄壁镇树林村冠山峰下，原名白茅寺，又称梦觉寺。寺始建于唐高宗年间（650～683年），明洪武二十四年（1391年）大加修葺，改名“白云寺”。

白云寺坐北朝南，现存主要建筑有山门、天王殿、大雄宝殿、左右配殿、东西陪楼、东西厢房、钟鼓楼及地藏王殿等，建筑面积4000平方米。大雄宝殿面阔五间、进深三间，悬山式灰瓦顶建筑，檐下施五踩重昂斗栱，构件有彩绘。现存建筑除大雄宝殿为明代外，其余均为清代建筑，但许多构件如斗栱、瓦件等，仍保留有早期风格。大殿内的清代壁画、彩绘及雕刻十分精美。

白云寺另存有宋碑一通，南宋砖塔一座，元代石塔两座，明代砖塔三座，寺院内外碑刻二十二块。其中元至元二十九年（1292

白云寺天王殿

白云寺大雄宝殿

年）"普照大禅师塔"，为喇嘛形石塔，塔基为二层须弥座，雕满飞天、佛像、卧狮和莲花。鼓形塔身雕两层佛龛，分别雕饰佛、菩萨、力士、天王等，为元代石雕的精品之作。白云寺院格局严谨完整，寺内中木、石建筑雕刻精湛，为研究宗教史和建筑史提供了珍贵的实物数据。

白云寺普照大禅师石塔

Located northwest of Baiyuan Temple Village, Bobi Town, Huixian City, the temple was first built in the Tang Dynasty, but the current standing buildings date from the Ming and Qing dynasties. Main buildings are: a main gate, two side gates, Middle Buddha Hall, a main hall, and east and west houses. The temple covers an area of 40,000 sq. m., and a floor space of 4,000 sq. m.

新郑轩辕庙

明至清

Xuanyuan Temple in Xinzheng

新郑轩辕庙位于河南省新郑市北关。包括轩辕庙和具茨山风后岭两部分。

轩辕庙位于新郑市北关轩辕路，是黄帝轩辕出生地和居住地。始建年代不详，从庙前明代砖桥知在此之前就已有庙。庙宇为清代建筑，坐北朝南，四合院落，现存大门、大殿、东西配殿。大门为硬山式黄琉璃瓦剪边灰筒瓦顶建筑，面阔三间，进深一间。大殿前有高大站台，大殿为前卷棚后硬山式绿琉璃瓦勾连搭建筑，面阔五间，卷棚进深一间，大殿进深二间，七架梁前对双步廊，卷棚五架梁，由穿梁相连。大殿前东西各有配殿三间。

庙前有明代隆庆四年（1571年）修建的砖拱券桥“轩辕桥”一座，清康熙五十四年（1715年）立“轩辕故里”碑一通。

具茨山风后岭，位于新郑市千户寨乡具茨山主峰。现存有石砌寨墙，宽2～4米，高2.5～5米，蜿蜒长达3千米。另有两座明代石殿、明代摩崖题记及明清时期

新郑轩辕庙大门

新郑轩辕庙正殿

碑刻。石殿为单檐歇山式灰筒瓦顶建筑，抬梁式石构架，三架梁前后对单步廊，檩枋、望板等构件均为石质。

新郑轩辕庙是全国唯一保存有明代以前实物的黄帝故里，保存的明代砖桥、殿宇、摩崖题记、石寨墙等具有重要的历史和文物价值。

Located on Xuanyuan Road, Beiguan, the City of Xinzheng, the temple (including related Ming-dynasty ruins at Fenghou Ridge, Juci Mountain) is said to be the place where Xuanyuan, or Yellow Emperor was born and raised. The time when it was founded is unknown. The current standing buildings date from the Qing Dynasty. Facing south, they include a main gate, a main hall, and east and west halls. In front of the temple is Xuanyuan Bridge, built in the 4th year of Longqing (1571 AD) in the Ming Dynasty, and a stele that reads 'Hometown of Xuanyuan', made and erected in the 54th year of Kangxi (1715 AD) in the Qing Dynasty.

新郑轩辕庙东厢房

千佛阁

明至清

Thousand-Buddha Tower

千佛阁位于焦作市武陟县木城镇南大街。千佛阁建于明嘉靖三十六年（1557年），清咸丰六年（1856年）重修，但保留了明代主要构件和建筑风格。现存有千佛阁、中佛殿、山门等建筑。

千佛阁，三重檐歇山回廊楼阁式绿琉璃筒瓦顶建筑，中下层面阔、进深各五间，上层面阔、进深各三间。七架梁结构。一层、二层檐下均施五踩双下昂斗栱，上层檐下施七踩三下昂斗栱。一层柱头有卷刹覆莲式柱础，为明代遗物。阁顶部扒砖上绘十八组天干地支阴阳五行八卦太极图。正脊中间置狮驮三重楼阁宝刹。

中佛殿，单檐悬山式绿琉璃瓦顶建筑，面阔三间，进深一间。七架梁结构，脊瓜柱两侧施叉手。前檐下施五踩双下昂斗栱，后檐下施三踩斗栱，其檐部缘头镶透雕卷云纹。

千佛阁

山门，单檐歇山式绿琉璃瓦覆顶建筑。面阔三间，进深二间。七架梁结构。檐下施五踩重昂斗栱前檐明间为乳钉板门，次间各置圆窗百寿花格窗棂。后檐明间为六抹隔扇门四扇。殿内中间供奉汉白玉雕弥勒佛像一尊，两侧为四大天王像。

另外，院内有明万历三十七年（1609 年）立石碑两通；一为“尊敬长上图”，一为“和睦乡里图”，均为武陟县知事秦之英撰文并书丹，周万书画，江以通刻石。后人称为书、画、刻之“三绝碑”。

千佛阁建筑既有佛教阁殿，又有道教庙宇，是明清时期释道合一的集中表现。建筑属地方手法，其梁架、斗栱形制存有不少袭古手法，为研究建筑史提供了重要实例，是我国南北方古建筑在中原地区融合的精华。

千佛阁斗栱

千佛阁翼角

Located on South Avenue in the town of Wuzhi County, the tower was first built in the 38th year of Jiaqing (1557 AD) in the Ming Dynasty and was rebuilt in the 6th year of Xianfeng (1856 AD) in the Qing Dynasty. Remaining buildings are Middle Buddha Hall and Thousand-Buddha Tower, whose total height is 16.6 meters.

阳台宫

第六批全国重点文物保护单位

明至清

Yangtai Palace

阳台宫位于济源市王屋山麓的王屋乡愚公村西。唐代著名道士、茅山宗师司马承祯于唐开元十五年（727年）创建。阳台宫依山而建，建筑面积3238平方米。建筑采用中国传统中轴线对称式布局，现存山门、三清殿、玉皇阁、东西配殿、白云道院等建筑。

三清殿面阔五间、进深四间，为明代单檐歇山殿堂式灰瓦顶建筑，木构件保留有许多宋元时期的营造手法。殿内明、次间有八角、圆形藻井共四组。玉皇阁建在高5米的台基上，面阔、进深各三间，为三重檐歇山楼阁式琉璃瓦顶建筑，梁架及一层的二十根雕龙石质檐柱均为明代遗物，部分柱子上刻有明代题记。另外宫内存有元、明、清时期的碑刻十一通。

阳台宫古建筑群体现了中原建筑的诸多地方特点，是研究中国古代建筑手法和道教历史的重要实物。

阳台宫山门

阳台宫玉皇阁

Located at the foot of Wangwu Mountain, Jiyuan City, the palace was built in the 15th year of Kaiyuan (727 AD) in the Tang Dynasty and was renovated many times afterwards. Remaining buildings are Main Gate, Daluo Sanjing Hall, Yuhuang Tower, east and west side halls and White Cloud Taoist Temple, which cover a floor space of 3,238 sq. m. The main buildings-Daluo Sanjing Hall and Yuhuang Tower-were built in the Ming Dynasty.

阳台宫玉皇阁龙柱

许昌文峰塔

明

Wenfeng Pagoda in Xuchang

许昌文峰塔位于许昌市文峰路中段许昌博物馆院内。始建于明万历四十二年（1641年），由许州太守郑振光创建，意欲振兴许昌文风。

塔为十三级楼阁式砖塔，平面呈八角形，通高50.03米。由塔基、塔身、塔刹三部分组成。塔基用青砖垒砌。塔身一层下部为青石须弥座，南侧辟门，塔门楣上嵌长方形青石匾额，正中阴刻行书“文笔耸秀”，进入塔心室可旋转登塔。室顶由砖质斗栱，九层檐下施三踩斗栱，其上收八角攒尖顶，各翼角用青石龙首口衔悬铃。塔刹为四重宝珠。塔内供奉千手千眼佛、白衣菩萨和文昌帝君等。

许昌文峰塔的斗栱、角梁、条砖升头木等建筑构件，均具有河南明代建筑地方特色，塔身的雕刻，对研究明代雕刻艺术具有参考价值。

许昌文峰塔

Located at Dongguan, Xuchang City, the pagoda was built in the 43rd year of Wanli (1641 AD) in the Ming Dynasty. Built of bricks in the pavilion style, the 13-storey pagoda has an octagon cross-section and a total height of 49.53 meters. It consists of four parts-the underground palace, the base, the body and the top.

许昌文峰塔局部

望京楼

第六批全国重点文物保护单位

明

Wangjing Tower

望京楼位于新乡市卫辉市汲水镇望京楼后街。又名崇本书楼，为明万历皇帝同母弟潞藩王朱翊镠于万历十九年（1591年）望京思母所建。

望京楼坐北朝南，平面呈长方形，长32米，宽19米，高23米，分内外两层。外壁用青石砌筑，内壁用大理石镶嵌。一层四面辟门，高大宽敞，中间无梁十字拱券顶。二层原有五间歇山式大殿“崇本书楼”，是供潞王父子读书写字的场所，已毁，柱础尚存；殿前现存“诚意坊”，四柱三楼庑殿顶，青石结构，坊身雕刻有“三龙戏珠”、“八仙庆寿”、“鹤鹿同春”、“童子拜寿”及对联等内容，雕琢精美。

望京楼形体高大，结构坚固，内砖外石，砌筑工整，具有典型的官式建筑风格。

望京楼

望京楼牌坊

望京楼内景

Located on North Gate Avenue in the urban area of Weihui City, the tower was built by Prince Lu in the 19th year of Wanli (1591 AD) in the Ming Dynasty. Facing south, it has a rectangular cross-section, measuring 32 meters long from east to west, 19 meters wide, and about 30 meters high. It is in the style of a beamless hall.

仓房香严寺

明

Cangfang Xiangyan Temple

仓房香严寺位于南阳市淅川县仓房乡西北4公里的龙虎二山之间。据寺藏碑记载：初建于唐代末年，大唐慧忠国师道场，国师入墓时，异香百里，经月不散，因此得名香严寺。

寺院坐北朝南，原有上下两座寺院，下寺于1970年淹没于丹江水库，上寺殿堂房舍基本保持原貌。寺院依山势而建，现存石牌坊、山门、韦驮殿、过厅、大雄宝殿、凝月轩（望月亭）、法堂、藏经阁等建筑，依次排列于中轴线上，组成五进院落，建筑面积4660平方米。

石牌坊，建于明代，三间四柱出头式牌坊。明间额枋上书“敕赐显通禅寺”，阴面题刻“大明唐府重建”、“嘉靖己亥年孟春立”。山门一间，硬山式灰瓦顶建筑。韦驮殿，面阔五间，进深三间，硬山式灰瓦顶建筑，五架梁对前后双步廊木构架。殿内分别彩塑关羽、韦驮、护法神等。过厅建在高台上，面阔、进深各三间，单檐歇山式灰瓦顶建筑，檐

仓房香严寺

仓房香严寺大雄宝殿

下施三踩斗栱，脊檩上书“大清光绪五年（1879年）三月”题记，过厅内有青石踏步十五级至大雄宝殿。

大雄宝殿面阔七间、进深五间，单檐歇山式灰板瓦顶建筑，七架梁前后对双步廊，檐下施三踩单昂异形斗栱，均出45度斜拱，象鼻昂；各构件均施旋子彩画；殿内四周壁上保存有清代彩色壁画403.93平方米，内容主要是有关于佛教方面的，也有部分道教内容，四壁还有许多小型佛龛，龛内藏玉、铁、木等不同材质的佛像。

凝月轩，又称望月厅，面阔、进深各三间，硬山式灰筒瓦顶建筑，一、二层檐下均施五踩双昂斗栱，轩内脊檩上书“大清光绪五年三月”，与过厅是同一时期建筑。法堂面阔五间、进深三间，硬山式灰板瓦顶建筑。

藏经楼，面阔七间，进深三间，二层硬山式灰板瓦顶建筑，木构件上均施彩绘，楼内墙壁绘有清代壁画。楼前东西两侧有文殊殿、普贤殿。另外还有静养院、后寮等清代建筑，宋至清时期的砖石和尚墓塔二十七座。

仓房香严寺曾经是豫西南最大的宗教活动中心，中州四大名寺之一。为中原建筑风格与南方建筑装饰特色相融合，是研究明清时期中原地方木构建筑法式的重要实物资料。大雄宝殿内的清代彩绘壁画，保存完好，是研究美术史、宗教史的珍贵资料。

仓房香严寺大雄宝殿内鎏金佛像

仓房香严寺过厅

仓房香严寺塔

Located west of Mogou Village, Xichuan County, the temple was built in the Tang Dynasty (618 ~ 907 AD) and was rebuilt many times afterwards. The current standing buildings date from the Qing Dynasty and cover over 4,200 sq. m. On the slope northeast of the temple there is a pagoda forest, which contains over 20 stone/brick pagodas built in the Ming and Qing dynasties.

仓房香严寺望月亭

悟颖塔

第六批全国重点文物保护单位

明

Wuying Pagoda

悟颖塔位于驻马店市汝南县汝宁镇西关村。塔因僧人悟颖主持修建而得名，又言冬至正午无塔影，故又称“无影塔”，明隆庆元年（1563年）重建。

塔为九级楼阁式砖塔，平面为六边形，高约25米。由塔基、塔身、塔刹组成。塔基系须弥座式，塔身南面辟塔门，一、二层有塔心室，塔心室砖砌叠涩穹隆顶。塔内砌筑有盘旋梯道可登顶。各层每面辟券门或圭形门，或设假门、假棂窗，或嵌砌佛像雕砖；每层塔檐下施砖雕五踩重昂斗栱，上承砖雕筒板瓦。顶为六边形刹座，其上置宝瓶状铁刹，刹顶施火焰宝珠。

悟颖塔结构坚固，设计合理，曾经历过十三次不同程度的地震安然无恙。塔的造型优美，图案雕刻精细，其建筑技艺对当今工程建造设计，仍具有重要的参考价值。

悟颖塔

Located at Nanguan in the town of Runan County, the pagoda was first built in the Northern Song Dynasty, and was rebuilt in the 1st year of Longqing (1567 AD) in the Ming Dynasty. Built of bricks in the pavilion style, it has 9 stories, a hexagon cross-section and a height of about 29 meters.

福胜寺塔

第六批全国重点文物保护单位

宋

The pagoda of Fusheng Temple

福胜寺塔位于南阳市邓州市城区大十字街西南角。建于北宋天圣十年(1032年)。据《邓州志》记载原为十三级，元末遭兵燹，剩下七层，明洪武初年(1368年)重修。

塔为七级楼阁式砖塔，平面呈八边形，高38.28米。由塔基、

福胜寺塔

福胜寺塔内壁砖雕

塔身、塔刹三部分组成。塔基座为须弥座，高3.4米，台明铺设浮雕宝相莲花方砖；束腰部分砌浮雕佛像砖，转角处砌浮雕力士神像。塔身南面辟拱券门通塔心室，一至二层、三至五层各为一个八角形塔心室，六至七层的塔心室为方形，砌砖叠涩藻井。一至二层有踏步可盘旋登塔，绕二层外檐平座进入塔壁西侧踏步攀登至四层，五层以上不可攀登。塔身外檐下施五铺作双抄斗栱，上承砖雕椽飞并出平座。塔身每层的内外壁面嵌砌各种砖雕，共两千多件，内容有坐佛、菩萨、天王力士、罗汉、伎乐、宝装莲花和各种花纹砖饰。1988年对该塔进行全面维修时，发现六边形地宫，内藏有金棺、银椁、象牙佛顶骨、鎏金双龙银壶、铁塔等，地宫南部正中砖砌须弥座上置大理石须弥座，束腰部分北面、东面刻《邓州龙兴寺大悲院地宫记》，落款为“大宋天圣十年二月二十五日记”，是建塔时间的重要依据。

福胜寺塔具有确切纪年，塔心室及地宫构筑精巧，是了解宋塔以及宋代砖结构的重要参照体。塔体斗栱及佛像花纹等砖雕，是研究宋代雕刻艺术及建筑艺术的重要资料。

福胜寺塔穹隆藻井

Located on Dashizi Street in the urban area of the City of Dengzhou, the pagoda was built in the Northern Song Dynasty (960 ~ 1127 AD). Built of bricks in the pavilion style, it has 7 stories, an octagon cross-section, and a total height of 36.70 meters. Stone chests, a golden coffin and a silver outer coffin have been unearthed in the underground palace.

河南府文庙

第六批全国重点文物保护单位

明

Confucian Temple of Henan Prefecture

河南府文庙位于洛阳市老城区文明街中段路北文明街小学院内。是奉祀孔子的庙宇。肇建年代失考。据《洛阳县志·艺文志之四重修文庙记》载，“嘉靖六年四月乙巳，……政通民和，乃饰修文庙”，可知早在明嘉靖六年（1527年）以前就已经存在。

河南府文庙现存戟门、大成殿、崇圣殿及东西廊庑等建筑。戟门为悬山式灰筒瓦顶建筑，面阔三间、进深二间，抬梁式木结构，七架梁分心用三柱。檐下均施五踩双下昂斗栱，梁架间施隔架科，为五彩斗栱，其结构分析，其始建年代当为金、元时期。戟门两侧各有硬山式灰筒瓦顶暖阁一间。大成殿前有站台，三面有踏步，正面两路踏步中间施石雕二龙戏珠御路，大殿为单檐歇山式灰瓦顶建筑，面阔五间，进深三间。檐下施五踩双下昂斗栱，有斗幽，阑额砍杀斜直两截；柱头正面顶部砍杀成斜面；梁枋皆施彩绘，因烟熏遮盖只隐约可见。戟门和大成殿的建筑时代从构造

河南府文庙前殿

河南府文庙大殿

风格看应为明初，其他建筑则被近代改造失去原貌。此外，还有“奉旨文武官员有等至此下马”等碑刻、石刻十余件。

文庙是孔子文化最具代表性的物化象征，在继承我国优秀传统文化方面有着不可替代的作用。同时其作为中国祠庙类的建筑自成一套完整的体例，是研究中国古代建筑最生动的例证。河南府文庙与历史上的府学、县学、贡院等合为一体，是研究中国古代教育及科考举士制度的实物例证。

大殿前石刻

The temple is located on Wenming Street in the old city of Luoyang. The time when it was first built is unknown. It was rebuilt in the 6th year of Jiaqing (1527 AD) in the Ming Dynasty. Facing south, it contains over 20 buildings, including Halberd Gate, Dacheng Hall, Chongsheng Hall, and east and west galleries and wing chambers, covering a total floor space of 1,444 sq. m.

祖师庙

第六批全国重点文物保护单位

明

Zushi Temple

祖师庙位于洛阳市老城区北大街中部。始建年代无考，为供奉道教祖师老子而建的建筑群，原有戏楼、大门、照壁、前殿、后殿等，殿内奉有祖师铜像，常有民间工匠拜祭，香火不断。

现存主要建筑有前殿、大殿、耳房，建筑面积341平方米。大殿面阔五间，进深三间，单檐歇山绿琉璃剪边灰筒瓦顶建筑，抬梁式木构架，七架梁后对双步梁，檐下施五踩双昂斗栱，木构件保持典型的元末明初的风格。

祖师庙是一座具有典型元末明初建筑风格的古建筑，对研究明代的道教建筑布局与道教文化，具有重要价值。

大殿外斗栱

Located on North Avenue in the old city of Luoyang City, the temple dates from the Ming Dynasty (1368 ~ 1644 AD). It contains 5 single-eave halls with overhanging gable roof covered by glazed tiles.

祖师庙大殿

洛阳山陕会馆

第六批全国重点文物保护单位

清

Shanxi-Shaanxi Guild Hall in Luoyang

洛阳山陕会馆位于洛阳市老城区九都东路。始建于清康熙年间（1662～1722年）。会馆系当时山西、陕西两地巨贾筹资修建，建筑面积1895平方米。

会馆坐北向南，整体建筑呈

洛阳山陕会馆正门

洛阳山陕会馆正殿

传统的中轴线对称分布，从南至北计有盘龙琉璃照壁、东西门楼、东西木构牌楼式仪门、山门、舞楼、拜殿、正殿及东西配殿、东西廊房等，另有碑刻十余通和石狮等。

东西门楼面阔、进深各一间。琉璃照壁位于会馆中轴线最南端，高7.6米，宽13.2米，自下而上由青石须弥座、壁身、硬山式绿琉璃瓦顶三部分组成。檐下施琉璃一斗三升斗栱与琉璃垂花柱，壁身南面为素面青砖墙，北面镶嵌琉璃砖雕“二龙戏珠”等图案，色彩绚丽，装饰繁复华丽。

东西仪门，东西向，为四柱三间三楼式木牌楼，悬山式绿琉璃筒瓦顶，面阔三间，明间檐下施九踩斗栱，两次间檐下施七踩斗栱，各跳均出45度斜拱。山门东西两侧筑八字砖墙与东西仪门相连，面阔三间，歇山式绿琉璃瓦顶，明间高于两次间，檐下枋间均施木雕驼墩、垂莲柱、雀替等。

舞楼又名戏楼，坐南朝北，二层，南面为庑殿式绿琉璃剪边灰筒瓦顶，面阔五间，北面为歇山式绿琉璃剪边灰筒瓦顶，面阔三间，南北正脊之间有一横向脊相连，成为“工字”脊；抬梁式结构，两架五架梁连在一起；前后檐下施三踩单昂斗栱；装饰达到无木不雕的地步，内容为“二龙戏珠”、戏剧人物、瑞禽猛兽、花卉等，并在木构件上存有清代旋子点金彩画等；屋面琉璃艺术构件均为清代烧制，釉质依然亮丽。

拜殿面阔五间，进深三间，歇山式绿琉璃剪边灰筒瓦顶建筑；七架梁前后双步廊用四柱木构架，

琉璃照壁

檐下施五踩重昂斗栱，琴面昂，每跳均出45度斜昂，梁架间施一斗三升隔架科斗栱。木构架上亦存有清代旋子点金彩画，保存完好。前檐柱础石为圆雕狮子驮仰莲；后檐清代隔扇门裙板上分别浮雕八仙及卷草等，雕工精湛。

正殿为悬山式绿琉璃剪边、黄琉璃枋心灰筒瓦顶建筑，面阔五间、进深两间；七架梁前出单步廊，檐下施五踩重昂斗栱，每跳均出45度斜昂；平板枋、挑檐檩和殿内梁、檩均为清代绘旋子点金彩画“龙、凤穿牡丹”，色彩依旧艳丽；前檐柱顶石为圆雕龙驮、虎牛驮莲花，并在莲瓣上分别刻有四种字体的“寿”字。

洛阳山陕会馆是豫西地区保存较为完整的清代早期建筑群之一。在建筑装饰艺术上非常讲究，盘龙琉璃照壁及砖、木、石雕工艺精湛、独具特色，舞楼、拜殿、正殿内梁枋上有大面积的、完整的清代彩绘，为中原地区面积最大、保存最完好的清代原始彩绘。现存建筑布局基本完整，布局与结构都有独到之处，对研究中原会馆建筑具有较高价值。

Located at No. 69, East Jiudu Road, the old city of Luoyang, the guild hall was built in the reign of Kangxi (1662 ~ 1722 AD) in the Qing Dynasty with donations made by successful merchants from Shanxi and Shaanxi. Main buildings are: a glazed screen wall with coiled dragons, east and west Yi gates in the style of wooden archways, a main gate, a Wu tower, a worship hall, a main hall, east and west side halls, and east and west gallery houses. The total floor space is 1,895 sq. m.

汝州文庙

清

Confucian Temple in Ruzhou

汝州文庙位于汝州市望嵩中路。又称学宫，初建于明洪武三年（1370年），后经历代修葺。明清时期，汝州文庙一直是汝州的最高学府，尤以收藏的二十块北宋徽宗大观三年（1109年）由汝州知州王采收集、筛选，精工细刻的《汝帖》最为珍贵。

文庙坐北朝南，建筑面积2885平方米。现存中轴线建筑有山门、大明坊、大成坊、大成殿、启圣宫、明伦堂等，东西廊房对称分布，多为硬山式灰板瓦顶建筑。大成殿前有站台和石狮，面阔五间，为单檐歇山式绿琉璃筒瓦顶建筑，檐下施五踩斗栱，并施彩画。

汝州文庙从平面设计到建筑格局，都是按照府级规模设计的，从单座建筑的力学设计到抗震性能都有一定的工艺水平，有较高的研究价值。

汝州文庙大成殿

汝州文庙附属建筑

汝州文庙附属建筑

Located on Middle Wangsong Road, Ruzhou City, the south-facing temple was first built in the 3rd year of Hongwu (1370 AD) in the Ming Dynasty and was renovated many times afterwards. Main buildings on the central axis are: Qisheng Palace, Dacheng Hall, Wenming Archway, Dacheng Archway and Minglun Hall. The total floor space is 2,885 sq. m.

朱仙镇清真寺

第六批全国重点文物保护单位

清

Mosque at Zhuxian Town

朱仙镇清真寺位于开封市朱仙镇老虎洞街。始建于明代，清乾隆三年(1737年)重修。

寺院采用四合院的建筑布局，坐西向东，建筑面积2666平方米。分前院和后院两部分，前院讲经授学，后院演习武术。建筑分布在中轴线上，有前大门、碑楼、卷棚、大殿、窑殿、后山门。大门为单檐歇山绿琉璃筒瓦顶建筑，卷棚、大殿及窑殿均为硬山式勾连搭绿琉璃瓦顶建筑，两侧厢房、沐浴室等，均为硬山式灰瓦顶建筑。寺内的木雕、石雕、砖雕艺术精湛，面积较大，主体建筑的构件上布满雕饰，题材广泛，内容丰富。图案雕饰动静兼备、栩栩如生。寺内存有清代石碑两通。

朱仙镇清真寺是一座保存完整，建筑艺术精湛的清代伊斯兰教寺院，是中国文化与伊斯兰教文化的巧妙结合，是研究清代伊斯兰教清真寺建筑的典型实例。

朱仙镇清真寺山门

朱仙镇清真寺礼拜大殿

碑楼及山门背面

Located on Laohudong Street, Zhuxian Town, Kaifeng County, the mosque was first built in the Ming Dynasty, and was rebuilt in the 3rd year of Qianlong (1737 AD) in the Qing Dynasty. Laid out like a traditional quadrangle, the mosque faces east. Buildings on the central axis are: front gate, stele tower, juanpeng (round ridge roof), main hall, mihrab, and back gate. The total floor space is 2,666 sq. m.

开封东大寺

第六批全国重点文物保护单位

清

Dongda Mosque in Kaifeng

开封东大寺位于开封市顺河回族区清平南北街。始建年代无考，明、清时期曾数次重修，现东大寺建筑为清道光二十六年（1846年）重建。

寺院坐西朝东，东西长160米，宽51米，建筑面积3447平方米。有大门、二门、卷棚、大殿、沐浴室及配殿、厢房等，均为硬山式灰瓦顶建筑，抬梁式木构架。寺内尚存有明代阿拉伯文《可兰经》古碑及重修清真寺碑。

开封东大寺是一处宗教设施齐全、一直延续至今仍作为传统宗教活动的场所。它是一处具有典型的明清时期特征的伊斯兰教古典式建筑群，对研究伊斯兰建筑与中国传统建筑的融合具有重要的参考作用。

可兰经文碑细部

开封东大寺二门

开封东大寺礼拜大殿

The mosque is located on North and South Qingping Street in the Hui nationality district at Shunhe, Kaifeng City. The current standing buildings were rebuilt in the 26th year of Daoguang (1846 AD) in the Qing Dynasty. Facing east, the mosque contains the following buildings: main gate, secondary gate, juanpeng, main hall, bath house, side halls and wing chambers. The total floor space is 3,447 sq. m.

开封东大寺沐浴室

陈元光祖祠

第六批全国重点文物保护单位

清

Ancestral Hall for Chen Yuanguang

陈元光祖祠位于信阳市固始县陈集乡陈集村。为了纪念唐代陈元光家族率府兵平抚泉州、潮州“蛮獠啸乱”而建，被称为“开漳圣王”祠堂，亦称“陈氏将军祠”。始建于唐天宝年间（742～755年），后经历代修葺。现存建筑均为清代，计有大门、正堂、配房、左右厢房及耳房。

祖祠整体建筑为四合院布局，坐北向南，均为硬山式青砖灰板瓦顶，砖、木、石结构，穿逗式木梁架，正堂梁架为四柱三间九界，从南至北依次为三界磕头轩、内四界、后双步三部分，与《营造法源》的“厅堂式”结构形式完全一致，证明穿逗式建筑结构在长江以北地区依然存在。祠东南600米处有陈氏祖茔。

陈元光祖祠建筑布局严谨，中轴线主体建筑突出，为典型的南方穿逗式木构架结构，是南方穿逗式建筑在河南存在的实物例证，是一组有较高历史、艺术价值的建筑群体。

陈元光祖祠

Located at Chenji Village, Chenji Township, Gushi County, the hall was built in the years of Tianbao (742 ~ 755 AD) in the Tang Dynasty, and was renovated many times afterwards. Currently it contains 31 houses built in the Qing Dynasty, with the general layout of a traditional quadrangle and a floor space of 740 sq. m.

太康文庙

清

Confucian Temple in Taikang

太康文庙位于周口市太康县城关镇黉学街，又称太康黉学。始建于汉代，元末兵燹被毁，明、清时期多次重修，现存拜殿和大成殿均为清代建筑。

太康文庙坐北向南。拜殿面阔五间，进深三间，单檐歇山式灰筒瓦顶建筑，檐下施五踩重昂斗栱。大成殿面阔七间，进深五间，前重檐歇山式绿琉璃筒瓦顶建筑，抬梁式与穿逗式结构相结合，七架梁前后对双步廊，檐下施五踩重昂斗栱。屋面前坡为重檐，加深了大成殿的深度，扩大了空间。四个翼角高挑，趋于南方建筑风格。

太康文庙大成殿为中原地区少见的南方建筑形式，梁架为南方穿逗式与北方抬梁式相结合，普拍枋、阑额、雀替上的镂空木雕，具有较高的艺术价值。大殿东西两山墙下部一米左右使用木质腰骨，腰骨以上无碱蚀，为古建筑防潮防碱提供了实物例证。

太康文庙大成殿

The temple is located on Hongxue Street, Chengguan Town, Taikang County. The time when it was first built is unknown. Facing south, it contains a worship hall and Dacheng Hall as its main buildings. Both were built in the Qing Dynasty, and cover a floor space of 462 sq. m.

长城（河南段）

The Henan Section of the Great Wall

河南省楚长城镇平段

河南省境内长城主要分布在豫北安阳、鹤壁、新乡等地的战国赵长城，豫中北新乡、郑州等地的战国魏长城，豫南南阳、平顶山、驻马店等地的春秋战国楚长城以及豫西北济源的北齐长城，共计1000余公里。

各个时期的长城均建筑在山岭之上，一般用石块砌筑而成，有关城、城墙、烽火台、战壕、营寨等遗迹。

河南楚长城南召段垛口

小顶山魏长城遗址

浮戏山魏长城遗址北段

The Great Wall in Henan province mainly include the Great Wall of Zhao state in Warring States Period ranged in Anyang, Hebi and Xinxiang, the Great Wall of Wei state in Warring States Period ranged from Xinxiang to Zhengzhou, the Great Wall of Beiqi Dynasty located in Jiyuan. All of them were about more than 1000 kilometers.

The Great Wall in various times were all built on the mountains, most of it was built of stons. There were some ruins, such as the city walls, the beacon-fire towers, the trenches, the military camps and so on.

石窟寺及石刻

Grottoes of Temple and Stone Carvings

石窟寺及石刻

Grottoes of Temple and Stone Carvings

河南文化遗产

全国重点文物保护单位

Brief Information on Major Historic Sites under National Protection in Henan Province

石窟寺及石刻

Grottoes of Temple and Stone Carvings

龙门石窟

第一批全国重点文物保护单位

北魏至唐

Longmen Grottoes

奉先寺卢舍那佛

奉先寺大卢舍那像龛

龙门石窟位于洛阳市南郊13公里的伊水两岸。是中国北方重要的佛教石窟群。石窟所在地两山对峙，伊水穿流，犹如天然门阙，故称“伊阙”。大大小小的佛龛密布于伊阙两岸的崖壁之上，南北绵延1000余米。

龙门石窟始凿于北魏孝文帝迁都洛阳（494年）前后，历经东魏、西魏、北齐、隋、唐、宋长达四百多年，共雕造窟龛二千三百多个，佛塔八十余座，造像近十一万尊，题记二千八百余品。主要洞窟有古阳洞、宾阳三洞、莲花洞、路洞、药方洞、潜溪寺、敬善寺、奉先寺、万佛洞和看经寺等。

古阳洞位于西山南部，是龙门石窟开凿最早、雕刻最华丽、造像题记最多的洞窟，高11.2米、宽6.9米、进深13.1米，平面为马蹄形，穹隆顶。正壁雕一佛二菩萨。洞窟雕满大小龛像，大部有施主造像发愿文，著名的“龙门二十品”中有十九品在古阳洞。

宾阳洞位于西山北部，由中、南、北三洞组成。宾阳洞平面为马蹄形，穹隆顶，正壁雕一佛二弟子二菩萨，高大威严。四壁满雕小龛，幽雅和谐，是北魏晚期石窟造像的经典之作。

莲花洞在西山中部偏南。因洞中藻井为一精美的浮雕大莲花而得名。开凿于北魏孝昌年间（525～527年），是北魏晚期开凿的大型洞窟。

药方洞位于西山奉先寺和古阳洞之间，因窟门两旁刻有古代药方而得名。开凿于北魏孝明帝时，历经北齐直到唐高宗、武则天时期仍有雕作。

潜溪寺在西山北部，前庭平面为方形，后室为马蹄形，高9.9米、宽9.8米、进深7.1米。正壁雕一佛二弟子二菩萨和二天王。是初唐时期的代表洞窟之一。

奉先寺远望

奉先寺位于西山南部，是龙门石窟最大的摩崖像龛。进深38.7米、宽33.5米。主像卢舍那大佛通高17.14米，头饰螺纹发髻，身披通肩式袈裟，结跏趺坐在束腰须弥座上。两侧二弟子、二菩萨、二天王、二力士。文殊、普贤二菩萨高13.25米。二天王高10.5米，左为北方多闻天王，身披铠甲，手持宝塔，足踏夜叉；右为南方增长天王，戎装甲胄。二力士上身袒露，下着战裙，高9.75米。在卢舍那佛座的左侧束腰部位有唐玄宗开元十年（722年）补刻的《河洛上都龙门山之阳大卢舍那像龛记》。

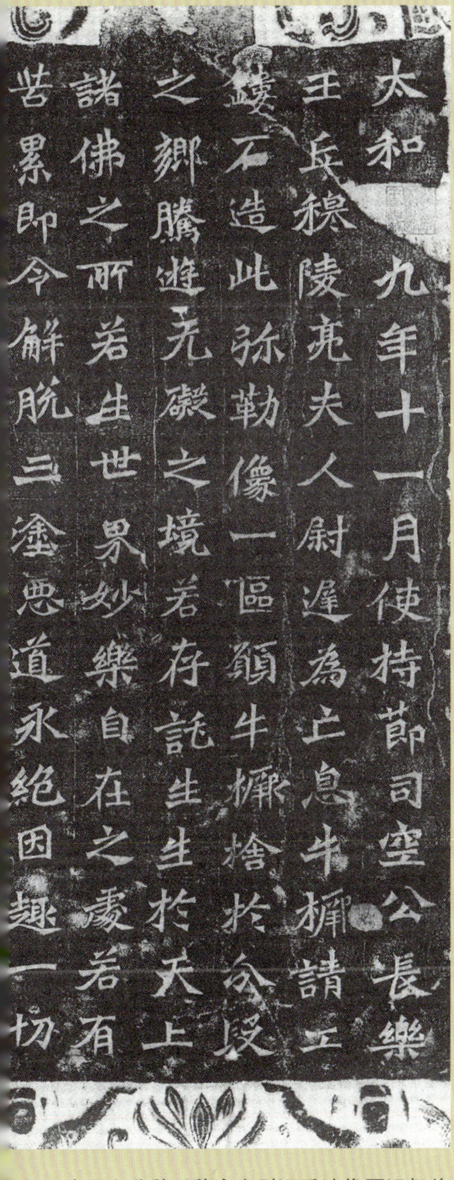

龙门二十品之北魏丘穆亮妻尉迟氏造像题记拓片

宾阳中洞如来三尊像

皇甫公窟北壁下部礼佛图

万佛洞位于西山中部。凿成于唐永隆元年（680年），平面为方形，平顶。

除了石窟造像，龙门石窟中的题记和碑刻，如“龙门二十品”和唐代褚遂良书《伊阙佛龛之碑》等，是我国古代书法艺术的珍品。

Located on Longmen Mountain on the banks of Yishui River in the southern suburbs of Luoyang City, the grottoes date back to the period from the Northern Wei Dynasty to the Northern Song Dynasty (386 ~ 1127 AD). They contain over 2,100 niches, nearly 100,000 Buddha statues, over 2,870 steles and inscriptions, and over 40 Buddhist pagodas. They were included on World Heritage List in Nov. 2000.

巩县石窟

第二批全国重点文物保护单位

北魏至宋

Grottoes in Gong County

巩县石窟，位于巩义市东北10公里大力山下伊洛河北岸。开凿于北魏时期，后经西魏、北齐、唐、宋各代，相继凿窟造像，共雕凿五个洞窟，佛像七千七百四十三尊。

第一窟，窟门面南，门上开方形窗，门外西侧雕力士一尊，高3.4米，力士像上方雕两排罗汉和一尊菩萨像。东侧雕一尊力士像，高3.36米，力士像上部残存一佛、一菩萨。窟平面为方形，高6米。窟顶雕方格平棊，靠中心柱的一周方格内雕飞天，其他雕莲花、卷草和化生。中心柱边长2.8米，四面各雕一佛龛，龛内雕

第一窟如来坐像

第一窟礼佛图

第一窟主佛

一佛二菩萨二弟子，正面佛座两侧各雕一狮子。中心柱上部和平基相接处各雕四个莲花化生。南壁窟门两侧雕上下三列礼佛图。

第二窟，除东壁一龛为东魏时所雕外，其余十个龛为唐代开凿。中心柱南面上下排列三龛，最下面一龛较大，内雕一佛二菩萨二弟子和二力士，分别立于莲花和莲蓬上。龛楣雕七佛和飞天，龛两侧雕二菩萨。

第三窟，平面呈方形，高4.25米，长宽各5米。窟顶雕方格平棊，靠中心一周方格内雕飞天，其他部位雕莲花、卷草和化生童子。中心柱宽2.22～2.38米，柱下方形基座高0.56米、宽2.78～2.92米。南壁雕上下三列礼佛图。

第四窟，形制和第三窟基本相同。窟门为拱形，门楣雕卷草纹，楣角雕龙头，门道两侧有唐代以后小佛龛。门内南壁东侧千佛龛下雕上下两列礼佛图。

第五窟，窟门为拱形，上窄下宽，楣脚雕龙头，门两侧有方

第三窟中心柱南向龛东侧上飞天

柱，下雕狮子柱础，门外两侧各雕一力士。窟平面近方形，唯四壁中部微向外凸，没有中心柱。高约3米，长宽各3.2米。

千佛洞，圆拱形龛楣，高1.5米、宽2.12米。后壁和两侧壁皆雕排列整齐的小佛龛，共计九百九十九尊，故称“千佛洞”。

巩县石窟共雕十八幅“帝后礼佛图”，其中第一窟最精美，东面三幅是以皇帝为首的供养人行例，西面是以皇后为首的供养人行列，均有比丘作前导。巩县石窟是中国北方重要的佛教石窟之一，其佛像和浮雕堪称古代雕刻的珍品。

Located east of Wan Village, Gongyi City, the grottoes date back to the period between the Northern Wei Dynasty to the Song Dynasty (386 ~ 1127 AD). There are 5 caves, 1,000 niches for Buddha statues, 3 statues carved in cliffs, 255 niches for statues, and 7,743 Buddha statues.

灵泉寺石窟

第四批全国重点文物保护单位

东魏至宋

Grottoes of Lingquan Temple

灵泉寺石窟位于安阳市西南30公里的宝山东南麓。灵泉寺始建于东魏武定四年（546年），原名宝山寺，隋开皇年间隋文帝杨坚取群山之泉及该寺高僧灵裕法师法号的首字，改宝山寺为灵泉寺。

灵泉寺坐落在宝山与岚峰山之间，坐北向南，原有山门、天王殿、三佛殿、观音阁、地藏王殿等建筑，至清末已成为废墟。唯北齐、唐代石塔及周围山崖上石窟造像保存基本完整。经调

灵泉寺石窟石雕塔林近景

灵泉寺石窟石雕塔林

查，灵泉寺石窟现存有石窟造像、摩崖石塔共二百零九处，北齐和唐代石塔各两座，和尚墓地一处。其中浮雕塔龛一百五十三座，被称为“宝山万佛沟塔林”，雕造于东魏至宋代，且多数塔龛都有雕凿年代和铭记。岚峰山的大留圣窟，由道凭法师开凿于东魏武定四年（546年），故亦称“道凭石堂”，为灵泉寺石窟中时代最早、规模最大的窟龛。宝山的大住圣窟由灵裕法师开凿于隋开皇九年（589年），为隋代石窟中的代表作。宝山上的道凭法师烧身塔，建造于北齐河清二年（563年），雕刻之精，堪称一绝。唐代双石塔位于灵泉寺旧址上，均为单层密檐式方形石塔，自下而上由基台、基座、塔身、塔檐、塔刹组成，东塔通高5.22米，西塔通高5.56米。寺院西百米处即和尚墓地，散存有众多的石刻。

灵泉寺石窟石雕佛塔

灵泉寺石窟大住圣窟门侧雕像

Located on both sides of the valley of Bao Mountain in Anyang County, the grottoes date back to the period between the Eastern Wei Dynasty to the Northern Song Dynasty (534 ~ 1126 AD). They are distributed in a range extending 1,000 meters east to west and 500 meters from north to south in Bao Mountain and Lanfeng Mountain. They contain 209 statues in niches.

千唐志斋石刻

第四批全国重点文物保护单位

西晋至民国

Qiantang Museum of Epitaphs

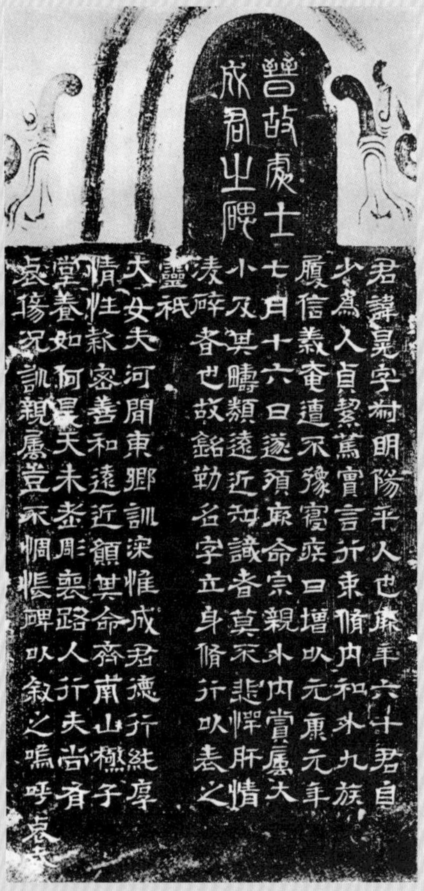

晋故处士成君之碑拓片（西晋元康元年）

千唐志斋石刻位于河南省新安县铁门镇，为我国最大的墓志石刻集中地。

斋中收藏有自西晋以来历代墓志石刻一千四百一十三件，其中，西晋志一件，北魏志两件，隋志两件，唐代墓志铭多达一千一百八十五件，宋志八十八件。20世纪30年代，张钫在洛阳北邙广泛搜罗墓志石刻，并在“蛰庐”西隅辟地建斋。

斋室包括一走廊、三天井、拱券式砖窑十五孔，将墓志石刻镶嵌于内外墙壁上。墓志石刻的内容涉及政治、军事、社会风俗、典章制度等各方面。特别是唐代墓志，自武德、贞观至天复、天祐无不尽备。记载了唐代三百余年文治武功及各种人物的社会活动，是研究唐代社会政治、经济、军事、文化、外交的珍贵资料，具有证史、纠史、补史的重要价值。

千唐志斋为我国史学研究的资料宝库，素有“中华志林”之称。其所藏郑板桥、董其昌、王铎、吴昌硕、康有为等书画石刻和历代造像、经幢、碑碣等，皆为艺术珍品。

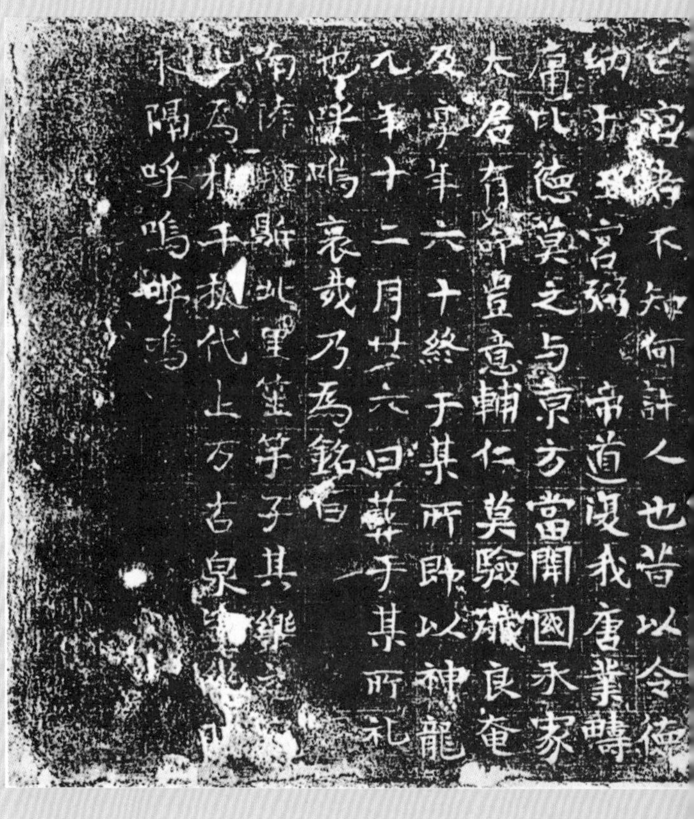

大唐亡宫九品墓志拓片（唐神龙元年）

Located in Tiemen Town, Xin' an County, the museum was built in 1932. It consists of a cave dwelling with 15 brick arches, three courtyards and a winding corridor. On the inner and outer walls are 1,413 pieces of relics collected by Zhang Fang, including epitaphs, paintings, calligraphic works and stone carvings, which date back to the period from the Tang Dynasty to the Qing Dynasty. In particular, 1,185 epitaphs were made in the Tang Dynasty.

鸿庆寺石窟

第五批全国重点文物保护单位

北魏

Grottoes of Hongqing Temple

鸿庆寺石窟位于义马市东南14公里的石佛村。

石窟坐西朝东，现存五个洞窟，南北横向排列在白鹿山下。自北向南依次编为1～5窟。窟内共有佛龛四十六个，大小造像一百二十余尊，佛传故事四幅，均凿于北魏时期。第一窟为塔柱窟，高5.4米、宽5.9米、进深7.5米，中心柱四面各有一大佛龛，正面下部与背面上部皆有浮雕画面，北壁上侧浮雕“出城娱乐”佛传故事，所雕楼台城郭中的五角形城门楼，是一座高层建筑，城门、城垣、城楼曲折相连，真实再现了北魏时期城楼建筑的形象；西壁中央雕菩提树，挺拔繁茂，周围群魔或持大刀、长矛，或持弓箭、盾牌，神态各异，是一组生动的浮雕画面，表现了释迦牟尼“降魔成道”的情景；南壁上层西段雕刻“犍陟吻别”、“礼佛图”。“犍陟吻别”雕菩萨半结跏于束腰圆座上，左足踏莲花座，白马犍陟前肢曲卧，引颈吻菩萨左足。“礼佛图”表现了高官贵族出行礼佛的盛大场面。

鸿庆寺石窟布局紧凑，规制严整，技法娴熟，是中原地区中小型石窟的典范。

鸿庆寺石窟1号窟外景

鸿庆寺石窟 1 号窟佛像

Located west of Shifo Village, the City of Yima, at the foot of a 30-meter-high sandstone hill, the grottoes date back to the period from the Northern Wei Dynasty to the Tang Dynasty (386 ~ 907 AD). The 4 grottoes that remain contain 46 niches and 121 Buddha statues.

鸿庆寺石窟 1 号窟南壁浮雕

小南海石窟

第五批全国重点文物保护单位

北齐 Xiaonanhai Grottoes

小南海石窟，位于安阳市西南25公里的善应村龟盖山南麓。因南临山泉“小南海”而得名。

小南海石窟现存洞窟三座，分别坐落在龟盖山南麓的崖壁上，开凿于北齐天保年间。其规模、题材和风格大同小异。西窟坐东面西，平面略呈方形，高1.76米、宽1.36米、进深1.76米，窟门作拱券状，门楣正中雕一朵莲花，两旁浮雕一腾龙，下雕两只金翅鸟，窟门两侧各雕一守门人，守门人之上各刻一尊倒立的裸体虎头人身。门左侧崖壁上，用减地法浅雕供养人像一组。窟顶作覆斗式，窟内造像皆为高浮雕，后壁正中为释迦牟尼像，佛高0.65米，其左右立胁侍弟子，高0.6米；南北两壁镌有胁侍菩萨和弟子立像三尊。中窟坐北向

小南海石窟1号窟

小南海石窟 2 号窟

南，窟前原有木结构建筑已毁。窟平面呈方形，高1.78米、宽1.19米、进深1.34米，窟门呈拱形，门两侧各雕一尊护法神立像。窟顶为覆斗状，莲花藻井。窟内西壁、东壁有高浮雕一佛二菩萨像，北壁为一佛二弟子像。南壁遍雕人物和花卉图案。东窟位于中窟东500米处的南海泉北岸，1999年整体搬迁到中窟之东8米处。该窟略呈方形，高1.79米、宽1.3米、进深1.2米。门外崖壁上镌刻佛、弟子、塔及菩提树组成的图案。窟内北壁正中为释迦牟尼佛坐像，东西两壁各雕三尊菩萨像。

小南海石窟的造像风格、雕刻技法与河北响堂山石窟相似，是研究佛教史及石窟艺术史的珍贵资料。

Located at Biegai Mountain, Zhuanghuo Village, Anyang County, the grottoes date back to the Northern Qi Dynasty (550 ~ 577 AD). The 3 grottoes that remain, one in the middle and the other two to the east and west of it, contain hundreds of stone statues.

小南海石窟浮雕

大丕山摩崖大佛及石刻

第五批全国重点文物保护单位

北朝至明

Great Buddha statue on a cliff and stone carvings at Dapi Mountain

大丕山摩崖大佛及石刻，位于浚县城区大丕山东天宁寺院内及其附近。

天宁寺始建于北魏太和年间（477～499年），时称“大丕山寺”，明代改称“天宁寺”。寺内现存后周显德六年（959年）《准敕不停废记》碑一通，记载了后周世宗柴荣颁诏灭佛，而天宁寺得以“准敕不停废”的史实。可知当时天宁寺及摩崖大佛的历史地位。

大丕山摩崖大佛，古称“大佛岩”，依山凿就，面向黄河，通高21.33米。佛为倚坐式弥勒造像，头饰螺髻，面相丰满，眉骨突起，左手扶膝，右手施无畏印。双脚踏于仰莲之上。身着双领下垂袈裟，内衣结带，衣纹疏朗。大佛楼面阔13.64米、进深14.76米、通高25.6米，硬山式木结构建筑。现存建筑为明正统十年（1445年）重建。以大佛为依托兴建的天宁寺，形成两条十字形中轴线，即以山门、藏经阁、大佛楼为东西轴线，以天王殿、三佛殿、十八罗汉殿、地藏殿为南北

大丕山摩崖大佛

大丕山天宁寺全景

轴线。总占地面积8000余平方米。据记载，大佛开凿于北齐，唐初雕成，为中原地区年代最早、造型最大的摩崖大佛。

摩崖大佛附近，现存历代石刻碑铭三百余块，其中北魏石兽，唐代"大丕山铭"、陇西尹公浮图、八棱经幢，后周《准敕不停废记》碑，宋代《康显侯告》碑，明代王阳明《大丕山诗》、王铎《再至青坛诗》等，均为不可多得的传世精品。千佛洞石窟现存造像九百六十余尊，多为唐代作品，是河南重要的石窟之一。

大丕山千佛洞

Located in Tianning Temple, in the town of Jun County, they were made during the period from the Northern Qi Dynasty to the Tang Dynasty (550 ~ 907 AD). Carved at the foot of the mountain and facing the Yellow River, the statue has a total height of 21.33 meters. In its vicinity are stone carvings made during the period from the Northern Wei Dynasty to the Ming Dynasty.

受禅碑与受禅台

第五批全国重点文物保护单位

三国 The stele of and the platform in memory of the acceptance of the abdicated throne

受禅碑与受禅台位于临颍县繁城镇内，是当时受禅过程的佐证。

受禅碑为三国魏黄初元年（220年）刻立。《公卿将军上尊号奏》碑，高3.7、宽1.1、厚0.33米，碑文正面二十二行，背面十行，每行四十九字，是四十六位

受禅碑

受禅台

公卿将军呈给魏王曹丕的奏章，力劝以曹代汉，建立魏国之事。《受禅表》碑，高3.7、宽1.1、厚0.3米。碑文二十二行，每行四十九字，详细记录了黄初元年冬十月二十九日，汉献帝在受禅台上禅让于魏王，魏王曹丕登基为魏国皇帝的事实。受禅碑呈圭形，额有穿，无花纹雕饰。石料为五色鲕状石灰岩，质地坚硬呈颗粒状。该碑不仅有历史价值，而且有着较高的书法艺术价值。史载：唐代李绰说此碑“王朗文，梁鹄书，钟繇镌字，谓之三绝”。当时著名的书法家颜真卿、徐浩、刘禹锡等都对受禅碑有过具体论述并学过它的笔法。从北宋开始，历代金石学家、书法家、书法理论家对两座碑多有评价。清末康有为称其“书家之盛，莫如季汉……于时卫敬侯出，古文实与邯郸齐名，笔迹精熟。今受禅表遗笔独存，鸱视虎顾，雄伟冠时”。

受禅台筑成于东汉延康元年，台上原有大殿等建筑。现仅存高台一座，台高13米，面积约8448平方米。

These are located at Fancheng Town, Linying County. The stele was made and erected in the 1st year of Yuanchu (220 AD) in the Wei Dynasty, with a height of 3.7 meters. The platform covers an area of 8,448 sq. m.

大唐嵩阳观纪圣德感应之颂碑

第五批全国重点文物保护单位

唐

Tang-dynasty stele of Songyang Taoist Temple

大唐嵩阳观纪圣德感应之颂碑

大唐嵩阳观纪圣德感应之颂碑，位于河南省登封市北2公里嵩山南麓书院村。是嵩阳书院的附属文物。

嵩阳书院为我国古代四大书院之一，原名嵩阳寺，始建于北魏太和八年（484年）。名儒范仲淹、司马光、程颢、程颐、朱熹等人先后在此讲学。现存书院保持了明末清初建筑布局，占地面积10000余平方米。

大唐嵩阳观纪圣德感应之颂碑位于书院大门外西侧10米处，唐天宝三年（744年）刻立。由基座、碑身、碑额、云盘、碑首五层雕石组成，通高9.02、宽2.04、厚1.05米，重达82吨，为河南现存最大、雕刻最好的石碑。碑趺用一块巨石雕成，四壁表面有线刻童子、卷草、宝相花和狮子等图案。又在束腰四面雕出十个门状像龛，正背面各三龛，侧面各两龛，龛内各雕神像一躯。碑身高3.82、宽2.06、厚1.04米。碑文由裴迥篆额，李林甫撰文，徐浩八分隶书，内容记述嵩阳观道士孙太冲为唐玄宗李隆基炼丹九转的故事。书法刚柔适度，笔力遒劲，是唐代隶书的代表作。

Located in front of Songyang Academy north of the City of Dengfeng, the stele was made and erected in the 3rd year of Tianbao (744 AD) in the Tang Dynasty. With a total height of 9.02 meters, it consists of a base, a body, a top part, yunpan, and five layers of stone carving on its top. The inscription on it records the story of Taoists at Songyang Taoist Temple concocting elixir for Emperor Xuanzong of the Tang Dynasty.

青天河摩崖

南北朝至唐

Cliff carvings at Qingtianhe

青天河摩崖位于焦作市博爱县寨豁乡青天河丹河峡谷内。由北魏摩崖和石佛滩隋唐摩崖造像组成。

北魏摩崖位于青天河景区内一座酷似天然大佛的山峰腰部绝壁上，面临丹河。石刻面积近2平方米，镌刻于北魏永平二年（509年）。摩崖以线刻观世音立像为中心，两侧刻题记，共四百三十二字。内容分为两部分，第一部分为《妙法莲花经·普门品第廿四》经文片段，第二部分记叙了当时修筑丹道的时间、经过、用工人数和镌刻摩崖石刻题记的原因等，最后为主持修路的

青天河摩崖全景

将官名单。

石佛滩隋唐摩崖造像在丹河峡谷南端石佛滩峭壁上，与北魏摩崖相距约30公里。开凿于隋大业十一年至十二年间（615～616年），初创时为隋朝皇家所封“同义寺”，唐代又开凿一批佛龛。20世纪50年代末修建焦太铁路时曾毁一批，现存佛龛五十九个，造像七十八尊，题记十方。造像有阿弥陀佛、弥勒佛、观音菩萨像等。

北魏线刻观世音和《观世音普门品》是国内最早佛经与图像相结合的石刻。题记内容则真实、准确地记录了当时修筑古丹道的情况，是研究北魏交通历史的重要资料。石佛滩隋唐摩崖造像反映了南北朝至隋向唐代过渡的特征，对于研究河南隋唐佛教艺术具有重要价值。

青天河摩崖近景

These include Northern Wei-dynasty cliff carvings and Sui-and-Tang-dynasty statues carved on cliffs at Shifo Beach. Located at Qingtianhe Scenic Area, the Northern Wei-dynasty carvings, covering nearly 2 sq. m., were made in the 2nd year of Yongping (509 AD). Carved on a cliff at Shifo Beach, the southern end of the valley of Dan River, the Sui-and-Tang-dynasty statues were made during the 11th and 12th year of Daye (615 ~ 616 AD) in the Sui Dynasty. There are 59 niches, 78 statues and 10 inscriptions.

西明寺造像碑

南北朝

Stele with statues at Ximing Temple

西明寺造像碑位于新乡县翟坡镇小宋佛村西北隅的新乡县历代石刻艺术博物馆内。

造像碑通高4.8米，整块青石雕刻而成。背光呈莲瓣形，正面雕一佛二菩萨，主尊为无量寿佛，胁侍为观世音和大势至，均跣足站立在狮子上；无量寿佛，右手施无畏印，左手提香包，身着褒衣博带式袈裟，内着僧祇支，

西明寺造像碑

胸前素带作结下垂；观世音立于左侧，左手持净瓶，右手握莲蕾；大势至双手合十捧一莲蓓立于右侧。背光背面线刻一帷幔，观世音坐于方形莲座上，前有侍女，后有菩提树，观世音在菩提树下做道场。佛像基座方形四面刻捐资人题记，下为宝装覆莲座。

西明寺造像碑不仅形体高大，整体雕刻线条细腻流畅，而且表现出典型的北魏晚期造像风格，是北魏晚期造像碑中的精品。

无量寿佛造像局部

Located in the northwest corner of Xiaosongfo Village, Zhaipo Town, Xinxiang County, the stele was made in the Northern Wei Dynasty (386 ~ 534 AD). It has a total height of 4.8 meters. Its back is in the shape of a lotus, and its front is adorned with one Buddha statue and two Bodhisattva statues.

西明寺造像碑局部

升仙太子碑

第六批全国重点文物保护单位

唐

Immortalized Crown Prince Stele

升仙太子碑位于偃师市府店镇府南村缑山之巅。为武则天于圣历二年（699年）赴嵩岳封禅途中，游幸新竣工的缑山升仙太子庙时，撰书镌刻的一通巨碑。

碑通高8米。螭首，首身一体，高6.70米，宽1.55米，厚0.55米，赑屃座高1.30米。碑额书“升仙太子之碑”，碑阳竖书，三十三行，行六十六字，约二千一百七十余字，行草相间，近章草，可以看出女皇武则天的个性和才华。碑文内容记述了周灵王太子晋升仙的故事，赞颂武周盛世，最后描述缑山升仙太子庙的风

清代乾隆重修碑

升仙太子碑碑亭

貌。落款为“圣历二年（699年）岁次己亥六月甲申朔十九壬寅建”。碑阴旁题“大周天册金轮圣神皇帝御制御书”，内容分三段，上部为武则天《游仙篇》及诸臣题名；中间为随行重臣武三思、王及善、苏味道、魏文中、狄仁杰、娄师德等人题名；其下刻神龙二年（706年）相王李旦题名题记。

升仙太子碑不仅是研究武周盛世的珍贵文献资料，而且其书法艺术被中外书法界誉为“华夏女子第一书”，在我国书法史占有重要地位。

Located on top of Nangou Mountain south of Fudian Village, the City of Yanshi, the stele was made in the 2nd year of Shengli (699 AD) in the Tang Dynasty. It has a total height of 8 meters. Its top is adorned with a dragon that is 6.70 meters high, 1.55 meters wide and 0.55 meter thick. The bixi (turtle-like mythological animal) base is 1.30 meters high. The top part is inscribed with the characters 'Sheng Xian Tai Zi Zhi Bei' (the stele of the immortalized crown prince).

崇唐观造像

第六批全国重点文物保护单位

唐

Statues at Chongtang Taoist Temple

崇唐观造像位于登封市北部中岳嵩山太室山南麓逍遥谷崇唐观老君殿内。崇唐观，原名“隆唐观”，唐调露元年（679年），高宗与武则天游嵩山到逍遥谷访名道潘师正，赐建“隆唐观”。后曾多次修葺。现存山门、老君殿、元始天尊石造像一尊及唐至清碑三块。

老君殿为清代建筑，硬山式黄琉璃筒瓦顶建筑，面阔、进深各三间，崇唐观造像供奉于老君殿内，为元始天尊坐像。造像雕于唐长寿二年（693年），通高2.8米，由莲花须弥座和造像两部分组成。天尊头饰发髻，身披道袍，身前置三足凭几，坐于束腰莲花须弥座上。须弥座束腰处雕刻伎乐，正面伎乐之上刻有“大周隆唐观敬造元始天尊像并左右二真人，长寿二年十月十五日毕功谨记”。

崇唐观外景

崇唐观元始天尊像

崇唐观造像座、题记

唐碑分别为唐垂拱二年（686年）立的“唐王征君之碣”碑，唐圣历二年（699年）“唐墨山中岳体元先生大中大夫潘师正碣文并序”碑；清碑为“重修老君殿金装神像碑”。

崇唐观造像是我国现存最早、保存最完整的道教元始天尊像，观内现存碑刻具有重要的历史、书法和艺术价值，是研究我国古代雕刻和书法艺术的珍贵实物资料。

They are in Laojun Hall, Chongtang Taoist Temple, in Xiaoyao Valley at the southern foot of Taishi Mountain, north of Dengfeng City. Built in the 1st year of Tiaolu (679 AD) in the Tang Dynasty, the temple contains Laojun Hall (built in the Qing Dynasty), a main gate, statues and steles.

元次山碑

唐

Yuan Cishan's gravestone

元次山碑位于平顶山市鲁山县城鲁山文庙院内。为唐代刺史、诗人元结（719～772年）墓碑。

碑铭原立于鲁山县城北青条岭泉坡元结墓地，明万历四十二年（1614年）将碑移于此并建保护亭。碑亭为方形攒尖顶灰筒瓦顶建筑，元次山碑立于亭内。

元结，字次山，卒于唐大历七年（772年）。颜真卿为元结撰写碑文并书丹，完成于唐大历七年（772年）或大历十年（775年）。

元次山碑碑亭

元次山碑

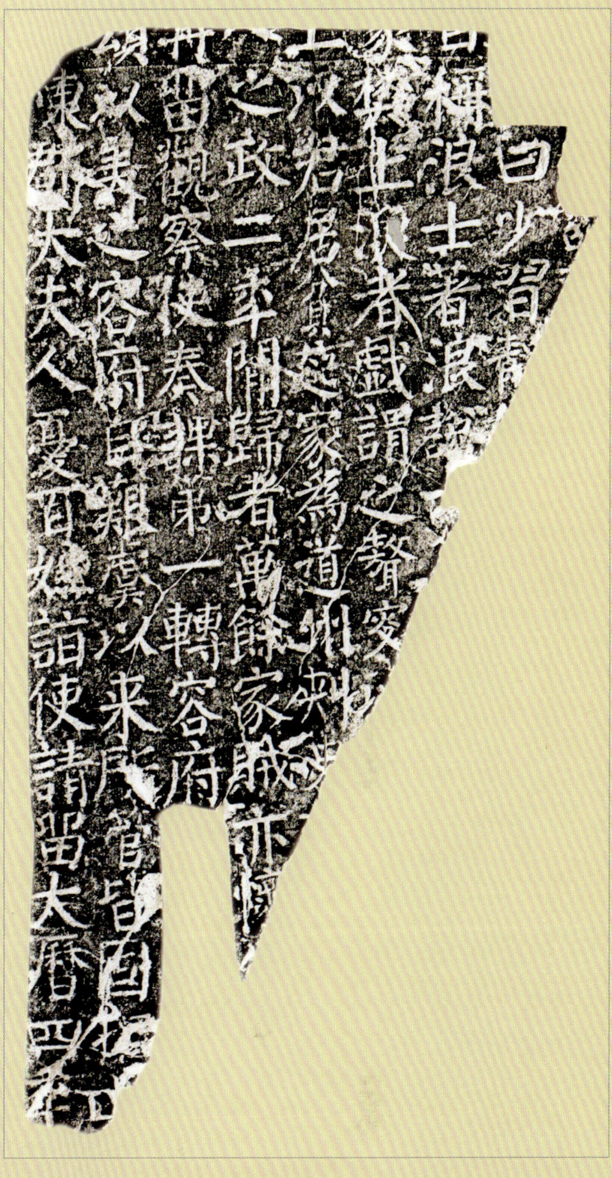

元次山碑拓片

碑为长方体，碑额已失，右下角残。四面碑刻，每行三十四字，正面背面各十七行，侧面各四行，共四十二行。全文共有一千三百七十八字，缺失二百三十字。

元次山墓碑是颜真卿六十多岁时的杰作，是颜书达到炉火纯青的作品之一，为国内仅存几方颜碑中的珍品，具有很高的历史、艺术价值。

Located in the compound of Lushan Confucian Temple in the town of Lushan County, this is the gravestone of Yuan Jie (Cishan by styled name; 719 ~ 772 AD). The epitaph was composed and written by Yan Zhenqing. In a cuboid shape, the gravestone has lost its top part, and its lower right corner is chipped. 230 characters in the 1,378-character epitaph have been lost.

云梦山摩崖

第六批全国重点文物保护单位

宋至民国

Cliff carvings at Yunmeng Mountain

云梦山摩崖位于鹤壁市淇县西南15公里云梦山。摩崖主要分布在云梦盆地的崖壁、水帘洞口、孙膑洞两侧、毛遂洞、舍身台、上圣庙、小峰门、五里井方圆5公里之内。有元、明、清历代的摩崖题记和摩崖碑刻大小共计二百二十品，碑刻三十三块，另有孙膑洞、毛遂洞、道教石塔、玉帝庙石牌坊、倒坐观音、将军庙、五里井石窟等。

云梦山摩崖较为集中，仅水帘洞口就保留了元代以来摩崖碑刻二十九方，有元代大文学家王恽撰写的《重修道院记》摩崖碑、明代御史孙征兰的狂草碑和通判窦文的行草碑。孙膑洞中有浅浮雕、线刻四十一幅八仙、戏曲人物故事，其中《白猿盗桃》、《孙膑下山》可谓上乘之作，对研究我国戏曲艺术有很高价值。舍身台摩崖题记，高6.9米，宽3.77

云梦山摩崖石刻

云梦山舍身台

孙膑洞

米，是河南省迄今发现最大的摩崖题记。道教石塔，创建于明代正德八年（1513年），呈正方形，密檐攒尖顶，塔身正中嵌有碑铭，是全真派李志和徒孙为其师丁尚立所建仙塔，是河南省仅有的道教石塔，为道教在云梦山活动的见证。

五里井石窟位于五里鬼谷中，为宋代开凿。洞窟开凿在距地面约10米的崖壁上，窟内正壁凿龛，原有释迦像被盗，四壁为千佛龛，龛内佛像姿态相同，高髻，身着偏衫袈裟，两臂下垂，掌心向上施禅定印。明成化十六年（1480年），在石窟下方创建华严寺。寺院已毁，现仅有殿基和殿内石供桌。

云梦山摩崖是了解当时社会和研究古代雕刻艺术的重要资料，具有较高的历史、文学和书法艺术价值。

Located at Yunmeng Mountain southwest of the town of Qi County, the carvings were made during the period from the Song Dynasty to the Republic Period (960 ~ 1911 AD). They are mainly found in a basin 3 km long and 1 km wide, and on cliffs in the mountain. There are 220 inscriptions and steles made in the Yuan, Ming, and Qing dynasties.

水帘洞摩崖题记

彼岸寺碑

第六批全国重点文物保护单位

宋 The stele of Bi'an Temple

彼岸寺碑位于漯河市郾城县黄河路西段第一实验中学院内。俗称“龙塔古篆”，刻立于北宋景德年间（1004～1007年）。

碑通高12.18米，由底座、基座、篆文碑、造像碑、碑顶构成。底座为八角形香水海池，池底刻海浪、蛟龙、亭台楼阁、高山流水及佛教故事等。基座为石雕须弥座，分为上、下两层，上层为四组佛龛浮雕四天王；下层为天龙八部、浮雕人物故事，四周为八根透雕蟠龙石柱。篆文碑为主体，高3.06米，平面四边形，上镌刻“重修许州郾城县彼岸寺碑铭”，正文小篆，记述了尉氏僧人契宗大师于太平兴国年间（976～984年）来此募资重修彼

彼岸寺碑

彼岸寺碑局部

岸寺的情况。上为盝顶，其上为受花台座，并浮雕伎乐仙人；再上为千佛造像碑，平面八边形，雕刻四百五十六尊罗汉和二十四尊佛像；碑顶砖砌密檐式八角攒尖顶，上覆灰瓦，檐下置仿木结构砖雕斗栱，上置宝瓶。

彼岸寺碑造型别致，雕刻精美，是我国宋代早期的佛教艺术珍品。

Located in the compound of Experimental Middle School on Yellow River Road, Yancheng County, the stele was made and erected in the Northern Song Dynasty (960 ~ 1127 AD). With a total height of 12.18 meters, it consists of a foundation, a base, a part inscribed with zhuan-style characters, a part adorned with statues, and a top part. The inscription records the rebuilding of Bi'an Temple in Yancheng County, Xuzhou. The statues are 456 Arhats and 24 Buddha statues. The top part has seven layers and is in close-eaves style.

刘碑寺碑

第六批全国重点文物保护单位

南北朝

The stele of Liubei Temple

刘碑寺碑位于登封市东南大冶镇刘碑村北。又名“刘碑”，北齐天保八年（557年）豫州刺史集刘氏居士筹资刻立。

该碑立于刘碑寺佛祖殿内，由一块青石雕成，碑体通高3.17米，宽1.46米，厚0.45米。由碑身、碑趺两部分组成。碑首雕有六龙盘绕，正中圆拱龛内一佛二菩萨；碑身中间刻一大佛龛，内一佛二弟子二菩萨；龛上为一菩萨，坐于菩提树下；大龛左右各为三小龛，龛中各为一佛二弟子；龛下有二弟子二力士，力士两侧各雕四只雄狮。碑阴上部为释迦多宝龛，龛下七佛八菩萨像，七佛下为二弟子奉博山炉，两侧各有四菩萨像。再下为造像碑记，正文为魏碑体，四十二行，行十三字，题记七例，字体圆浑遒劲。碑身侧面，上部为龛，内有一立佛二弟子，龛下线雕螭龙、云气、追逐射猎等图案。碑趺平面呈长方形，正面和左右侧面有十二尊高浮雕神王像，座背面为线雕射猎图。此外，寺内现存建筑有火神殿、老君殿等，均为清末硬山式青砖灰瓦顶建筑。

刘碑寺碑年代确切，内容丰富，雕刻精细，是中原地区北齐时期造像中的精品，对于研究北齐造像风格、佛教题材以及书法艺术都具有重要意义。

刘碑寺碑碑额正面

刘碑寺碑

Located north of Liubei Village, Daye Town, southeast of Dengfeng City, the stele was erected in the 8th year of Tianbao (557 AD) in the Northern Qi Dynasty. It has a total height of 3.17 meters. The body and the base were carved separately; the body has 7 niches in it. The top is adorned with a coiled dragon. The base is in a rectangular shape.

唐兀公碑

第六批全国重点文物保护单位

元　Tangwugong Stele

唐兀公碑位于濮阳县柳屯镇杨什八郎村南，唐兀氏墓地的南部。元至正十六年（1356年）立。

碑为青石质，盝顶上施火焰宝珠，檐下雕有斗栱，碑身正四方柱体，宝装覆莲瓣圆形碑座下连方趺。通高3.2米。碑身高1.7米，四周雕刻相近，额篆一周“大元赠

唐兀公碑

敦武校尉军民万户府百夫长唐兀公碑铭”，碑文镌刻于碑身四面，魏碑体，共七十二行，每面十八行，满行四十二字。碑文记述：唐兀氏是元代党项族之姓，始祖唐兀台原住贺兰山，西夏人，元朝初年，唐兀公随蒙古军队南征北战，收金破宋，多次获得功赏，曾参加元与南宋之间著名的襄樊战役，元灭南宋后，带军籍到开州濮阳县定居，开荒垦田，开办义学，受到当地人民爱戴，其后代卜茔于什八郎村；还详细记叙了唐兀氏自始祖唐兀台至唐兀闾马、达海、崇喜几代以后数辈人的子女嫁娶情况，从第四代起更姓“杨”，逐步融入汉民族，是不可多得的研究民族大融合的实物资料。

唐兀公碑是研究元代政治、经济、文化、军事，尤其是中华民族大融合的重要资料，其盝顶形式是研究元代建筑不可多得的例证。

唐兀公碑远景

Located north of Yangshibalang Village, Liutun Town, Puyang County, the stele was erected in the 16th year of Zhizheng (1356 AD) in the reign of Emperor Shun in the Yuan Dynasty. It has a quadrangular prism body and a hip-roof head. It has a total height of 3.2 meters, with the body measuring 1.7 meters high.

古遗址
The Site of The Ancient City

古遗址

The Site of The Ancient City

河南文化遗产

全国重点文物保护单位

Brief Information on Major Historic Sites under National Protection in Henan Province

古遗址

The Site of The Ancient City

仰韶村遗址

第一批全国重点文物保护单位

新石器时代 Yangshao site

仰韶村遗址是新石器时代遗址，仰韶文化的命名地，位于渑池县北7.5公里处的仰韶村，发现于1921年。

最早发现并确定仰韶遗址的是瑞典地质学家、考古学家安特生（1874～1960年）。1918～1921年，安特生及其助手先后三次赴渑池县仰韶村，由调查寻找脊椎动物化石而发现大量磨制石器。1921年4月，安特生亲临调查，发现许多冲沟壁上显露大片灰层和许多袋形灰坑，并在其中采集到磨制石器和彩陶片。经中国地质调查所报请中国政府批准，安特生于当年10～12月在此进行大规模发掘，共发掘十七个地点，获得了大批珍贵文物。

仰韶村遗址面积约30万平方米，文化层堆积厚达4米。遗址、遗物非常丰富，包含仰韶文化、河南龙山文化和东周文化等不同文化遗存。1951年中国科学院考古研究所进行了发掘，发现的陶器有鼎、鬲、盆、豆、罐、钵、尖底瓶等，部分为彩陶。石器有斧、锛、刀、镞、环。骨器有针、锥等。仰韶遗址的发掘，确认了中国石器时代的存在，影响巨大，意义深远。此后，将在黄河中游广大地区发现的同类史前文化遗存均命名为“仰韶文化”，这是中国近代考古学史上出现的第一个考古学文化名称。

地质学家、考古学家安特生

仰韶村遗址出土彩陶盆

渑池仰韶村遗址

仰韶村遗址

仰韶村遗址全貌

The site is located at Yangshao Village, Mianchi County, the City of Sanmenxia. It dates from the middle and late periods of the Neolithic Age (circa 3,000 ~ 4,000 BC). It covers an area of 300,000 sq. m. It was first excavated in 1921. Yangshao Culture, named after the site and characterized by painted pottery, is famous all over the world.

郑州商代遗址

第一批全国重点文物保护单位

商 A Shang-dynasty city site at Zhengzhou

郑州商代遗址位于郑州市区，东起凤凰台以东，西到西河口以西，北到花园路北段，南到二里岗及陇海铁路，面积约25平方公里。

郑州商代遗址1950年秋首先发现于二里岗。多年来经多次发掘，在中部发现了一座商代前期夯土城垣。郑州商城东墙长约1700米、北墙长约1690米、西墙长约1870米、南墙长约1700米，周长为6960米。城墙均由夯土筑成，北墙东段、东墙、南墙西段和西墙少部分还保留在地面之上，其余皆在今地面之下。城墙底宽20～30米，残高约1～2米，最高处约4～5米。

城内外发现了丰富的遗迹。在城内中部偏北、中部偏东和东北部一带，发现数十座夯土建筑基址，有些夯土基址面上还保存有柱洞或柱基槽和石柱础，表明这里是宫殿区。在宫殿区内发掘了10号房基，南北长34米、东西宽10.2～10.6米。夯土地坪上保存有7排圆形柱洞，每排2～13个，其下为料礓石筑成的柱础，房基西壁还残存部分墙基。发掘的15号房基，东西长65米、南北宽13.5米，地坪面上有南北两排柱础槽，每排多达27个，槽中部有圆形木柱痕，槽底部有石柱础（河

郑州商代城墙

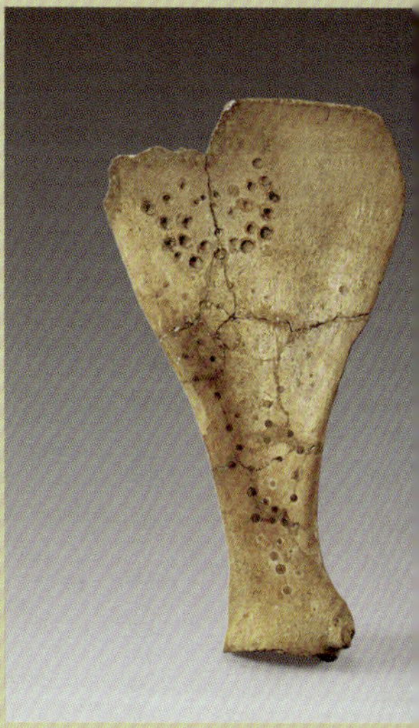

郑州商城出土卜骨

郑州商城北大街宫殿遗址发掘现场

卵石或红色砂岩），柱础槽外侧还有小型擎柱。可以复原为重檐顶带回廊的大型宫殿。发掘的16号房基，南北长38.4米、东西宽31.2米，地坪上有三排平行柱基槽，自西侧转向南侧，其余部分被破坏。推测原建筑应有较宽的回廊与重檐，或许为堂一类的建筑。

两处铸铜作坊遗址内，发掘出当时进行生产操作的地坪，出有大量坩埚残片、红烧土块、炼渣、木炭和数以千计的铸造各种青铜器的陶范。在大量陶范中，包括铸造铲、斧、刀、凿、锥等工具范，镞、戈等兵器范，方鼎、圆鼎、鬲、爵、觚、尊等容器范。显示了相当的生产规模。

在张寨南街青铜器窖藏坑内，出土两件大型铜方鼎和一件铜鬲。在向阳回族食品厂青铜窖藏坑内出土十三件青铜器，包括大方鼎、大圆鼎、扁足圆鼎、牛首尊、羊首、提梁卣、觚、中柱盂、盘。在南顺城街青铜窖藏坑内出土十二件青铜器，其中有大

郑州商城出土玉璋

郑州张寨出土兽面纹方鼎

郑州商城出土陶斝

方鼎、斝、爵、簋、戈、钺，几乎包括郑州商城绝大部分的青铜器种类。

在郑州商城内外，除了发现包括窖藏坑和墓葬内出土的大量的青铜器外，还有许多陶器、原始瓷器、玉器、石器、骨器、象牙器、蚌器和刻字卜骨，反映了当时深厚的文化底蕴，有着重要的历史、科学和艺术价值。

The site is located in the urban area of the City of Zhengzhou. It dates from the early Shang Dynasty (circa 1450 ~ 1600 BC). It covers an area of about 25 sq. km. And its center is the capital city, with a circumference of about 6,960 meters. The northeastern part of the city is occupied by a palace. Outside the city, there are handicraft workshops for making bronze, pottery and processing bones, and there are also some grave yards. A great number of heritages, such as bronze wares, pottery, porcelain and jade wares, have been unearthed.

殷墟

第一批全国重点文物保护单位

商

Yin Ruins

殷墟，是商王朝最后一个都城遗址，位于安阳市西2.5公里小屯村及其北面的洹水两岸。遗址东西长6公里、南北宽4公里，面积24平方公里。自宋代以来，这里就不断发现青铜器，到清代末年发现有甲骨出土，被断定为商代晚期的甲骨文卜辞。经过调查，于1908年找到了出土地点——安阳小屯，殷墟自此被确认。

1928年秋，前中央研究院历史语言研究所成立，同年10月至1937年6月，先后由董作宾、李济、郭宝钧、梁思永主持对殷墟进行过十五次发掘，河南省政府亦派何日章到殷墟发掘三次。共出土甲骨两万七千多片，还有大量的陶器、骨器、蚌器、石器、玉器、青铜器等珍贵文物。特别是1939年春，武官村村民挖出重达875千克的司母戊鼎，更是引起国内外对殷墟的重视。殷墟还发现有仰韶文化、龙山文化和殷商文化层，殷商大墓、建筑基址、车马坑、窖穴等重要遗迹，为商史和安阳殷代古都的研究增添了实物资料。

殷墟出土司母戊铜鼎

司母戊铜鼎铭文

殷墟妇好墓出土嵌绿松石夔鋬象牙杯

殷墟妇好墓出土虎纹铜钺

出土青铜器、玉器、石器、宝石制品、骨器、蚌器、象牙器、陶器共1928件。另有红螺2件，阿拉拉绶贝1件和货贝6880余枚。这些随葬品制作精美、纹饰细腻、用途广泛，是不可多得的艺术珍品。

殷墟是中国第一个有文字记载并经甲骨文及考古发掘所证实的商代晚期都城遗址。它的发现、发掘和研究，取得了显著的成果。殷墟考古在中国考古学史上具有重要的地位。

殷墟宗庙宫殿遗址鸟瞰

殷墟妇好墓出土跽坐玉人

殷墟武官村大墓出土虎纹石磬

殷墟妇好墓出土妇好爵

Located in Xiaotun Village northwest of the City of Anyang, these are the ruins of the capital city of the late Shang Dynasty (circa 1046 ~ 1300 BC), covering a total area of about 30 sq. km. Important remains are palace foundations, imperial mausoleums, aristocrats 'tombs, commoners' tombs, pits of sacrificed humans, and workshops for making bronze and processing bones. A great number of bronze wares, jade wares, bone wares, pottery wares and inscribed bones and tortoise shells have been unearthed. It was included on World Heritage List in July 2006.

郑韩故城

第一批全国重点文物保护单位

东周

The site of the capital of Zheng and Han

郑韩故城位于新郑市城区的双洎河（古洧水）和黄水河（古溱水）交汇处。

西周末期，郑国从林（今陕西省华县一带）迁都于此。周平王东迁洛邑以后，郑武公在此建都。周烈王元年（公元前375年），韩哀侯灭郑，韩国自阳翟（今河南禹州市）迁都于此。秦王嬴政十七年（公元前230年）秦灭韩后，此城大部废弃。因郑、韩先后在此建都，所以称为郑韩故城。

城址外城墙略呈不规则的三角形，因状如牛角，当地民众俗称“牛角城”。城墙为夯筑而成，经过多次加修。地面以上的墙体北城墙与东城墙大部分保存，高15～18米、基宽40～80米。东城墙依黄水河走势略微弯曲，长约5900米，北城墙长约5000米，外侧尚存三处马面。南城墙有两道，双洎河以南的城墙东部高5米、宽约20米，呈断续状，西部仅残存望母台至侯家台一段城墙基础；双洎河以北的城墙东段大部分被河水冲毁，有少量残存，

郑韩故城东城墙及护城河

其西端与隔城墙相连接。隔城墙向北接北城墙，长约4500米，将故城分为东西两部分，除一些地方有高约1.5米的地上墙体，其余大部分为城墙基础，还有巨石垒砌的基础。西城墙被双洎河冲刷和两汉时期大规模的烧窑起土破坏早已无存。经多年持续的考古调查和发掘证明，北、东和双洎河以南的城墙为春秋时期郑国所筑，即文献所记载的郑国都城的“郭城”；战国中期韩国沿用东、北城墙，放弃双洎河的南城墙，增筑河北与隔城墙，形成战国时期典型的西王城东郭城的布局。

城内遗迹除西城梳妆台高台建筑为地面以上建筑，其余均为地下遗址。东城内手工业作坊较多，主要有春秋时期郑国铸铜作坊遗址，有战国时期韩国的制骨、制玉、铸铁、制陶、铸钱等作坊遗址。还发现有宫殿基址区、祭祀遗址、公族墓地、贵族墓地、平民墓地等郑国遗址和墓地，粮仓遗址、夯土基址等韩国遗址。1923年在郑伯大墓中出土青铜器达七百多件，其中最精美的器物是莲鹤方壶。

新中国成立以后，故城内外不断有重要考古发现。如2001～2002年在郑国公族墓地北端发掘春秋大型车马坑1座，清理出各

郑国祭祀遗址15号礼器坑

郑国祭祀遗址1号乐器坑

郑韩故城出土车马坑

式葬车22辆，发掘国君中字形大墓1座。在南北墓道中清理出三十多辆葬车，数量之多、形式之多样、规格之高，国内罕见。2002年在东城区的东北部发掘战国时期大型官营制陶遗址，清理出大型作坊6座、陶窑5座与许多制坯流程工作台池，完整地再现了当时大型官营制陶作坊的场景，并可填补制陶工艺的一些学术空白。在东周制陶遗址中出土了大量的各式陶器与支垫工具，不仅可以作为郑韩故城乃至中原地区东周陶器断代标尺，而且对研究战国时期陶器支烧工艺有着重要意义。

郑韩故城出土莲鹤方壶

Located in Chengguan Town, Xinzheng City, the site was the capital of Zheng and Han, two states in the Eastern Zhou Dynasty (circa 770 ~ 221 BC). With a circumference of about 20 km, the city wall consists of an east section and a west section. Major sites are palace foundation, tombs, large storage cellars, and workshops for making iron and pottery and processing bones. Ritual wares, musical instruments and weapons made of bronze have been unearthed.

汉魏洛阳故城（含辟雍碑）

第一批全国重点文物保护单位

东汉至北魏

The site of Luoyang City in the Han and Wei dynasties (including Piyong Tablet)

汉魏洛阳故城是东汉、曹魏、西晋、北魏四朝都城，位于洛阳市东15公里偃师市与孟津县交界处，北靠邙山，南临洛河。

1954年开始对汉魏洛阳故城进行勘探和发掘，基本查明了城垣、门阙、街道格局、护城河、金墉城、宫城区、殿、台、仓、厩等遗存；还查清了永宁寺、灵台、太学遗址和刑徒墓地的情况。洛阳故城周长约14公里，城址为不规则的南北长方形。东墙、西墙和北墙断断续续保留在地面上，南墙被洛水冲毁，仅余部分墙基。

据文献记载，洛阳故城在东汉、魏、晋建都时有十二门，门皆有双阙。北魏建都后，对旧门进行修缮和改建，并在城西墙北段新开承明门。依魏晋之名，西门四座，自南向北为西明门、西阳门、阊阖门、承明门；北门两座，一曰大夏门，一曰广莫门；东门有三座，自北向南分别是建春门、东阳门、青阳门；南面有四座城门，自东向西为开阳门、平昌门、宣阳门、津阳门。经发掘已找到城门十座，因南城墙被洛河水冲毁，南面诸门已无迹可寻。城内共发现东西向街道四条，南北向街道四条。宫城位于

汉魏洛阳故城城墙

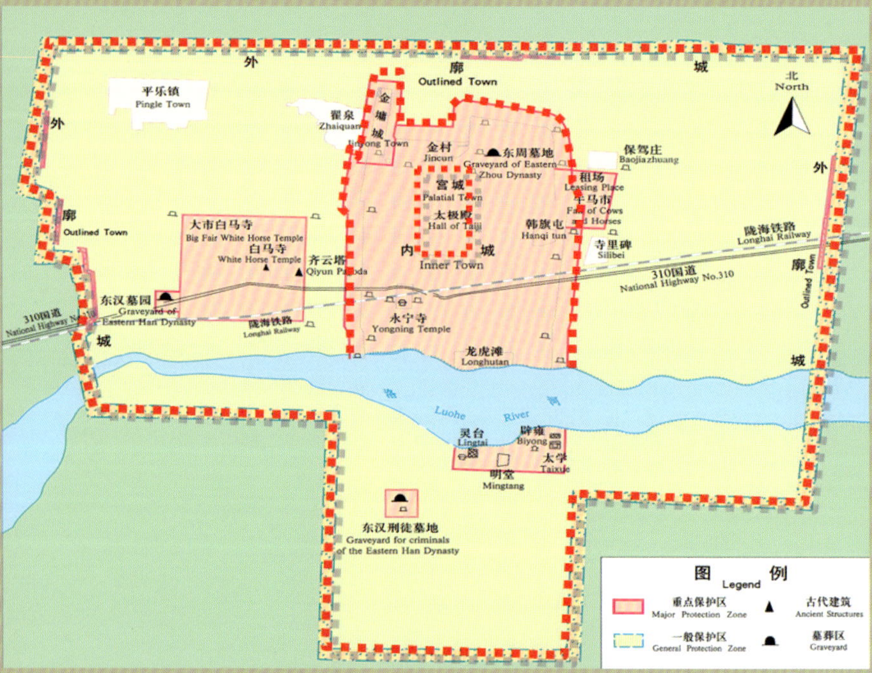

汉魏洛阳故城平面图

永宁寺出土泥塑供养人头像

城内中北部，南北长1398米、东西宽660米，占全城总面积的十分之一左右。宫城内发现夯土台基二十余处，比较密集，应是宫殿基址。其中一处夯土台基高出地面4米左右，东西长100米、南北宽60米，是北魏太极殿遗址。在东北隅发现东汉和曹魏时期的太仓、武库，西晋时期的太子宫、北魏时期的太仓、河南尹官署等建筑基址。与文献记载相符。

在洛阳城内外，还有永宁寺、灵台、明堂、辟雍、太学、刑徒墓地等重要遗址。永宁寺是北魏时期最为豪华壮丽的皇家寺院。永宁寺遗址南北长301米、东西宽212米。发掘出土了许多造型生动的泥塑佛像等文物，并得知永宁寺木塔建筑在百米见方的夯土基础之上，塔高约合136.71米。这样高的木塔，在我国古建筑史上是罕见的。灵台，是当时研究天文、气象的专用建筑。灵台遗址面积达40000平方米，周围有墙，其中心建筑是一座残高8米余的夯土台，南北长41米、东西宽31米，台的四周有上下两层平台建筑遗址。灵台是当时全国最大的国家天文台，使用时间长达二百五十年之久。明堂即天子太庙，是封建皇帝祭祀祖先或接受臣属朝拜的地方，在灵台遗址之东。遗址系夯筑台基，近正方形，南北长近400米、东西宽386米，中心部分是一座南北长64米、东西宽63米、高2.5米以上的方形夯土台基，应是明堂的主体建筑。

汉魏洛阳故城东汉灵台

辟雍碑，位于河南省偃师市佃庄乡东大郊村，1931年出土于东大郊村北的西晋太学遗址中。碑身和碑额系用一块整石雕成，高3.22、宽1.1、厚0.3米。1974年又在太学遗址中发掘出碑座。碑首约占碑身的三分之一，碑额为蟠龙伏绕，正面竖排隶书“大晋龙兴皇帝三临辟雍皇太子又再莅之盛德隆熙之颂”，碑的正文有隶书三十行，每行五十五字，该碑刻凿于晋咸宁四年（278年）十月。据碑文记载，太学创建于东汉建武五年（公元29年），学生最多时达三万余人，至西晋时仍有万余人，来自十五个州，七十多个县，还有四名西域学生。碑文详细记述了太学要“勤学务礼，遵修旧典”，“敦礼明化以序为先”。同时记述了晋武帝司马炎三次、皇太子司马衷两次亲临辟雍巡视，考察学生的“德行”、“通艺”，并行赏赐的情况。碑阴分排依次刻写了学官、博士、礼生、弟子等人的职别、郡籍、姓名。题名列二十一种名称，其中有博士、助教以及弟子、门人、散生等四百余人的郡籍姓名。碑文采用晋隶，字体比较灵活，具有独特风格。

永宁寺出土泥塑供养人

永宁寺塔基遗址

The site is located at the juncture between the Yanshi City and Mengjin County, and dates from the period from Eastern Han Dynasty to the Northern Wei Dynasty (25 ~ 533 AD). It was the capital city of the Eastern Han Dynasty, the Wei Kingdom (during the period of the Three Kingdoms), the Western Jin Dynasty and the Northern Wei Dynasty. It has a circumference of about 14 km. Discovered ruins include streets, palaces, government offices, temples and blocks

Located in Dajiao Township east of Yanshi City, Piyong Tablet was made in the 4th year of Xianning period of the Jin Dynasty (278 AD); it records facts about the imperial college in the Western Jin Dynasty.

平粮台古城遗址

第三批全国重点文物保护单位

新石器时代

The site of the ancient city of Pingliangtai

平粮台古城遗址，是一处新石器时代遗址，坐落在淮阳县城东南4公里大朱庄西南台地平粮台上。

1979年在此挖土时发现一柄“越王”剑，由此引起文物考古部门的重视，随即进行了抢救性发掘，在一座甲字形楚墓中发现了一柄“巴蜀”剑和五件铜鼎及大批玉器。同年9月，发现了龙山文化的高台建筑，台上用土坯砌墙，排列有序。1980年在台的四周发现夯土痕迹，在东、西、南、北墙及拐角分开探沟、探方十四个，通过发掘判明，平粮台古城遗址是一座河南龙山文化城址。

平粮台龙山文化古城遗址平面呈正方形，有南北二门，城墙每边长205米，面积50000平方米。城墙上部宽8～10米、下部宽13.5米、残高3.65米，用小版筑堆筑法建成。发掘面积4532平方米，共清理房基29座，灰坑260座，墓葬211座，陶窑3座，车马坑1座。

平粮台古城遗址的年代，根据地层关系共分五期，第一期是大汶口文化晚期，第二至第四期是河南龙山文化，第五期是二里头一期文化。根据地层叠压关

平粮台古城遗址发掘现场

平粮台古城遗址

平粮台遗址出土陶水管

平粮台古城遗址出土陶甗

系，平粮台古城的墙压在大汶口文化晚期地层之上，东城墙直接压在龙山文化平粮台二期的灰坑H61之上，而平粮台三期的南门卫房（F13、F14）下，还有一层门卫房和陶水管道尚未发掘，因此平粮台古城的建城年代应早于平粮台三期文化的年代，从打破东城墙内坡的H75出土的木炭碳十四测定，年代为距今4500年。

平粮台古城遗址是我国发现较早、保留较好的古城址之一，对于研究我国古代城市的发展、文明的起源有重要的意义。

Located in the southwest corner of Dazhu Village, Huaiyang County, this Longshan-culture site dates from the late Neolithic Age (2000 ~ 3000 BC). It is in a square shape, each side measuring about 185 meters. It covers an area of over 34,000 sq. m.

二里头遗址

第三批全国重点文物保护单位

夏商

Erlitou Site

二里头遗址位于偃师市西9公里外的洛河故道（在今洛阳南）以北。

整个遗址包括二里头、圪当头、四角楼、寨后、辛庄五个自然村，面积3平方公里。二里头遗址坐落在伊河与洛水之间，土质肥沃，地势平坦，自然环境十分优越。1959年夏在偃师、登封、禹县一带调查“夏墟”时发现了二里头遗址。此后经多年调查与发掘，发现了许多重要的遗迹和遗物。二里头遗址的1号、2号宫殿，皆由主体殿堂、围墙（廊庑）、庭院和大门组成，布局严谨，主次分明，其平面安排开创了我国宫殿建筑的先河。殿堂下面有台基，宫殿墙基里使用木骨，在檐柱外面用小擎檐柱支撑屋顶出檐，这些都是早期宫殿的建筑手法。在1号宫殿的殿堂附近和庭院中，发现一些以人为牺牲的祭祀坑；2号宫殿的殿堂后面有大墓。在宫殿遗址中没有发现明显的居住生活迹象，推测这里可能是王室的宗庙建筑，在这里举行祭祀和其他政治活动。

二里头遗址出土的青铜器有刀、锛、凿、锥、鱼钩等生产工具，有戈、镞、戚等兵器，有鼎、罍、爵等容器，有铃等乐器，有圆牌铜器，有盾形镶嵌绿松石片的铜牌饰等；玉器有玉刀、玉璋、玉戈、玉钺、玉铲、玉柄形饰、玉版、玉琮、玉筒等。此外，还发现有石磬、陶埙等乐器，青蛙、羊头等陶制艺术品，又有麻布、海贝和陶文符号等。出土量最多的陶器中，除了传统的泥质灰陶和夹砂灰陶，又出现了一些新品种，如印纹硬陶、釉陶、原始瓷器、白陶、黑陶等，代表了当时

二里头遗址平面图

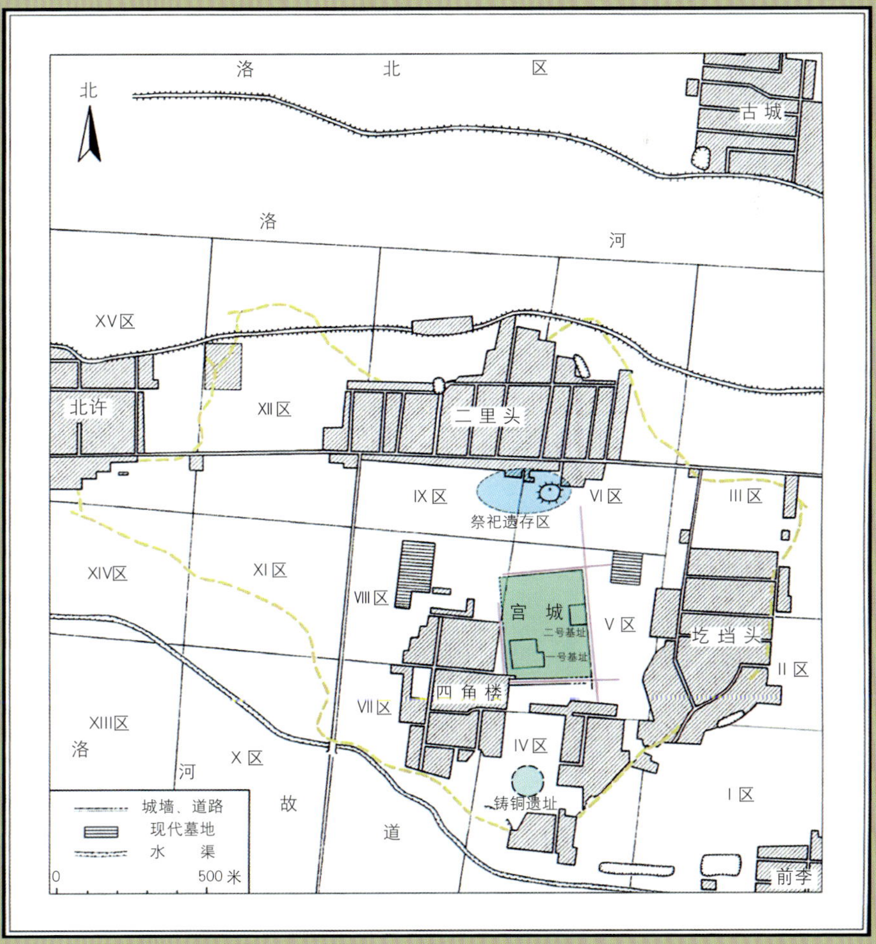

二里头遗址出土铜爵

二里头遗址出土绿松石龙

二里头遗址出土嵌绿松石兽面铜牌饰

二里头遗址出土石钺

二里头遗址出土陶爵

较高的生产工艺水平。

二里头遗址在中国考古学上占有重要地位，由于其长期作为夏代王都所包含的极大信息量而被称为“探讨我国文明和国家起源最前沿的遗址”；并因其丰富的遗迹遗物具有典型性和代表性，被命名为二里头文化。二里头文化主要分布在河南和山西西南部，在陕西、湖北、安徽也有少量发现，其影响可达四川、江苏、浙江和内蒙古一带。

Located to the south of Erlitou Village, Yanshi City, this was the capital of the middle and late Xia Dynasty (1880 ~ 1600 BC). It covers an area of 3.5 sq. km. 'Erlitou Culture' was named after it.

尸乡沟商城遗址

第三批全国重点文物保护单位

商

Shixianggou Site of a Shang-dynasty city

尸乡沟商城遗址，是迄今发现的最早的商城之一。遗址位于偃师市，北依邙山，南临洛河，西南距二里头遗址6公里，东接今偃师市，处于河洛之间的平原上。

城址平面近长方形，全城总面积约为190万平方米。城墙全部用夯土筑成，残高2米左右。现已发现七座城门，其中东西两边各三座，北边一座，还发现若干条纵横如织的大道，均与城门相连。在大道之间分布着一些建筑物的遗迹，有四处规模甚大。高庄村边地势隆起，传是汤都西亳的“亳”地。塔庄村北有一条横贯东西的慢坡低洼地带，当地百姓称之为尸乡沟，遗址因此而命名。

尸乡沟商城由多重城圈相套合，大城之内有小城，小城之内有宫城，布局严谨。宫城内发现

尸乡沟商城宫殿基址

尸乡沟商城遗址出土陶鬲

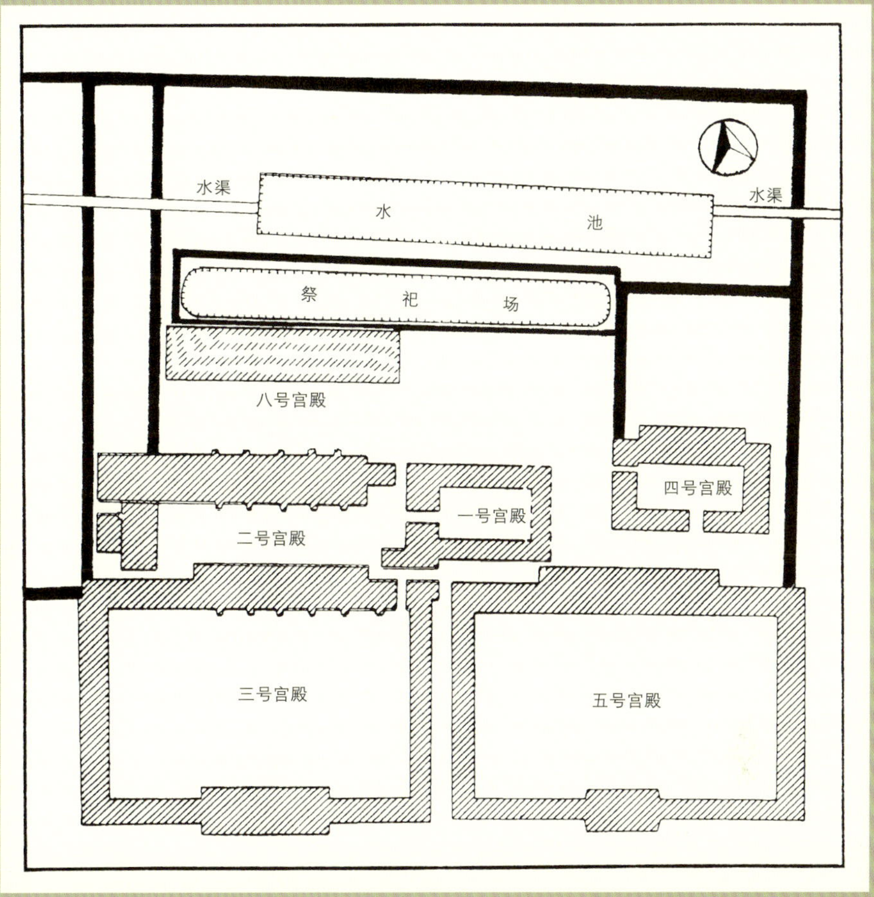

尸乡沟商城宫城遗址平面图

尸乡沟商城遗址出土大口陶尊

多座宫殿基址，宫殿建筑规模宏大，有的面积达数千平方米，周围往往有高大的院墙。宫城西南另有一个由围墙环绕的基址群，成排成列地分布着九十六座建筑基址，据推测可能是王室仓储之所。在城门和各宫殿基址下，多发现有排水和供水管道，宫城北部还发现有用石块砌成的面积达2000多平方米的大型蓄水池，可能为供游乐的池苑。

尸乡沟商城遗址，并非二里头夏代都城的延续，而是重新选址兴建的一座新的都城，比二里头夏都的规模更大，布局更为合理，更便于军事防守，并增加了游乐设施，更合于王都的要求。尸乡沟商城遗址的发现，对于研究我国古代文明和城市的发展历史，具有十分重要的意义。

尸乡沟商城遗址

尸乡沟商城遗址航拍图

尸乡沟商城宫殿遗址水池及东侧水道

Located at Dahuaishu Village, Yanshi City, this was the capital of the early Shang Dynasty (1600 ~ 1500 BC). It covers an area of about 1.90 million sq. m. Discovered ruins are palaces, gardens with ponds, sacrifice ground, streets and smelteries.

隋唐洛阳城遗址

第三批全国重点文物保护单位

隋唐

The site of Sui-and-Tang-dynasty Luoyang City

隋唐洛阳城遗址位于洛阳市内。

洛阳城始建于隋大业元年(605年)。隋定东都十五年，唐东都三百年，五代后梁都十四年，后唐都十三年，后晋都二年，共历五个朝代三百四十四年。

1954年以来，对城址进行了大规模勘探和发掘，基本探明了城址的范围和城内布局。城址包括外郭城、宫城、皇城、东城、含嘉仓城、圆壁城、曜仪城、夹城以及纵横如织的街道、市井等。城内布局经过精心设计，井然有

隋唐洛阳城平面图

隋唐洛阳城遗址出土建筑构件

隋唐洛阳城北城墙

序，其规模仅次于都城长安。

外郭城平面略呈南北长方形，周长27.5公里。据文献记载，除西垣无城门之外，东南北垣各有三座城门。已发现南垣中门定鼎门（隋曰建国门），其东2255米为长夏门，其西1060米是厚载门（隋曰白虎门）。东垣有建春门（隋曰建阳门）、上东门（隋曰上春门）、永通门。北垣原有二门（安喜、徽安），因破坏严重，其门址尚未找到。

皇城位于外城郭内西北部，南城的东南部被洛河水冲毁仅存西段540米，唯右掖门址尚存。东墙长1115米，有宣耀门。西墙长

隋唐洛阳城遗址圆形建筑

1670米，有宣辉门与宣耀门相对。

宫城在皇城内北部，南面正门即应天门，其东有明德门，西有长乐门。北面正中即玄武门，其西有嘉豫门。诸门址均已探明。城内还发现有最北面的陶光园、西北角的九洲池和东南角的东宫基址。

含嘉仓城，是隋唐东都洛阳城内一座贮藏粮食的大型粮仓，创建于隋大业元年（605年），唐代继续使用。仓城为南北长方形，南北城墙均长612米、宽17米、残高1.5米。总面积43万平方米。该城有四座城门，东为仓东门，西为仓中门或称圆璧门，北称德猷门，南曰含嘉门。城内东北部和南半部保留密集的仓窖，已探出二百八十七个，按其分布情况推测应有四百多个。

隋唐洛阳城内有繁密的街道、市井和里坊，在洛河以南已掘出街道十二条，还有明教、乐和、尚贤、归德、崇仁、里仁等坊，南北顺城街、西市等。在洛河以北探明三条东西方向的顺城街，以及通远坊、兴艺坊、积德坊和温雄坊等。隋唐洛阳城遗址的考古工作，对研究中国古代城市发展史具有重要意义。

隋唐洛阳城含嘉仓遗址

隋唐洛阳城白居易故居鸟瞰

The site is located in the eastern part of the urban area of Luoyang City and its southern suburbs. The city started to be built in the 1st year of Daye period (605 AD), in the reign of Emperor Yang of the Sui Dynasty. It was used as the capital in the Sui and Tang dynasties, and in the Liang, Tang and Jin dynasties in the Five Dynasties period. As archeological findings show, it contains an outer city, an imperial city, a palace city, a yaoyi city, a yuanbi city and a hanjiacang city. It has a circumference of about 27.5 km.

北宋东京城遗址（含繁塔、延庆观）

第三批全国重点文物保护单位

北宋

The site of Dongjing City in the Northern Song Dynasty

(including Po Tower and Yanqing Taoist Temple)

北宋东京城遗址位于开封市。

城址分外城、内城和皇城三重城墙。外城，又称新城、罗城，是京师防御的第一道屏障，呈东西略短、南北稍长的长方形。东墙长约7660米、西墙长约7590米、南墙长约6990米、北墙长约6940米。四面城墙距今开封市现存的明清城1.3～2公里，在西城墙南段的试掘表明，外城墙为版筑而成。现存顶部宽4米、底部宽达34.2米、高8.7米，城墙外的护城壕宽约40米、深11米。据文献记载，外城共有城门十二个，水门六个。

繁塔

繁塔砖雕佛像

目前已探明十余座，多为直门两重或屈曲开门的瓮城门。按照分布位置，南墙的三处分别为南薰门、戴楼门和蔡河水门，东墙两处可能为新曹门和汴河下水门旁边的拐子城，西墙的五处应为新郑门、汴河上水门、固子门、万胜门和金水河门。内城，又称里城、旧城或阙城。整个内城略呈正方形，其南墙位于今城南墙北约300米的东西一线，北墙位于龙亭大殿北约500米的东西一线，内城的东西墙叠压在今城东西墙下面，四墙总长11550米左右。其面积较现存的开封明清城墙略小。文献记载内城的十座城门，只有朱雀门遗址和汴河西角子门遗址的位置大致确定。朱雀门为内城正南门，位于今大南门以北300米处的中山路路面下，已知缺口宽约150米。汴河西角子门位于现存的明清城西墙南门北侧，南距明清城墙西南角约920米。皇城，又称宫城、大内，是皇帝生活议政的场所。经过考古勘探，皇城略呈东西短、南北长的长方形，周长2521米，南墙位于今午朝门处的东西一线，北墙位于今龙亭大殿后墙的东西一线，东西墙分别位于今潘、杨两湖的东西岸，城墙夯筑而成，内外均匀用青砖包砌，据文献记载，皇城有六座城门，因多是被现代建筑物所压或浸没在湖水下，目前只在明周王府紫禁城东、南、北三墙遗址下发现三处城门或缺口，可能分别为宋皇城的三座城门。在宋城内，还清理了御街、州桥、汴河、金明池等遗迹，出土了瓷片、钱币、砖瓦等遗物。

繁（音婆）塔，位于河南省开封市东南1.5公里的天清寺旧址上。据载，后周显德二年（955年）在繁台之上建天清寺，宋太祖开宝年间（968～976年）重修天清寺，并在寺内建塔，名“兴慈塔”。因繁台周围多居住繁姓，故俗称“繁塔”。寺院建筑已毁，唯塔独存。

延庆观玉皇阁

繁塔为六角形楼阁式砖塔，原为九层，据载宋末元初繁塔曾遭雷击，上部六层毁，清代初年在残留的三层塔身上修建七级小塔，形成现今的特殊形式。由于黄河泛滥，塔基没入地下，露于地面的高度为31.67米。底层塔身有明清时期的封护墙脚，一层南北各辟圆券门，能入内而互不通。南面塔心室为六角形，仅供佛像而已。北面塔心室内设有东西对称的砖砌梯道，通过内壁盘旋而上至第三层。外壁每层檐下均有仿木构建筑的砖雕斗栱，二、三层有平基可绕塔而行。南北一至三层开圆券门，二层东南和西南各辟平券门。内外塔壁镶嵌有一百零八种佛像雕砖，据考证雕砖均为宋代造型。

繁塔内外尚存宋、明、清碑刻和题记二百余方。其中《金刚般若波罗蜜经》、《十善业道经要略》、《大方广圆觉修多罗了义经》三经刻石均为北宋书法家赵安仁书丹，楷书方正庄重，浑厚有力。另有捐施者题名刻石。

延庆观，位于河南省开封市西南隅。延庆观原名“重阳宫”，是为纪念道教全真教创始人王喆而修建的。建于金大定年间（1161～1189年），后屡有重修，明洪武六年（1373年）改名延庆观。明清之际屡遭兵火水患，现仅存玉皇阁。

玉皇阁坐北面南，通高18.8米。阁分三层，下层平面为方形，青砖砌造，外部为四坡顶，南面中间辟圆券门，门两侧辟直棂铁窗，东窗铁棂上铸有“大明永宁王大府镇国中尉雪窗重修玉皇阁三官无梁宝殿铁窗门户两扇，嘉靖二十八年九月吉日”题记，铸于1549年。室内下方上圆呈穹隆顶，四角砌出斗栱，顶部饰砖雕菊花、葵花等八种花卉图案。中层为实体，平面呈八角形，阁顶作琉璃八角攒尖式，正中安置铜质火焰宝珠。经鉴定，玉皇阁下部为元代风格，上部为明代重修。

Located in the urban area and environs of Kaifeng City, the site dates from the Northern Song Dynasty (960 ~ 1126 AD). It is divided into an outer city, an inner city, and a palace part. It has a circumference of 29 km.

Sitting on Fan Platform in the southeast corner of Kaifeng and built in the 7th year of Kaibao period (974 AD) of the Northern Song Dynasty, Po Tower is a hexagon tower built of bricks in the pavilion style.

Yanqing Taoist Temple is located on Yanqingguanqian Street, Kaifeng. It started to be built in the Jin Dynasty (1115 ~ 1234 AD). Remaining buildings are Yuhuang Pavilion, juanpeng, front hall and flank halls.

钧台钧窑遗址

宋

The Jun-kiln site at Juntai

钧台钧窑遗址位于禹州市老城内钧台附近。是宋代汝官哥定钧五大瓷窑之一钧窑的遗址。

钧瓷始烧于唐代，至宋代鼎盛，北宋时曾一度成为宫廷用品，禁止民间私藏。目前在禹州境内已发现唐代窑址七处，宋代窑址四十余处。钧台钧窑遗址分为官用和民用两大烧造区，东部以烧官用瓷为主，西部以烧民用瓷为主。窑址东西长约1100米、南北宽约350米，总面积约38万平方米，文化层厚1～2米。1974年以来经全面钻探和重点发掘发现，该窑址的烧造规模和产品质量均为禹州诸钧瓷窑址之冠。在发掘出的十一座瓷窑中，一般都是就地挖筑的土质窑，有的在窑门和烟囱口部垒砌小砖。除烧造天目瓷的窑门朝西外，其他窑门都向北。窑炉修筑比较集中，有的呈一线排列，有的三窑鼎立，中间设作坊与各窑相通。窑炉有圆形、马蹄形和长方形。烧造区发现的窑具有桶状匣钵、直壁漏斗状匣钵、锯齿状支烧、铜刀、鹿角抿子等。出

钧台钧窑遗址1号窑炉

钧台钧窑遗址出土钧瓷六足花盆

土的瓷器产品种类繁多，釉色主要有天青、月白、紫红、碧蓝、米黄诸色。特别是窑变，红紫相映，光彩夺目。器物造型有各类花盆和盆奁，还有钵、碗、尊、鼓钉洗及高足碗等。产品胎质细腻致密，造型端庄规整，釉色光亮浑厚，一般器物底足满釉，盆类底足为刷釉，器表有蚯蚓走泥纹或开片，盆类按照器形的大小排列。

神垕镇西南部的钧窑遗址是钧窑的中心窑场之一，2001年重点发掘了白峪河北地、下白峪等四处窑址，揭露面积650平方米，共清理出八座窑炉，其中五座保存完好，还有三座石砌澄泥池，一座灶，五处窑前工作场所，出土数十万片瓷器残件和窑具，其中完整或可复原的器物达数千件。这次发掘所获得的新资料，填补了我国北方地区民间烧制钧瓷的一项空白，对研究钧窑及唐、宋、金、元时期钧窑的发展史有着重要的意义。

Located in the northeastern corner of the urban area of the City of Yuzhou, the site dates from the Song Dynasty (960 ~ 1126 AD); it covers an area of 380,000 sq. m. Remains brought to light are 16 furnaces, 28 ash pits and a number of workshop sites. The kiln was one of the five most famous kilns in the Northern Song Dynasty. The Jun Kiln site at Shenhou is located in an area containing seven villages, including Liujiamen in Shenhou Town. It was mainly used to make Jun-kiln porcelain.

西山遗址

第四批全国重点文物保护单位

新石器时代

Xishan Site

西山遗址出土彩陶钵

西山遗址出土彩陶壶

西山遗址是一处新石器时代仰韶文化晚期遗址，位于郑州市北郊23公里的邙山区田村。

遗址平面近圆形，面积约10余万平方米。在遗址中发掘清理出新石器时代城址及大批房基、窖穴、灰坑、墓葬，遗址内涵以仰韶文化和龙山文化早期遗存为主，另有少量周代遗迹。遗址中出土铜、陶、玉、石、骨、蚌、角等类遗物五百余件。城址东西宽约200米，现存西墙残长约64米，北墙呈弧形，全长约210米。城墙采用当时先进的方块版筑法，在内外两侧挖沟，就地取土，在经过平整的高低错落的生土基面上夯筑起建。墙宽约5～6米，城角处宽约8～10米，残存长1.5～2米、宽1.3米左右，夯层厚3～4厘米，夯窝经局部揭示为圆形，底倾斜不平，深0.3～0.5厘米，初步推断为集束棍夯。在城墙筑造中，已经使用夹板、穿棍和立柱。

西山城址距今约5300～4800年间，它的发现，将我国古城产生的年代向前推进约八百至一千年，对于探讨我国夯筑技术和早期城市的起源，具有重要的科研价值。

Located in Sunzhuang Village, Guying Town, the City of Zhengzhou, the site dates from the middle and late Neolithic Age (5300 ~ 2070 BC). It covers an area of about 100,000 sq. m. The site of a city dating from the late period of Yangshao Culture was discovered in its northeast.

西山遗址北门城台瓮棺发掘现场

西山遗址西门北侧城墙发掘现场

王城岗及阳城遗址

第四批全国重点文物保护单位

新石器时代至东周

The sites of Wangchenggang and Yangcheng

王城岗及阳城遗址位于登封市告成镇附近。王城岗为龙山文化晚期城址，阳城为东周城址。

王城岗遗址的东城大部分被西移的五渡河水冲毁，遗址的西城保存较好，北城墙东段已被山洪冲毁，北城墙西段外侧，还有一条与城墙平行的壕沟。南城墙东端有一段宽约10米的缺口，很可能是西城的南门。西城的西北城角和西南城角保存较好，西城墙长约92米、南城墙长82.4米。王城岗东西两城的建筑方法相同，都是先挖城墙的基础槽，在基础槽内填土，逐层夯筑。从地层叠压关系看，城墙基槽夯土上面被河南龙山晚期文化层所压，城墙基槽夯土内所包含最晚的陶片亦属河南龙山文化晚期，城墙基槽夯土层下面压有河南龙山中期文化层。由此可知，王城岗遗址城墙基槽夯土的年代应是河南龙山文化晚期。在城内发现许多当时的生活垃圾坑，在西城中部和西南部较高的地方，发掘出一些断断续续的夯土遗存，很可能是建筑的遗存。城址内还出土陶器、石器、骨器、蚌器等大量遗物。还出有一

阳城遗址南城墙

王城岗遗址发掘现场

件青铜残片，残高5.7厘米、残宽6.5厘米、壁厚0.2厘米，器表有烟熏痕迹，表明为实用容器。残片左端还留有一小段合范缝，说明了铸造工艺已经有了一定的进步。经化验，证实是铜锡合金的青铜铸件。在一件泥质黑陶薄胎平底器的外底上，刻划有一个“共”字，其字形结构与商代甲骨文和西周金文相似。城址、青铜器、文字、奠基坑等遗存的发现，表明已经进入文明社会。

王城岗龙山文化晚期城址经碳十四测定为公元前2070年左右，其年代属夏代初期，其地望在夏代阳城范围之内。城址虽小，城墙基槽夯筑方法也很原始，但这种现象正符合中国古代城垣建设由小到大，从原始趋向成熟的发展规律。因此，王城岗城址的发现对探索夏文化是一次重大的突破。不少学者认为王城岗城址是夏代初年的都城。近年在王城岗遗址西北城角外侧旁边，又发现一道东西向城墙，长约370米，与王城岗城址很可能同为一体，城址的范围增加六七倍，作为夏都阳城的理由就更充足一些。

1997年5月，在登封告成镇东北的平坦高地上，发现了一座南北纵长方形的东周城址，发掘证实这里是春秋战国时期的阳城遗址。阳城遗址位于王城岗遗址以东约1公里处，遗址南北长约2000米、东西宽为700米，总面积为1.4平方公里。北城墙保存最好，地面上尚有8米高，北墙中段有一宽13米的缺口，可能就是北城门。城外有宽约60余米的

王城岗遗址出土鬶口杯

王城岗遗址出土陶杯

护城壕。而东城墙、西城墙和南城墙只有断续几段城墙夯土保留在地面之上。在城内中部偏北，发现一处大型建筑基址，地面上还有成片的铺地砖，并堆积有大量的砖块、板瓦、筒瓦、瓦当等建筑构件和一些陶片。在建筑基址西侧断壁上，还发现地下埋有自西北向东南套接的陶水管道。城内出土遗物丰富，有铁器、铜器和大量的陶器。在一些陶豆、陶釜、陶瓮、陶盒、陶罐、陶碗和陶量上，还刻印有“阳城”、“阳城仓器”等戳记和其他各种陶文符号。这些陶器少数属于春秋晚期，多数属于战国时期。

Located west of Gaocheng Village, the City of Dengfeng, Wangchenggang Site dates from the late Neolithic Age (3000 ~ 2000 BC). The ruin of a castle and a city dating from the late period of Longshan Culture were discovered. The site covers an area of about 300,000 sq. m.

Yangcheng Site is located in the northeast of Gaocheng Village. It is 2,000 meters long from north to south, and 700 meters wide from east to west. Remains of large buildings have been found. Many of the remains discovered bear the characters 'Yang Cheng' , which shows it to be the Yang Cheng city of the Han State in the Warring States Period.

羑里城遗址

第四批全国重点文物保护单位

新石器时代、商、周

The site of Youli City

羑里城遗址是一处蕴含丰富的龙山至商周时期文化遗址，位于汤阴县城北4公里的河村东。城址呈土台状，高出地面约5米、南北长106米、东西宽103米，面积约10918平方米，文化层厚7米。经初步考古钻探和对出土器物的分析，可知遗址上层是商、周时期的文化层，出土有陶鬲、罐、豆等陶片；下层为龙山文化层，出土有陶鼎、瓮、盘、盆、罐和骨针、蚌镰等生活生产用具，器物表面有篮纹、绳纹、方格纹等纹饰，并发现有白灰居住面房基和红烧土等遗迹。

羑里城还是先秦时期的国家监狱。据文献记载，里，狴犴也。夏曰夏台，殷曰羑里，周曰囹圄，皆圜土。圜土，即用土筑成圆形的专门囚禁罪犯的建筑物。由此可知，它是我国遗存下来的时代最早的国家监狱，有着重要的历史价值。殷商时期，纣王听信谗言，将西伯侯姬昌囚禁于此达七年之久。后来姬昌被其次子姬发（即周武王）追谥为周文王。“文王拘而演周易”即是此地，后人为纪念姬昌在羑里城遗址上修建了文王庙。现存文王庙为明清两代所建，坐北面南，计有正殿五间、演易台两间、山门三间。庙前建有演易坊，坊后右侧立明代“周文王羑里城”石碑，左侧立“禹碑”一通。文王庙已成为人们朝敬先贤周文王的圣地。

演易坊

演易亭

Located west of Qilipu Village, Tangyin County, the site dates back to the period from the late Neolithic Age to the Eastern Zhou Dynasty (3000 ~ 221 BC), and covers an area of over 10,000 sq. m. Most of the remains reflect Longshan Culture, and the rest reflects ancient cultures in the Shang and Zhou dynasties. Historical records point to it as the place where King Wen of Zhou State was imprisoned by Di Xin (King Zhou) in the late Shang Dynasty.

蔡国故城

第四批全国重点文物保护单位

西周、春秋

The site of the Cai-state capital

蔡国故城，为现在驻马店市上蔡县县城所在地，是西周蔡国的都城。据史书记载，公元前11世纪周武王灭商，封其五弟叔度于蔡，建立了蔡国，因此叔度也被称为蔡叔度。由于蔡叔度和被分封在管的管叔、分封于霍的霍叔三国肩负了监视殷朝遗民的重任，故称三国为“三监”。因此，蔡国在当时是一个重要的诸侯国。后由于管蔡二叔挟武庚作乱，被周公削去封国，直到其子蔡仲时才得以复国。蔡国故城也就是在这一时期修建起来的。

故城遗址平面略呈不规则的长方形，北城墙长2113米、东城墙长2490米、南城墙长2700米、西城墙长3187米，全城周长10490米。除了东城墙一部分为现代建筑所覆盖外，其他三面城墙直到今天仍保存完好。其残高多在3～15米之间，顶部宽18～88.5米，底部宽为23～95米。在北城墙上还保留有烽火台和部分马面。城外是宽约70～120米、深约5～10米的护城河。城墙上有多处豁口，经发掘和考证，可以确定为城门的共有四处。蔡国故城不仅城墙规模巨大，而且城内布局规整。宫殿区位于城西南部

蔡国故城北城墙烽火台

蔡国故城出土铜鼎

蔡国故城出土陶鬲

一个高于周围6～7米的高台地上，东西长1200米、南北宽1000米，面积达120万平方米。宫殿区内随处可见遗留的筒瓦、板瓦等建筑构件。在城内除了平民生活区，围绕宫殿区还分布有制陶、制骨和铸铜等手工业作坊区。

蔡国战略地位十分重要，蔡国故城曾作为蔡国国都达五百年之久，是国内现存较为完整的先秦列国都城之一。由于它南邻荆楚，后又为强楚所并，故在这里中原文化与楚文化融为一体，形成了自己独具特色的地方文化。

Located in Lugang Township, Shangcai County, the site dates from the Zhou Dynasty (1046 ~ 221 B.C.). Roughly rectangular, the city wall has a circumference of about 10.49 km. Ruins discovered are palaces, workshops, smelteries and cemeteries. To the west of it is Wolonggang Hill, a cemetery for Chu-State nobles in the Warring States Period.

酒店冶铁遗址

第四批全国重点文物保护单位

战国、汉

Iron Smelting Site at Jiudian

酒店冶铁遗址位于西平县西部和舞钢市的中、东部。是古文献记载的中国最早的冶铁作坊遗址之一，也是战国时期最著名的兵器冶铸基地。据勘查，在今舞钢市北部有铁矿点三十余处，分布在山前丘陵和山前平原，部分属于露头矿，占河南铁矿总量的76.3%。丰富的铁矿资源，为这一区域从东周时期就出现的众多冶铁作坊提供了易采易用的原料。古冶铁作坊遗迹中，一部分集中分布在今西平县的酒店乡和芦庙乡相邻地带，其中酒店冶铁遗址做过小面积的试掘，出土了大量炼炉壁残块、炼渣，以及部分属于战国中晚期的盆、罐、瓮、板瓦等陶器残片。在遗址的南部（潭山水库南岸），清理了一座保存较为完好的属战国中晚期的冶铁炉。该冶铁炉位于今潭山水库岸边的一座小土丘顶部南侧，炉体为井状竖炉，利用小土丘的南坡挖成，由炉基底、炉缸、炉腹和风沟组成，炉体东北部总残高2.17米。炉的结构、形制和筑造方法等明显具有战国中晚期的时代特征，其结构与湖北铜绿山春秋时期冶铜炉近似。

据考证，中国的生铁冶铸技术始于春秋时期，在战国时期得到快速发展和初步普及，极大地促进了当时社会生产力的发展，引发了社会各方面的进步，使中华古文明出现了一个空前繁荣的局面。

Located in the south of Jiudian Village, Xiping County, the site dates back to the period from the Warring States Period to the Han Dynasty (475 BC ~ 219 AD), and covers 110,000 sq. m. An elliptical smelting furnace was discovered, and ruins include the remainder of the furnace wall, iron ores and ceramic urns and pots.

酒店冶铁遗址冶铁炉

戚城遗址

春秋

The site of Qi City

戚城遗址位于濮阳市城区内。

戚城遗址的城垣基本呈方形，东西稍宽，周长1520米，面积14.4万平方米，残存城墙最高处为8.3米，最厚处为16.5米。城墙东、西、南、北四面中部各有一缺口，其宽度均在30～40米之间，为城门遗迹。城内地面平坦，遗物比较丰富，发现裴李岗文化、仰韶文化、大汶口文化、龙山文化、商、西周、春秋、战国、汉代的房基、灰坑和文化层。城墙上部的夯土层中含有龙山文化和商周时代的绳纹陶片，下部含有较多的仰韶文化、龙山文化和商代文化遗物。城垣以东36米与80米处有东、西两土丘，均呈长方形，原高约6米左右，人工夯筑。西土丘较小，曾遭损毁。今东土丘长20米、宽16米、高4.6米，其夯层土色、包含物与城墙下部相同。1981年曾对西土丘地面部分和东土丘周围钻探。地面下也为夯土，深2米余，夯土下有灰土。由此可见，两土丘与城垣当属同一时代，应为戚城的附属建筑物。参照各种文献及考古资料，此夯土台应是当年的会盟台基址。

戚城遗址城墙

戚城遗址城墙断面

戚城遗址地下文化遗存相当丰富，裴李岗文化遗存扩大了对裴李岗文化分布地域的认识，为研究裴李岗文化及其北部的磁山文化的关系提出了新的实物资料。仰韶文化遗存与其南面不远的出土蚌壳摆砌龙虎图案的西水坡遗存遥相呼应。其中发现的大汶口文化遗物，为研究华夏集团与东夷集团的关系提供了线索。龙山文化及商代文化遗存，为研究戚城本身的形成，及夏商之际濮阳一带的历史提供了实物依据。西周春秋时代的文化遗存是戚城文化内涵的主体，它为研究这一时代本地区的历史，尤其是湮没不详的卫国历史，以及春秋时期各诸侯国的关系，具有无可替代的历史和科学价值。

Located to the north of Qicheng Village which is south of the urban area of Puyang City, the site dates from the Spring and Autumn Period (770 ~ 476 BC). In a square shape, it has a circumference of 1,520 meters, and covers an area of 144,000 sq. m.

裴李岗遗址

第五批全国重点文物保护单位

新石器时代 Peiligang Site

裴李岗遗址位于新郑市西北8公里裴李岗村西北，双洎河北岸拐弯处的台地上。遗址面积20000平方米，高出河床25米，是一处重要的新石器时代早期文化遗址。

1977年对裴李岗遗址进行了试掘，1978年进行第二次发掘。探明裴李岗遗址以西河李水渠为界，以东是居住区，以西是氏族公共墓地。文化层简单，文化内涵有早晚差异，墓葬的随葬品多寡不同，表明居住在这里的先民以农业生产为主，并出现猪、羊家畜的饲养。

1979年对裴李岗遗址进行了大面积发掘，发掘面积2157平方米，发掘清理墓葬八十二座、灰坑三座，出土文物四百余件，其中石器有磨盘、磨棒、铲、斧、镰、刀、弹丸等，陶器有鼎、罐、壶、盆、碗、钵、盘、瓢形器和陶猪头、羊头等。有集中的墓地，墓葬分布密集，排列有序。均为长

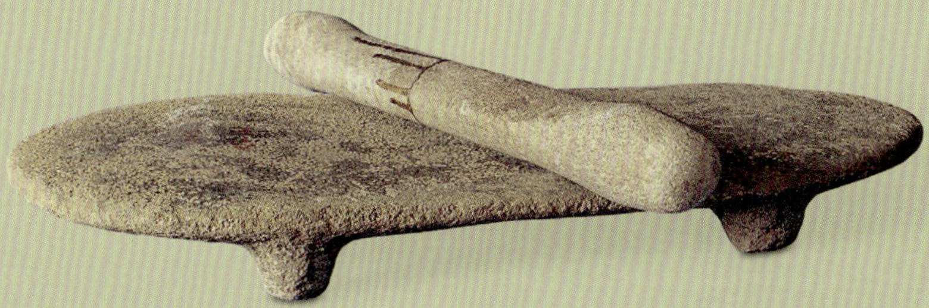

裴李岗遗址出土石磨盘

裴李岗遗址出土三足陶钵

裴李岗遗址出土双耳陶罐

裴李岗遗址全景

方形土坑竖穴墓，头向南，多为单人一次葬，少数为合葬，仰身直肢，随葬品一至十件不等，有两座墓的形制较大，随葬有松绿石珠。经人骨鉴定，凡随葬石磨盘、磨棒、陶鼎、罐、壶的墓是女性，凡随葬石铲、斧、镰的墓均系男性，说明生产已出现男女分工。石器以磨光为主，制作精致，也有少数打制石器。陶器的特征更为突出，手制，胎壁厚薄不匀，初出土时陶质松脆。陶胎多呈红色或橙红色，个别呈灰褐色，泥质陶无纹饰，夹砂陶的纹饰有篦点纹、划纹和乳钉纹。

根据碳十四测定的数据，结合地层关系，裴李岗遗址的年代为距今9000～7000年，是我国新石器时代文化早期遗存。据此命名了裴李岗文化。

Located in Peiligang Village, Xinzheng City, the site dates from the early Neolithic Age (6000 BC). It reflects Peiligang Culture, which existed in the Central Plains in the early Neolithic Age.

贾湖遗址

第五批全国重点文物保护单位

新石器时代

Jiahu Site

贾湖遗址位于漯河市舞阳县北舞渡镇贾湖村东，整个遗址平面呈不规则圆形，其最长径东南—西北向长约280米，最短径东北—西南向宽约250米，总面积为55000余平方米，是目前发掘面积最大、出土文物最为丰富的裴李岗时期文化遗址，距今年代约在9000～7800年之间。

1983～2001年对贾湖遗址先后进行了七次发掘，清理出房址、陶窑、墓葬、瓮棺葬，出土了大批珍贵的文物。当时的人们已经栽培了水稻，说明此遗址的经济结构有别于以种植粟和黍为主的黄河流域。许多灰坑里发现了大批动物骨骼，大致可以分为哺乳类、鸟类、爬行类、鱼类和蝌鲃等类，说明当时渔猎业的发达和人们生活的多样性。遗址中房屋的分布十分密集，其中数量最多的是平面呈椭圆形的半地穴式房子，其次是圆形和不规则形，少量为方形或近方形。出土的陶器以红陶为主，多为泥质灰陶、夹砂陶和夹炭陶。火候较低，种类丰富，表面

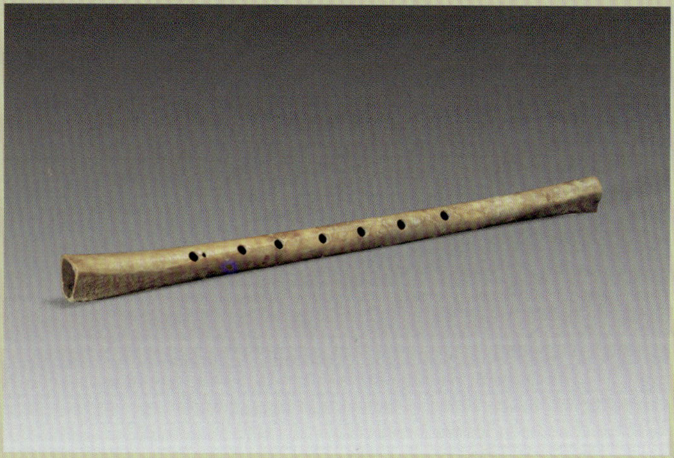
贾湖遗址出土骨笛

贾湖遗址出土龟甲

贾湖遗址发掘现场

贾湖遗址出土稻谷

饰有绳纹、方格纹、席纹、网纹和刻划纹。生产工具以石器为主，其次还有骨、角、牙制品。部分墓葬里还发现了牙饰、骨环、骨叉形器、契刻骨板。随葬有叉形器、龟甲以及骨笛的墓葬应代表着死者高贵的社会地位和身份。

在贾湖遗址中重要的收获还有骨笛的发现，这些骨笛多为墓中随葬品，个别出土于灰坑中。墓主多为男性。骨笛有五孔、六孔、八孔、两孔和七孔的，都是用丹顶鹤的尺骨制成。经过测音，已经具备七声音阶结构，是当今世界上年代最早、个数最多、仍可演奏的乐器实物。其中最为精美的一只两孔骨笛，通身饰满精美花纹，据推测可能作测音用。这些骨笛的出土，为音乐史研究提供了重要的实物资料。

Located east of Jiahu Village, Wuyang County, the site dates from the early Neolithic Age (6000 BC), and covers an area of 55,000 sq. m. Typical heritages include symbols engraved on tortoise shells, bone wares and stone wares, and a number of bone flutes made of leg bones of birds of prey, so that this site is part of the Peiligang Cultural Site.

八里岗遗址

第五批全国重点文物保护单位

新石器时代

Baligang Site

八里岗遗址，位于邓州市城郊乡白庄村北湍河南岸二级阶地上，是一处重要的新石器时代文化遗址。

遗址现存面积约60000平方米，文化堆积十分丰富。上部遗存因遭后期的严重破坏，以残破灰坑为主，分属屈家岭文化、石家河文化和八里岗四期文化。下部为仰韶时期遗存，堆积厚，延续时间长，内涵丰富，主要遗迹有房址、窖穴和墓葬，其遗存分属于仰韶早期半坡类型和仰韶中期庙底沟类型。已清理墓葬一百余座，有多人二次合葬墓和单人一次葬墓两种。随葬品以陶器为主，骨器次之，石器少见。陶器多为明器，基本组合为鼎、罐、钵和器座等。除墓葬外，另有与之同一时期的墓祭坑和圆形房址等。

仰韶中期庙底沟类型聚落遗存主要是房屋建筑基址，流行由数套单元房相连而成的长屋和排房式村落布局。发掘区内房址被规划成东西长南北分列的两组三排。遗物以陶器为主，另有少量骨器和石器。陶器以泥质与夹砂红陶为主，褐陶次之，少量灰陶和黑陶。纹饰较少，有少量细绳纹、指甲戳印纹、指窝纹、附加

八里岗墓葬M120

八里岗房址F34、F35

堆纹和镂孔等。另有少量彩陶，纹饰主要有宽带纹、回旋勾连纹和双三角叶纹等。陶器基本组合为钵、罐、鼎、盆或器座。

八里岗屈家岭文化遗迹有袋状窖穴。遗物以陶器为主，石器与骨器少见，陶器以泥质和夹砂灰陶为主，灰褐陶次之，另见少量泥质红陶和黑陶。纹饰主要为旋纹和附加堆纹，有少量镂孔。彩陶较少，饰网格纹、宽带纹或晕染式纹样。器类基本组合为鼎、壶形器、杯、盆、钵、双腹碗、罐和豆等。

石家河文化遗迹有袋状或锅底状灰坑，遗物有盆、豆、杯、甑和鬶等。

八里岗四期文化遗存主要为袋状灰坑。陶器器类有罐、釜、豆、杯、盆等，为龙山时代晚期遗存，具有一定的地方特色，同时也受到以王湾三期文化为代表的中原地区龙山遗存的较大影响。

Located at Baligang, Baizhuang Village, Dengzhou City, the site dates from the middle and late Neolithic Age (4000 ~ 2000 BC), and covers 90,000 sq. m. The most typical heritages unearthed are long rows of houses. Apart from Yangshao-culture remains, it contains remains of Qujialing Culture, Longshan Culture and Shijiahe Culture.

北阳平遗址

第五批全国重点文物保护单位

新石器时代

Beiyangping Site

北阳平遗址位于灵宝市阳平镇北阳平村以西。

遗址南北长近2000米、东西宽约400～500米，现存总面积达90万平方米，为灵宝铸鼎塬及其周围仰韶文化聚落群中规模最大的遗址。遗址的主要遗存为仰韶文化中期庙底沟类型时期的文化堆积。遗迹有房址、灰坑与墓葬。房址可分为地穴式和半地穴式两种，口部呈长方形或不规则形，以硬土作居住面，有的经火烧呈青灰色。

出土的遗物有陶、石、骨和角器等。陶器以泥质红陶为主，其次为夹砂褐陶，另有泥质灰陶、泥质黑陶、夹砂红陶和夹砂黑陶。磨光与素面陶较多。纹饰中以细绳纹占绝大多数，还有少量旋纹及附加堆纹。有一定量的

北阳平遗址全景

北阳平遗址地层

彩陶，主要饰红衣黑彩，也有少量白衣和红彩，仅个别器物施内彩，极少数器物将彩陶和绳纹同施于器表。彩陶纹饰有圆点、勾叶、弧线三角、垂帐和条带纹等。器形以盆、罐、钵和小口尖底瓶最为常见，其余还有鼎、釜、灶、瓮、缸、壶、杯、盘、器座、器盖、陶球、陶环、纺轮和人头像等。石器多为磨制，个别打制。器类有斧、刀、镞、球、珠和细石叶等。骨、角器有簪、匕、锥等。试掘还出土有动物遗骸，猪约占总数的95%以上，其余有少量兔、鸡、鸟、鼠、熊等，表明猪是当时人们主要的肉食来源。

遗址还有东周文化堆积，发现的遗迹有灰坑和墓葬。其中灰坑因平整土地被破坏，仅存底部，情况不详。墓葬皆为长方形竖穴墓，底略小于口，四壁修整光滑，底部四周留有生土二层台，单椁，单人单棺或双人各单棺一次葬。遗物有陶罐、豆、鬲及铜带钩、铁带钩、水晶环、贝饰等。

Located at Beiyangping Village, Lingbao City, the site dates from the middle Neolithic Age (4000 ~ 3000 BC). Covering nearly 900,000 sq. m, it consists of over 30 Neolithic sites, with the feature of being the center of the middle and late Yangshao Culture.

庙底沟遗址

第五批全国重点文物保护单位

新石器时代

Miaodigou Site

庙底沟遗址为新石器时代仰韶文化庙底沟类型的命名地，位于河南省三门峡市西南3公里的青龙涧南岸。

庙底沟遗址发现于1953年，1955年进行了全面调查。其内涵分为二期，总面积24万平方米。从1956年起陆续进行了考古发掘，发现仰韶文化房基两座，窖穴一百六十八座，残墓一座。两座房基的结构基本相同，都是南北向的方形浅竖穴，根据发掘的平面布局，可以复原成四面坡屋顶的房子。这里出土的仰韶文化陶器经复原的有六百九十多件，按用途可分为容器、炊具、工具、装饰品和玩具等。容器和炊具都是当时的日常用具，如盘、碗、盆、鼎等，多是红陶，纹饰除素面或磨光外，还有彩绘、线纹、弦纹等。其中最有代表性的是彩陶，由于该期文化主要彩绘图案以花瓣纹为主，而异于其他同期文化，故命名为仰韶文化庙底沟类型。

庙底沟遗址鸟瞰

庙底沟遗址出土彩陶钵

庙底沟遗址出土彩陶钵

仰韶文化层上面还压有龙山文化早期堆积，也称为庙底沟二期文化。由于该期遗存特征不仅保留有明显的仰韶文化因素，而且出现了龙山文化诸多的早期器形，因此该期文化属仰韶文化向龙山文化过渡的遗存。庙底沟遗址的发现，解决了仰韶和龙山文化的分期，更重要的是解决了仰韶和龙山文化间的过渡关系，为研究中国古代文化发展提供了重要的实物例证。

Located at Miaodigou Village, Sanmenxia City, the site dates from the middle Neolithic Age (4000 ~ 3000 BC), and covers 240,000 sq. m. The most typical remains unearthed are various kinds of leaf patterns. It reflects the transition from Yangshao Culture to Longshan Culture.

大河村遗址

第五批全国重点文物保护单位

新石器时代

Dahe Village Site

大河村遗址位于郑州市东北郊的柳林镇大河村西南约1公里的慢坡土岗上。1972～1987年先后进行过二十一次发掘，揭露面积达4738平方米。

遗址平面呈椭圆形，南北长700余米、东西宽600多米，总面积40余万平方米，文化层厚达7～12.5米，为郑州附近规模最大、堆积最厚的新石器时代遗址。遗址中包含仰韶、龙山、二里头和商等四个时代的堆积，其年代跨度长达三千三百多年，记载了仰韶文化到商代前期漫长的发展过程。其中最丰富的是仰韶文化遗存，可分为七期，涵盖了仰韶文化从产生、发展到消亡的全过程，前后延续二千四百年之久，为中原地区仰韶文化树立了一个典型的分期标尺。有研究者依据该遗址将仰韶文化相关遗存命名为“大河村类型”或“大河村文化”，成为豫中地区同时期文化的代表。

大河村原始聚落的布局已基本探明。房址集中在遗址的中心地带，形成居住区，大量窖穴分布在房屋周围；遗址中部偏东有一处饲养牲畜的圈栏；两处公共墓地位于遗址北部的边缘地带。

大河村遗址出土彩陶双连壶

大河村遗址房基

大河村遗址出土白衣彩陶钵

在该遗址发现的众多遗迹中，最为重要的是保存完好的连间房屋建筑，墙壁之中的木柱痕与芦苇束痕清晰可见。遗址出土完整或可复原的陶、石、骨、角、蚌等各类遗物约五千件，其中最引人注目的是大批造型精美、色彩绚丽、种类繁多、纹样复杂的彩陶。形制奇特的彩陶双连壶、饰有各种天象纹的彩陶钵等器物均为新石器时代彩陶器中的珍品。

除中原系统的文化堆积，遗址中还发现了属于东夷文化体系的大汶口文化，以及属于苗蛮文化系统的屈家岭文化遗存，显示了中原古文化与邻境诸原始文化之间的交流与相互关系，也是我国古代文化大融合的考古学实证。

Located at Dahe Village, Zhengzhou City, the site dates back to the period from the middle Neolithic Age to the Shang Dynasty (5000 ~ 1500 BC), and covers about 300,000 sq. m. Most of the remains unearthed reflect Yangshao Culture, while the rest reflect Longshan Culture, Dawenkou Culture and Qujialing Culture.

孟庄遗址

第五批全国重点文物保护单位

新石器时代至商、周

Mengzhuang Site

孟庄遗址位于辉县市孟庄村东侧的台地上。

遗址平面形状呈椭圆形，总面积约30万平方米。1992～1995年对孟庄遗址进行了考古发掘，发掘面积达5000余平方米。遗址包含的文化内涵十分丰富，有裴李岗、仰韶、龙山、二里头、二里岗、商代晚期、西周以及东周等多个历史时期的文化遗存。其中龙山、二里头、商代三个时期先后叠压的城址的发现最为重要。

裴李岗文化遗存主要位于遗址南部，发现的遗迹只有灰坑，出土较多遗物。仰韶文化遗存在整个遗址内都有分布，主要遗迹有长方形房基、灰坑、儿童瓮棺葬等，并出土丰富的遗物。龙山文化遗存的重要遗迹有城址、房基、水井、墓葬、灰坑等。城内还发现夯土基址、长方形房基、水井以及数百座灰坑，在这些遗迹中出土了大量的遗物，为研究该城的年代、性质提供了可靠的资料。

龙山城址的上面叠压着二里头时期的城址。城内发现的重要遗迹有圆形半地穴式房基、长方形水井以及圆形、椭圆形窖穴等，城西北部、西南部发现了两

孟庄遗址出土陶钵

孟庄遗址龙山城址东北角

处墓地，共二十余座，还出土有丰富的遗物。二里头时期的城址上面是殷墟时期城址。城内的重要遗迹有长方形地面式房基、长方形水井以及圆形、椭圆形窖穴等，城西北部、西南部还发现了一些墓葬，均为长方形土坑竖穴墓，多数墓内有随葬品。

西周时期的文化遗存，目前发现的主要遗迹是灰坑、陶窑、墓葬等，出土遗物一般为鬲、罐、豆或簋、罐、豆组合，主要为泥质灰陶和夹砂灰陶，年代应为西周中晚期。

东周时期的文化遗存较少，其中春秋时期的文化层仅保留一些埋藏较深的灰坑、水井、墓葬等遗址。出土遗物主要为绳纹陶器。战国时期文化遗存有灰坑、陶窑、墓葬等。战国时期的墓葬主要分布于遗址的西南部Ⅷ区内，一般都为长方形土坑竖穴墓，葬式为仰身屈肢。辉县一带自20世纪50年代以来，发现了不少战国时期的大墓，如固围村大墓等，但一直没有找到与大墓一致的遗址，孟庄战国遗址的发现为寻找这一时期遗址提供了重要线索。

Located east of Mengzhuang Village, Huixian City, the site dates from the late Neolithic Age (2400 ~ 1000 BC). It contains the unearthed remains of a Longshan-culture city, which continued to be used in the Erlitou-culture period and the Shang Dynasty.

◀ 孟庄遗址发掘现场

古城寨城址

第五批全国重点文物保护单位

新石器时代

Guchengzhai Site

古城寨城址位于新密市东南35公里的古城寨村。城址总面积约17.65万平方米。外侧南、北、东三面都有新石器时代遗址。其中城西南部是仰韶文化遗址，其北面被龙山时代城址所压；城北、城东均是龙山文化遗址。城址内外的新石器时代文化遗址约30万平方米。城墙内出土的龙山文化陶片，可辨器形有深腹罐、高领瓮、斝、鼎、折腹盆、钵、碗、杯、刻槽盆、甗、豆、鬶、盉、觚、壶、盘、缸、器盖和陶纺轮等。

在城址内清理出龙山文化晚期的一座夯土基址（F1）和一座围绕F1的廊庑式建筑（F4）。F1位于城址中部偏东侧，为夯筑高台建筑，坐西朝东，南、北、东三面均有回廊。南北长28.4、东西宽13.5米，面积383.4平方米。

古城寨城址遥感图

古城寨城址北城门

古城寨城址F1大型房基

在房基上各排柱洞中的中心柱洞内都置有柱础石。房基上的六排柱洞把房子分隔成面阔七间。

龙山文化第一期遗存的年代与禹州瓦店一期相当，早于王城岗一期文化，为龙山文化早期。第二期遗存的年代相当于王城岗三期文化，又可分为前后两段。第三期遗存相当于王城岗四期文化。第四期遗存相当于王城岗五期文化，年代已接近新密市新砦遗址的新砦期。

古城寨龙山文化城址从选择到布局，明显受龙山文化中晚期

古城寨城址廊庑奠基坑狗骨

古城寨城址F4廊庑基址

城址的影响，特别是受王城岗城址的影响。古城寨地近夏人活动的中心地区，是新石器时代晚期文化与夏文化分界的重要标志之一。特别是城垣与大型建筑（宫庙）基址的发现，揭示了夏商文明的基本特征，成为研究我国古代文明形成、国家产生的重要佐证。

Located at Guchengzhai Village, Xinmi City, the site dates from the late Neolithic Age (circa 2300 BC). It reflects Longshan Culture. The remaining city wall measures over 7 meters high, and the remains of the city cover an area of about 180,000 sq. m. In its northeast are the remains of palace foundations.

府城遗址

第五批全国重点文物保护单位

商

Fucheng Site

府城遗址为商代早期城址，位于焦作市西南郊约10公里的府城村西北部台地上，距今约为3600年左右。遗址平面略呈方形，西城墙现存高度约2～3米、长约280米、宽4～8米。北墙保存长度为284米、高度约2～3米。

宫殿位于城内的东北部，该区域分布有大面积夯土基址，已发掘的四处夯土基址之间有叠压打破关系，其中1、2号基址保存较好。

1号夯土基址平面为长方形，南北长70米、东西宽55米。基址在汉代和西周文化层之下，分南北两个院落，中间为正殿。前殿位于南院的南部，与两边的配殿连为一体，南北宽约75米，在西南拐角处保留有向外漫出的夯土。正殿位于前后两院之间，南北宽148米，东西已发掘部分的长度为117米。北院发掘出的有西回廊和北殿（后殿）。西回廊基

府城遗址1号宫殿东部

府城遗址 1 号宫殿北门

府城遗址 1 号宫殿西部夯土

槽宽41米。二号基址叠压着1号基址的北殿，基址为长方形，坐北朝南。已发掘部分南北长12.5米、东西宽6.5米，为地面式建筑。建筑方法是先挖一基槽，基槽内的夯土是十分纯净的浅黄色土，居住面上铺有一层含有料礓石粒的黄色土层，夯砸后作为居住面，然后再立木柱，建造房子的地上部分。在紧邻1号基址北殿边缘的一个长方形窖穴，出土了大量完整陶器，有鬲、圜底深腹罐、大口尊、深腹盆、小口高领瓮、大口缸等。这些陶器的特征与郑州二里岗下层的同类器物基本相同。

Located at Fucheng Village, Jiaozuo City, the site dates from the Shang Dynasty (16th-11th century BC), and covers nearly 100,000 sq. m. In the middle of it there is a city, city wall and palace foundations. The city was built in the Shang Dynasty, and continued to be used in the Warring States period and the Han Dynasty.

番国故城遗址

第五批全国重点文物保护单位

东周

The site of the Fan-state capital

番国故城遗址，是东周时期番国（又称鄱国）都城所在地，位于信阳市固始县城关。

遗址分内城、外城两个部分。外城平面呈不规则的四边形，其西墙长3735米，北城墙全长2325米，最长的东墙全长达5800米，南城墙长仅1000多米。全城周长达13.5公里。其中除了东城墙的南部和南城墙已被破坏，其余部分保存较为完好，多数墙体残高仍在4～5米左右，墙的顶端宽15～20米。内城位于城内的东北角，其东墙、北墙分别和外城的东墙、北墙共用一道城墙，此处城墙特别坚固，墙基宽厚，多数在30～40米之间。西墙长1950米、墙基宽20米、高3.8米。南墙长920米、墙基宽29米、高5米，残存四段。内城全长为6.9公里。

近年来有关番的青铜器多有出土，如1974年信阳县长台关乡东周墓的青铜盘、青铜匜，1976年信阳县吴家店乡春秋早期土坑墓中出土的青铜鼎、青铜盘等。1978年河南固始侯古堆1号墓出土了一套编钟，共计九件，每钟上都有铭文，但铭文中原有的人名都被铲掉了，再在原来的位置上刻以“鄱子成周”。此墓规模巨大，随葬物丰富，且十分精美。墓内出土有九鼎，应是番国夫人墓葬。

番国故城遗址

Located in the town of Gushi County, the site dates from the Eastern Zhou Dynasty (770 ~ 221 BC), and covers nearly 100,000 sq. m. It the middle of it, ruins of a city have been found. It is divided into an inner city and an outer city; the inner city has a circumference of 6.5 km, and the outer city has a circumference of 13.5 km. There is a cemetery in its southeastern corner.

城阳城址

第五批全国重点文物保护单位

东周

The site of Chengyang City

城阳城址位于信阳市长台关乡苏楼村西。

遗址平面呈方形，总面积约68万平方米。分为内城和外城。内城在外城的西南隅，平面形状作不甚规则的梯形，东垣长500米、西垣长325米、南垣长524米、北垣长530米，合计周长达1879米，面积约20万平方米。在内城的西半部，至今仍残存有一片高大的夯土台基，有可能是当时重要建筑的基址，或即宫殿区。外城东城墙长640米、北墙长770米，西墙在内城西垣的北端又向北延伸422米，南墙在内城的北墙的东端又向东延伸406米。包括内城的东、南、西三垣，外城周长达3587米，面积约48万平方米。

所有城垣均系夯土筑成，残存高度在5米左右。内城处在整个遗址的最高点，外城东侧则距淮河不远，因此整个城址的位置十分险要。又因南控著名关隘长台关，城阳城的军事用途十分明显。

信阳长台关7号楚墓墓室全景

信阳长台关 7 号楚墓彩绘漆豆出土情况

城阳城址西城墙

据《战国策》记载，在公元前 278 年秦将白起率大军攻破楚国都城郢都之后，楚顷襄王率部将楚国的政治军事中心北迁至城阳。信阳长台关故城就是楚顷襄王留掩的城阳城旧址，因此城阳城遗址自古以来又有“楚王城”之称。城阳城址附近，明清以来就不断有重要文物出土。

1957年在城阳城遗址的西南角外侧附近发掘了两座属于战国时期的大型木椁墓，出土了一千多件明显具有楚文化风格的珍贵文物。长台关楚墓的发掘，丰富了河南楚文化研究的内容，在某些方面填补了考古学上的空白，为城阳城址的深入研究提供了丰富的资料。

Located at Chenglizhuang, Sulou Village, the City of Xinyang, the site dates from the Eastern Zhou Dynasty (770 ~ 221 BC). Divided into an inner city and an outer city and irregularly shaped, it covers a total area of 2.50 million sq. m. It was at one time the temporary capital of the State of Chu.

古荥冶铁遗址

第五批全国重点文物保护单位

汉

The Iron Smelting site at Guxing

古荥冶铁遗址是一处兼具冶铁和铸造的汉代大规模官营冶铁作坊遗址，位于郑州市西北24公里的古荥镇西墙外。

遗址南北长400米，东西宽300米，面积12万平方米。1975年进行了部分发掘，发掘面积1700平方米，清理出两座冶铁高炉炉基，是迄今发现我国古代最早、最大、结构最完整并首次科学发掘的特大椭圆冶铁高炉炉基。以炉基为中心还清理出大积铁块、矿石堆、炉渣堆积区以及与冶炼有关的遗迹水井、水池、船形坑、四角柱坑、窑等。出土了一批耐火砖和铸造铁范用的陶模，还有铁器、陶器、石器等。两座炉基东西并列，间隔14.5米。炉门向南。一号炉基础坑略呈南北长方形，长约17米、宽约13米；二号炉基础坑则大致为方形，边长13米。基础坑一般用黄土分层夯填，夯层厚5～10厘米。此外还清理出炉缸基槽与耐火材料土基床，用耐火土夯筑炉体的炉缸、炉前工作面以及紧靠工作面

古荥冶铁遗址发掘现场之一

的炉前坑。清理出的积铁块有九块，最大的重20余吨。积铁料块上遗留的木炭说明当时炼铁还主要是使用木炭作燃料。出土铁器中有犁、犁铧、铲、锛、钁、臿等农具，均为铸造；此外还有凿、齿轮、矛等。在部分陶模和十余件铁器上发现有“河一”字铭，因而判断古荥冶铸遗址当是汉代河南郡铁官的第一号冶铸作坊。

古荥冶铁遗址在我国古代冶金史研究领域，特别是在汉代冶铁史研究领域占有极为重要的地位，遗址所揭示的冶铁规模之大和技术水平之高，充分说明了在汉代处于三大手工业中主导地位的冶铁业已达到空前的发展高度，成为繁荣的汉文明最为重要的物质基础之一。

古荥冶铁遗址发掘现场之二

It includes the ancient Yingyang city and the Guying iron smelting site. The ancient city of Yingyang is located at Guying Town, Zhengzhou City. It dates from the Han Dynasty (206 BC ~ 220 AD). In a rectangular shape with the south and north sides longer than the east and west ones, it covers 12 sq. m.

The Iron Smelting site is located beyond the west wall of the ancient Yingyang city, containing the remains of a smeltery in Henan Prefecture in the Han Dynasty. Some of the iron wares unearthed are inscribed with two characters- 'He YI' .

黄冶三彩窑址

第五批全国重点文物保护单位

唐

Tangsancai kiln site at Huangye

黄冶三彩窑址位于巩义市东北约6公里的站街镇黄冶河两岸。

窑址总面积约23万平方米。1972年和1976年对窑址进行试掘，发现十余个窑址和作坊遗迹，出土一大批三彩器皿、俑、窑具、模具和建筑构件等。器皿多为炉、盆、罐、枕、碗、盘等生活用品，俑和小型玩具则有小儿骑马俑、人骑骆驼俑、马、象、卧狮等。釉色有黄、棕、蓝、白、绿等互融、互间、互点的多种釉彩，自然流淌交融，斑驳灿烂；也有黄、绿、红、淡青、蓝等单色釉；还有珍贵的绞胎、绞釉器。

窑址存在三个相叠压的文化堆积层。第一层厚1.8米，发现“咸平元宝”铜钱一枚。第二层厚0.5米，出土器物有三彩三足炉、碗、盆、三彩埙、三彩俑等，数量大、品种多，色彩鲜艳，光泽晶莹。另有“开元通宝”铜钱一枚。第三层叠压在三彩层之下，厚0.2~0.6米，出土器物有瓷盆、罐、瓶、盘等，瓷胎纯净，火候较高，胎骨厚重，器形较大，釉色有白、黑、淡青、鳝鱼黄等。第三层为隋代窑址，第二层是唐代窑址，上层即宋代窑址，充分证明了唐三彩是由隋代白瓷、黑瓷、青瓷逐步发展而来的。同时发现的窑具有匣钵、支具、垫饼等；模具有小型艺术品的模具，如凤首壶、马、象、雀、人骑骆驼、猴头埙模等，大型器物附

黄冶三彩窑址6号窑炉

黄冶三彩窑址出土唐三彩水注

黄冶三彩窑址唐代早期瓷器埋藏坑

属装饰贴花模具，如翼狮、海石榴、榕花、炉足模等，建筑构件模具，如云雀小瓷砖、山茶花模等。窑炉主要分布在遗址的东部和南部黄冶河两岸，目前已发现窑炉十多处，其窑室平面呈马蹄形，平底，窑室内径1.25米、深1.3米、顶高1.1米、口宽0.96米，窑室周壁用五至六层耐火砖砌成。窑内壁呈暗灰色，外部为暗红色烧土，厚约0.4～0.5米。

黄冶三彩窑址是目前发现的唐代烧造三彩制品时代最早、规模最大、产品种类最多、烧造工艺最高、持续时间最长的一处窑场，对研究唐三彩的制作工艺、陶瓷艺术以及中外文化交流等，具有重要价值。

Gongyi Kiln site is located in Tiejianglu Village and Baihe Village, Gongyi City. It dates back to the period from the Northern Dynasties to the Song Dynasty (386 ~ 1271 AD). At first it produced celadon, but in the Sui and Tang dynasties it produced white porcelain.

The Tangsancai kiln is located at Huangye Village, Gongyi City. It dates back to the Tang Dynasty (618 ~ 906 AD). It mainly produced Tangsancai, or Tang tri-colored glazed pottery. Many remains of workshops and kilns have been discovered, and a great number of kiln tools and articles made of Tangsancai pottery have been unearthed.

清凉寺汝官窑遗址

第五批全国重点文物保护单位

宋

Ru Kiln site at Qingliangsi

清凉寺汝官窑遗址，是北宋时期专为宫廷烧制御用瓷器的官窑遗址，位于宝丰县大营镇清凉寺村及村南台地上。遗址面积共计101.5万平方米。

汝窑是宋代五大名窑之一，产品为青瓷。汝瓷胎质细腻坚硬，釉色青幽润泽，以天青色最为珍贵。其烧制工艺为满釉支烧，支钉细小如芝麻状。据文献记载，汝窑烧造时间很短，因此传世品极少。因釉料中搀加玛瑙，产生出高贵独特的釉色，更增加了其在历史上的价值和神秘感。为了寻找汝窑遗址，考古工作者经历了半个多世纪的周折，最终断定其在宝丰县清凉寺。1987年，在此进行了首次发掘，发掘面积200平方米，发现典型御用汝瓷十余件，之后经过四次大规模发掘，每次都有较大的收获。1998年在一村民院内发现耐火砖墙和御用瓷片，经钻探和发掘，初步确认了汝官窑中心烧造区的具体位置和范围。2000年在中心区开始大面积发掘，取得了重大成果。

这次发掘，清理出烧制御用瓷器的窑炉十五座，大部分保存基本完整。窑室周壁用耐火砖垒砌，一般由窑门、火膛、窑床、隔墙和烟囱组成。窑炉形制大致可分作马蹄形和椭圆形两种。同时探明有作坊、排水沟、灰坑及汝瓷

清凉寺汝官窑遗址出土淡天青釉三足盘

清凉寺汝官窑窑炉遗址

清凉寺汝官窑遗址御用汝瓷残器堆积

窖藏，内涵十分丰富。出土器物的种类比较齐全，有碗、盘、杯、壶、碟、罐等生活用品，有文房用具及瓷枕、瓷玩、瓷雕等工艺品。

该窑址的发现，不仅找到了宋代的汝官窑址，为传世汝瓷鉴定提供了可靠依据，而且从地层上确定了汝官窑的具体烧造年代，对于深入探讨汝官窑的发展历史和制作工艺，有着重要的意义。

Located at Qingliangsi Village, Baofeng County, the site dates from the Northern Song Dynasty (960 ~ 1126 AD), and covers 1.015 million sq. m. It is divided into an area of government-run kilns and an area of privately run kilns. In the government-run kiln area, sky blue glaze and kiln tools have been unearthed.

鹿邑太清宫遗址

第五批全国重点文物保护单位

宋、金

The site of Taiqing Palace in Luyi

鹿邑太清宫遗址，是唐宋时期皇家祭祀老子的地方，为一处包括宋金建筑基址、碑刻及明清建筑的大型遗址群，位于鹿邑县城东5公里的太清宫镇。

鹿邑为老子故里。太清宫祭祀老子的遗存始于汉，盛于唐宋，延续至今。太清宫遗址由隐山遗址及太清宫、洞霄宫遗址三部分组成。太清宫镇现存有“唐开元神武皇帝道德经注碑”、“大宋重修太清宫之碑”、“金续修太清宫碑”等重要碑刻，以及清代重建的太极殿、圣母殿等。1997年和2000年，对隐山遗址及太清宫、洞霄宫遗址先后进行了两次发掘，初步探明了唐宋时期太清宫的规模与建筑基址。太清宫范围约1.5平方公里，中心殿址就在今太极殿之下。史载太清宫唐时分前后两宫，前宫有午门、御道，中央是太极殿，两侧为七元殿、五岳殿、南斗殿、虚元殿。经钻探发现，以太极殿为中心，向南300米、向北200

鹿邑太清宫遗址太极殿

鹿邑太清宫遗址老君台

鹿邑太清宫遗址御碑

米、东西700米的范围内都有建筑遗迹。在后宫"洞霄宫"遗址进行了钻探和局部发掘。洞霄宫以圣母殿为中心，分宫殿区和一般区，宫殿区的前区为宗教活动区，中路自南向北依次为照壁、踏道、山门、前殿、大殿、中门、回廊、后殿。发掘出了宋金时期的回廊、中门、西配殿、后寝殿等重要基址和大批建筑构件。

太清宫遗址内现存唐、宋、元碑刻二十余通，著名的有"唐开元神武皇帝道德经注碑"，宋真宗御碑"先天太后之赞"，元"圣旨碑"、"执照碑"等。

鹿邑太清宫祭祀老子的遗存时代早，跨度大，文化内涵丰富，具有很高的历史、科学和艺术价值。

Located at Taiqinggong Town, Luyi County, the site dates back to the Tang, Song and Jin dynasties. It was the place where sacrifices were offered to Lao Tzu in the Tang and Song dynasties. Main remains are building foundations and stone tablets dating from the three dynasties. There still remain some buildings dating from the Ming and Qing dynasties.

织机洞遗址

第六批全国重点文物保护单位

旧石器时代 Relics at Zhiji Cave

织机洞遗址位于荥阳市城区以南20公里的崔庙镇王宗店村北约1公里处的大路山西坡。遗址主要分布于织机洞洞内及洞前斜坡上，总面积约300平方米。洞内堆积厚约24米，可分为23个沉积层。其中发现用火遗迹17处，出土石制品6000余件（其中石器近1600件），哺乳动物化石和鸟类化石也相当丰富，已获标本达万余件。石器种类有刮削器、尖状器、石锥、砍砸器、石锤和雕刻器等，其中以刮削器和尖状器为最多。石制品以小型居多，原料简单，打片方法以锤击法为主，修理工作以砸击法最为普遍，但比较粗糙。织机洞遗址的石器组合，是已知中国北方分布最南、石制品最丰富的一处遗存。

织机洞遗址中发现有中更新世动物群中的典型动物肿骨鹿、中国鬣狗。根据伴生的哺乳动物群看，织机洞遗址的年代应为中

织机洞遗址全景

织机洞遗址出土尖状器

织机洞遗址出土刮削器

更新世中、晚期。织机洞遗址的发现，对研究人类的起源和旧石器时代南北文化的交流等，具有十分重要的学术价值。

织机洞遗址，是我国北方地区继北京周口店之后旧石器洞穴遗址的最重大发现，也是首次发现在一个洞穴遗址内既有旧石器又有新石器遗存。它对研究现代人类的起源和旧石器时代南北文化的交流等，具有十分重要的学术价值。

Located at Wangzongdian Village, Yingyang City, the relics date from the late Paleolithic Age (70,000 years ago), and are mainly distributed in Zhiji Cave and the slope in front of it, which cover a total area of about 300 sq. m. 17 traces of the use of fire have been discovered, and over 6,000 relics have been unearthed.

杨台寺遗址

第六批全国重点文物保护单位

新石器时代

Yangtaisi Site

杨台寺遗址位于驻马店市区西北约10公里的杨台寺旧址处。遗址位于高出周围地面7米左右的台地上，面积约11万平方米。西北距汝河4公里，有一条小河从遗址西部自南向北流过。

从遗址西部深沟和断崖上可见文化层2～5米，已发现有灰坑、房基柱础、陶灶等重要遗迹和大量红烧土及陶片。从遗址范围内地表采集到的陶片和遗物看，其文化内涵有仰韶文化、屈家岭文化、石家河文化、龙山文化及二里头文化遗存。典型器物有白衣红黑彩陶罐、指甲纹鼎足、鸭嘴形鼎足、器盖、陶豆、陶罐、陶碗、红陶钵、澄滤器等。质地有泥质、夹砂、夹蚌三种。陶色有红、黑、灰、棕、黄色。纹饰多为素面，兼有篮纹、弦纹、镂孔和附加堆纹。生产工具有石斧、石镞、石镰、陶纺轮等。装饰品有陶环。

该遗址文化内涵丰富、保存完好，是淮河流域上游同时期遗址中较为典型的一处。该遗址地处我国南北文化的交汇地域，对研究中原地区的文化与江汉文化的关系有着重要意义，另外，对研究豫南地区乃至淮河流域上游新石器时代早、中、晚期文化的继承关系及发展序列，具有重要学术价值。

Located at the site of Yangtai Temple southwest of Yanglou Village, Zhumadian City, the site contains relics that date from the middle and late Neolithic Age (approximately 4500 years ago). They are distributed on a 7-meter-high mound that covers about 80,000 sq. m.

杨台寺遗址

瓦店遗址

第六批全国重点文物保护单位

新石器时代

Wadian Site

瓦店遗址出土陶罐

瓦店遗址出土陶刻槽盆

瓦店遗址位于禹州市火龙镇瓦店村东部和西北部的台地上。颍河由遗址的北面、东面转而流向东南。

遗址南北长1500米，东西宽300米，面积约45万平方米。文化层厚2～3米。自1979年发现，至1998年先后共进行了五次较大规模的考古发掘，发掘面积约7000平方米。瓦店遗址主要包含有龙山文化早、中、晚期遗存，其中以晚期（王湾三期文化晚期）遗存为主。从遗址地面存有的大型建筑基址和奠基坑遗迹，以及精美的陶酒器、玉鸟、玉璧、玉铲和大卜骨等器物看，该遗址在河南龙山文化晚期（王湾三期文化晚期）中属于较高规格。瓦店遗址文化层厚度一般在2米，最厚处达4米。文化内涵丰富，主要遗物有：陶鼎、罐、甑、盆、斝、鬶、觚、瓮、刻槽盆、钵、碗、缸、器盖、豆、圈足盘、罍、陶环、石刀、镰、骨锥、卜骨、龟甲以及玉鸟、玉璧、玉铲等，并存有大量的房基、灰坑、墓葬、灰沟、奠基坑、窖穴等。而遗物中又以陶酒器、玉器、大卜骨为代表性器物。从出土遗物及遗址的规模看，瓦店遗址是中原地区龙山文化时期最重要的遗存之一。

Located at Wadian Village, Yuzhou City, the site contains relics dating from the late Neolithic Age (4120 BC), and covers an area of about 450,000 sq. m. Most of the relics reflect Longshan Culture.

石固遗址

第六批全国重点文物保护单位

新石器时代

Shigu Site

石固遗址外景

石固遗址位于长葛市区西南12.5公里的石固镇岗河村西，石梁河与胜天湖河故道交汇处的台地上。遗址面积约105000平方米。

石固遗址包含裴李岗和仰韶时期的文化遗存，已清理出裴李岗文化的房基、灰坑、墓葬等，发现仰韶文化的房基、灰坑、墓葬，以及龙山文化的灰坑等重要遗迹。遗址文化堆积厚1.3～1.7米，其中仰韶文化一、二期文化层内涵特殊，系目前中原地区首次发现。该遗址还出土了石磨棒、石磨盘以及鼎、罐、碗、钵等陶、石、蚌类器物11890件，其中裴李岗时期的器物8632件，仰韶时期的器物3258件，经碳十四测定，该遗址年代距今约7400～4500年。

石固遗址的发现证明河南中部地区的仰韶文化是由裴李岗文化演变而来的，从而解决了两者间的发展、继承关系。填补了裴李岗文化和仰韶文化之间的某些缺环，解决了长期以来悬而未决的仰韶文化的渊源问题。

Located at Ganghe Village, Shigu Town, Changge City, the site dates from the early and middle Neolithic Age (7400 ~ 4500 BC) and covers 105,000 sq. m. It contains relics reflecting Peiligang Culture and Yangshao Culture.

郝家台遗址

第六批全国重点文物保护单位

新石器时代

Haojiatai Site

郝家台遗址位于漯河市源汇区孙庄乡石槽赵村东北约800米处的台地上。是一处龙山文化、二里头文化遗存，遗址年代距今约4700～4100年。

郝家台龙山文化城址，平面呈长方形，面积约30000平方米，东城墙中部有城门。发现的主要遗迹有夯土城墙、长方形排房房基、陶窑、水井、灰坑、墓葬等，出土了大量陶器、石器、骨器、蚌器等。郝家台遗址文化特征明显，它代表了分布在嵩山以东淮河水系的沙河、颍河流域的龙山文化类型，遗址面积大，文化堆积厚。郝家台龙山文化城址的房基多数为长方形排房，普遍使用土坯筑墙，建于平地或高台之上，也有少数圆形房址。尤其是城址内的建筑基址的布局，比较规范、规模宏大，有的建筑物下用人奠基。郝家台龙山文化城址的年代经碳十四测定、树轮校正为距今4606±121年。它的发现，标志着古老的氏族社会的结束，文明时代的开始，对研究我国古代国家的起源具有重要价值。

Located at Shicaozhao Village, Luohe City, the site dates from the late Neolithic Age (4700 ~ 4100 BC). It is 2 to 3 meters higher than the ground around it and covers about 65,000 sq. m. Ruins of a Longshan-culture city have been discovered in its southwest.

郝家台F18排房

郝家台遗址出土陶鼎

王油坊遗址

第六批全国重点文物保护单位

新石器时代 Wangyoufang Site

王油坊遗址

王油坊遗址位于永城市西25公里酂城镇王油坊村东。遗址东西、南北皆长约100米，现存文化层厚度一般为3米左右，地表已成为耕地。

经考古发掘清理出比较完整的龙山文化房基20座、灰坑44个、石灰窑3座。房基有半地穴式、地面圆形建筑、方形连体几种形式，并出现了土坯砌墙技术和房基下用成人和儿童奠基的现象。

出土陶器主要是泥质灰陶，少数蛋壳黑陶、白陶、红陶等，还有夹蚌壳陶。陶器多为轮制，亦有手制。器形主要有：深腹罐、鼎、甗、直领瓮、豆、圈足盘、筒形杯、平底盆、器盖等。纹饰主要是绳纹、篮纹、方格纹。另外，还出土了大量石、骨、角、蚌器等。龙山文化可分三个层次，出土器物变化明显，各有特点。

王油坊遗址中的龙山文化特征明显，是具有代表性的一种文化类型，考古界已定其为王油坊类型。该遗址丰富的文化遗存，为研究古代人们的生产、生活和中国建筑发展史都提供了珍贵的依据，具有重要的历史价值和科学价值。

Located at Wangyoufang Village, the City of Yongcheng, the site dates from the late Neolithic Age (4450 BC) and covers about 10,000 sq. m. The culture it reflects is named 'the Wangyoufang type of Longshan Culture'.

李庄遗址

第六批全国重点文物保护单位

新石器时代

Lizhuang Site

李庄遗址（又称山台寺遗址）位于商丘市柘城县申桥乡李庄村。该遗址面积2.18万平方米，文化层厚4米，文化内涵有：龙山文化、岳石文化、商代晚期、东周时期的遗存，其中尤以龙山文化最为丰厚。龙山文化遗迹中发现有较大的夯土台基；房址有圆形、方形和长方形，其中以F2的五间排房最为壮观；牛坑1座，坑内埋有完整和不完整的牛骨架9具，鹿下颏骨1副，这是迄今所见龙山文化时期埋牛最多的一例；水井1座，井口的四角上各有一个柱洞，表明井口之上原有井亭之类的建筑；灰坑68座，形制有方形、圆形和不规则形等几种；不完整的木栅栏遗址1座，它是由23个小柱洞连成一段弧线，中间有一宽约2.5米的豁口。此外，还清理残窑1座，灶址2处。

李庄遗址全景

李庄遗址出土陶罐

李庄遗址出土陶盆

经过整理，复原完整的陶器有265件。器种有炊具鼎、甗、甑、深腹罐等，容器有盆、瓮、大口罐、钵、盉、鬶等；陶色有灰、灰褐、黑、橙红等，其中以灰陶为主，其次是褐陶、黑陶；纹饰有篮纹、绳纹、方格纹、旋纹、刻纹、云纹、波浪纹、叶脉纹、菱形纹、三角纹、同心圆纹等。另有较完整的石、骨、蚌、陶等质地的小件器物320余件。

李庄遗址的发现对研究商文化的起源和用牛祭祀等问题具有重要价值，同时也为研究和探索豫东地区的龙山文化补充了珍贵的实物资料。

Located north of Lizhuang Village, Zhecheng County, the site dates back to the period from the late Neolithic Age to the Shang Dynasty (3600 ~ 1046 BC) and covers about 30,000 sq. m. It mainly contains relics of Longshan Culture.

王湾遗址

第六批全国重点文物保护单位

新石器时代

Wangwan Site

王湾遗址位于洛阳市涧西区红山乡王湾村北。是一处性质多样、分布密集且布局严整的新石器时代遗存，面积约8000平方米，文化层厚3米左右，内含仰韶文化、仰韶文化向龙山文化过渡时期和龙山文化三期。丰富的文化内涵和明显的地层叠压关系及大量的实物数据，对于探讨仰韶文化的发展去向和河南龙山文化的渊源具有重要意义。由于王湾遗址出土的陶器多，地层明确，从早期到晚期陶器的发展演变脉络清楚，对陶器分期断代具有重大的意义。

王湾遗址是一处最早发现的具有代表性的遗址，根据其文化性质，遗址中的仰韶文化可定为仰韶文化王湾类型，龙山文化定为龙山文化王湾类型，解决了仰韶文化向龙山文化过渡阶段的性质问题。

王湾遗址首次发现在仰韶文化中用石块铺砌的墙基和挖槽等现象，对于研究当时人类居住房屋的建筑结构、防潮措施等方面提供了重要实物资料。遗址中发现的房基、墓葬、陶窑和大量生产工具、生活用具，对研究当时的聚落形态及生产力发展水平都具有重要科学价值。

王湾遗址近景

王湾遗址出土小口尖底瓶

王湾遗址出土彩陶钵

王湾遗址出土镂孔黑陶豆

Located at Wangwan Village, the City of Luoyang, the site dates from the middle and late Neolithic Age (7,000 years ago ~ 3965 ± 95 BC). Covering 45,000 sq. m., it has a 3-meter-thick layer of cultural relics with a dense distribution of ash pits.

鹿台岗遗址

第六批全国重点文物保护单位

新石器时代至周

Lutaigang Site

鹿台岗遗址位于杞县裴村店乡鹿台岗村。西距县城12公里，南距惠济河0.5公里。

遗址北高南低，平面呈梯形，东西宽132米，南北长180米，总面积23760平方米，文化层厚约2～8米，自下而上依次为：仰韶文化、河南龙山文化、先商文化、岳石文化、早商文化、春秋时期文化，属村落居住址。遗址原来面积很大，后被挖掉大部分，东、北两面遭受破坏，现形成高6米的断崖。出土器物有陶器、骨器、石器、蚌器、牙角器、铜器等，其中以生产工具和生活用具为主。生活用具又以陶器为主，陶质分夹粗砂、夹细砂和泥质三类；陶色分灰、褐、黑（黑皮）、红、白五种。纹饰主要有直线、弧线、网格纹、三角纹、篮纹、绳纹、方格纹、弦纹、联珠纹、刻划纹、曲尺纹、布纹、乳钉纹、镂孔、箍状堆纹、附加堆纹、云雷纹、红色彩绘、卷云纹，另有素面和磨光陶器。

Located west of Lutaigang Village, Qi County, the site dates back to the period from the late Neolithic Age to the Spring and Autumn Period (3000 ~ 475 BC) and covers 14,000 sq. m. It contains relics of Yangshao Culture, Longshan Culture, pre-Shang Culture and Yueshi Culture.

鹿台岗遗址

新砦遗址

第六批全国重点文物保护单位

新石器时代至夏

Xinzhai Site

新砦遗址位于新密市东南22.5公里刘砦镇新砦村的梁家台、苏沟、煤土沟等范围内。遗址面积约100万平方米。

新砦遗址是一处设有外壕、城壕和内壕三重防御设施，中心区建有大型建筑的城址。城址总面积约100万平方米。它是河南省迄今为止发现面积最大的一处龙山文化时期的城址。这对于寻找早期夏都遗址、探讨城址和二里头遗址的年代与性质，探讨夏代都城和夏王朝的诞生以及中国古代文明的起源，都具有十分重要的意义。通过对新砦遗址的发掘，发现了河南龙山文化晚期与二里头文化一期之间的过渡文化层，由此被定名为“新砦期”。这一重大发现，填补了河南龙山文化晚期向二里头文化早期过渡的空白。

新砦遗址城墙与护城河遗迹

新砦遗址出土陶鼎

新砦遗址出土深腹罐

Loated west of Xinzhai Village, Xinmi City, the site dates back the period from the late Neolithic Age to the Shang Dynasty (3000 ~ 1046 BC) and covers about 1 million sq. m. The ruins of a large city have been discovered, which dates back to the period from the late Longshan-culture Period to Xinzhai Period, with an outer moat and an inner moat. Foundations of large rammed-earth buildings have been found in its center.

唐户遗址

第六批全国重点文物保护单位

新石器时代至周

Tanghu Site

唐户遗址位于新郑市观音寺镇唐户村南的溹水河与石洞寺河交汇的台地上。遗址南北长约1400米，东西宽500米，面积约52万平方米。

通过考古调查和试掘，了解到遗址的西北部属裴李岗文化，文化层厚2米，中部偏北和东部属仰韶文化，文化层厚约3米，一部分直接叠压在裴李岗文化层之上。遗址的中部偏南是以龙山文化为主的分布区域，文化层厚2～4米。南端为夏、商文化遗存，两周时期墓葬在遗址中部均打破仰韶文化层。唐户遗址中的文化遗存十分丰富，其中属于裴李岗文化遗物有石磨盘、磨棒、石铲、石镰、石斧。陶器有深腹罐、三足钵、壶等，均为夹砂红陶和泥质红陶；仰韶文化的陶器有钵、盆、碗、罐、鼎、釜、小口尖底瓶、大口尖底瓶、纺轮等，以泥质红陶为主。石器有斧、铲、凿、锛、刀镞及研磨器；骨器。另外还发现房址和墓葬；龙山文化的陶器有钵、碗、盆、罐、豆、杯、器座等，为泥质黑陶，另出土有蛋壳黑陶；新砦期文化中以新砦

唐户遗址发掘现场

唐户遗址房屋基址

唐户遗址出土三足钵

二期陶片为主，可见器形有罐、盆、瓮、碗；西周、春秋贵族墓葬出土一批青铜器、玉器、金器、铁器等，为研究郑国历史、郑国青铜器提供了十分重要的数据。

唐户遗址中铁器的发现，说明在春秋时期中原地区已能铸造和使用较先进的铁制生产工具了。

Located south of Tanghu Village, Xinzheng City, the site dates back to the period from the early Neolithic Age to the Zhou Dynasty (6000 ~ 221 BC) and covers about 100,000 sq. m. It contains relics that date back to the period from the early Peiligang-culture period to the Zhou Dynasty.

蒲城店遗址

新石器时代至汉

Puchengdian Site

蒲城店遗址位于平顶山市卫东区东高皇乡蒲城店村北。遗址面积约20万平方米，文化层厚2～4米，文化遗存十分丰富。

蒲城店遗址是一处具有新石器时代龙山文化、夏代二里头文化早期、西周、春秋、战国、汉、宋、明各个时期文化特征的大型遗址。其中尤以龙山文化和二里头早期文化为主，遗址中发现有房址、壕沟、灰坑、墓葬、水井、灶等遗迹。其中二里头文化早期的房址最为重要，其面积大、数量多、排列有序，在长170多米，宽20米的范围内发现20余处房址，房间1～6间不等，反映从原始社会的群居生活到奴隶制社会一家一户生活的转变。

蒲城店遗址发现的龙山文化和二里头文化城址各一座，对于研究豫中南地区新石器时代晚期及二里头文化早期的文化面貌具有特别重要的价值。

蒲城店遗址M40

蒲城店遗址房基

Located north of Puchengdian Village, Pingdingshan City, the site dates back to the period from the late Neolithic Age to the Xia Dynasty (3000 ~ 1600 BC) and covers a total area of about 14,000 sq. m. City ruins dating from the Longshan-culture period and the Erlitou-culture period have been discovered.

大师姑城址

第六批全国重点文物保护单位

夏至商

Dashigu Site

大师姑城址位于荥阳市广武镇大师姑行政村、郑州市高新技术产业开发区沟赵办事处岗崔村一带（其中绝大部分在荥阳市境内）。索河自西南折向北从城址西部穿过。城址呈东西长、南北窄，总面积约51万平方米。

城址由城垣和城壕两部分组成。城垣现存部分均在地表以下，距地表1米左右。城垣现存顶部宽7米，底部宽16米，残高3.75米，夯土筑成，其结构较为复杂，是经过多次的续建和修补而成的。目前已发现的墙垣主要为南墙西段及东段、东墙部分地段、西墙北段和北墙西段，总长度近800米。城垣的外侧约6米处为城壕。城壕开口距地表深1.4～2.6米，壕深2～2.8米，现存宽度为5～9米，城壕现周长为2450米，复原长度为2900米。城址内的文化堆积以二里头文化二、三期和四期偏早阶段的遗存为主，主要有灰坑、灰沟、房基、墓葬和大量的陶器等。另外，在城垣和护城壕之间，还发现一处和护城壕平行分布的大型早商环壕。

大师姑城址是我国迄今为止发现的唯一一座二里头文化大型城址。城址的发现填补了我国夏代城址考古的空白。

大师姑城址出土陶鬲

大师姑城址出土陶簋

大师姑城址索河流经处

Located at Dashigu Village, Guangwu Town, Yingyang City, the site dates from the Xia Dynasty (2070 ~ 1600 BC) and covers about 510, 000 sq. m. Ruins of an Erlitou-culture city have been discovered.

小双桥遗址

第六批全国重点文物保护单位

商

Xiaoshuangqiao Site

小双桥遗址位于郑州市西北约20公里的石佛镇小双桥村西南部。北至索须河，南至连霍高速，东至岳岗村，西至后庄王村，面积144万平方米。小双桥遗址是一处商代都城（敖都），是商王朝政治、经济、文化、军事的中心。

小双桥遗址先后发掘面积近20000平方米。发现夯土建筑基址多处，其中一处为高台型（原讹传为周勃墓），位于遗址东北部，黄色细沙土掺褐色黏土逐层夯打而成，夯土层厚0.08～0.12米，夯窝清晰，圆形圜底，直径0.03～0.06米。夯土层上部发现大面积的红烧土堆积，含丰富的烧土块、草拌泥块和木骨泥墙的墙体、墙皮，堆积厚达1米。夯土层平面略呈长方形，东西长50米，南北宽40米，面积约2000平方米，夯土厚度达12.8米左右，夯基中间有深2～3米的基槽。

祭祀坑分人祭和牲祭两种。人祭坑发现4处，牲祭坑数量较多，出土遗物十分丰富。

陶器种类有鬲、盆、簋、觚、爵、缸、刻槽盆、中柱盂、甑、瓮、大口尊等。石器有铲、镰、刀、斧、圭等，还发现十多枚海贝，以及原始青瓷尊片、青铜器、卜骨等。同时还出土有能反映商代礼乐制度的大石磬和长方形石圭。采集

小双桥遗址夯土台基

小双桥遗址出土铜建筑构件

小双桥遗址出土陶鬲

的2件青铜建筑构件尤为重要，其中一件平面呈“凹”字形，高18.5厘米，正面宽18.8厘米，侧面宽16.5厘米，两侧各有一个6×4.2厘米的长方孔，壁厚0.6厘米，重6公斤，正面饰单线饕餮纹，侧面在长方孔四周为一组龙虎斗象图，龙、虎形象生动，象为艺术变形。据分析应是宫殿正门两侧枕木前端的装饰性构件，根据器物推测，该建筑规模很大，非商王莫属。这种青铜建筑饰件为国内首次发现，其造型独特，纹饰繁缛，为商文化中少见的精品。

小双桥遗址更重要的是在陶器表面发现了朱书陶文约8字。这些文字均书写在陶缸表面的绳纹之间，书写工具应为毛笔，颜料为朱砂，与殷墟出土的甲骨文和朱书文字一脉相承。这是我国目前发现的商代最早的书写文字。郑州小双桥遗址的发现为郑州商城性质的进一步探讨和研究提供了重要线索。

小双桥遗址牛角坑

Located south of Xiaoshuangqiao Village, Zhengzhou City, the site dates from the Shang Dynasty (1600 ~ 1046 BC) and covers about 150,000 sq. m. Foundations of rammed-earth buildings and a number of sacrifice pits have been unearthed.

宋国故城

西周

The site of the Song-state capital

宋国故城位于商丘市睢阳区。是周初周成王封微子于宋时期的都城，也是商末周初的政治、经济、文化中心之一。

经对宋国故城遗址的钻探和发掘，确定了城墙的方位、大小和基本结构。第一部分夯土距地表6.9米，出土两块橙黄色的战国陶鬲口沿，一隋代的四系瓷罐（四系残失），罐口覆盖青瓷碗，还清理出一唐代砖窑，窑内留有少部分砖、白色瓷碗和三彩碎片，另外出土有板瓦、筒瓦及五铢钱等。因此，断定第一部分夯土的年代当属汉代。第二部分被第一部分叠压，出土战国陶鬲口沿和数块陶片，年代最晚者为春秋时期，所以第二部分夯土的年代，上限应为春秋时期，下限至战国。第三部分夯土的颜色为深灰褐色，表明最初在筑城时，曾取用了附近古遗址的土层，故夯土内包含了大量

的灰土和陶片。陶片多为绳纹，器种有高直领罐、矮直领罐、小口罐、盆、厚胎圜底器等，这些陶片的时代绝大多数不晚于西周，所以第三部分夯土的年代下限不应晚于春秋时期，而上限或有可能推至商末周初。从勘探结果看，宋国故城的四面城墙都很直，但城墙的走向不是正南正北，东墙和西墙走向偏东北和西南，而南墙和北墙则偏东南和西北；东南角和西北角为钝角，而西南角和东北角为锐角。东墙长2900米，南墙长3550米，西墙长3019米，北墙长3252米，面积10.2平方公里。

宋国故城是我国历史上具有代表性的一处都城，具有较高的历史价值和科学价值。

Located in Suiyang District, Shangqiu City, the site dates from the Zhou Dynasty (1046 ~ 221 BC). In a roughly rectangular shape, it covers about 10.2 sq. km. Ruins of 5 city gates and a moat beyond the city wall have been discovered.

宋国故城城墙遗迹

卫国故城

东周

The site of the Wei-state capital

卫国故城位于淇县县城。建于春秋时期，作为卫国都城长达400余年。

城址平面呈长方形，南北长2250米，东西宽1650米，城墙宽70米，面积约420万平方米。地面现存城墙四段，即西城墙三段，北城墙一段，共长1150米。城内宫殿区、墓葬区尚未进行全面钻探，情况不详。城内现有商代摘心台遗址、西坛村学校战国冶铁遗址，在东城墙南段外侧的东关村东头发现一处春秋时期的制骨作坊。卫国是当时170多个诸侯国中之大国。故城城址之大，城墙之宽，在东周古城址不多见，具有很高的历史研究价值。

卫国故城可能是文献记载中的“朝歌故城”，经对卫国故城进行的局部考古发掘，初步了解该城址在春秋战国时期曾多次修补增筑。故城约废弃于西汉早、中期。有关卫国故城原为殷代故都的问题，仍待进一步探索。

卫国故城西城墙

Located around the county town of Qi County, the site dates from the Zhou Dynasty (1046 ~ 221 BC). It is in a rectangular shape, measuring 3,100 meters from north to south, and 2,100 meters from east to west. There are ruins of smelteries, bone-processing workshops and cemeteries in and outside the city.

卫国故城北城墙

黄国故城

第六批全国重点文物保护单位

东周

The site of the Huang-state capital

黄国故城东城墙

黄国故城位于潢川县隆古乡。黄国故城保存完整，城平面近长方形，东城墙长1750米，西城墙长1550米，南城墙长1650米，北城墙长1720米，面积2.8平方公里。

黄国故城城墙最高处为7米，低处3米，基宽59米，四周城壕最宽处为36米，深2米，从城墙断面夯窝及遗物看，年代应与历史记载相符。

故城西南1000米处的高坡上，为墓葬群，据勘探，这一带分布有几百座中、小型墓葬。

公元前262年楚封黄歇为令尹（相国），并获春申君封号，系战国“四君子”之一，潢川留有春申君衣冠冢和“楚春申君”残碑一块。多年来，黄国故城和墓葬区域出土了许多青铜器、陶器。1966年在潢川隆古乡高稻场村出土了13件青铜器，其中铜簠器身呈长方形，满饰蟠螭纹，器底铸两行八字铭文。1975年潢川上油岗磨盘山出土了春秋早期的3件青铜器，其中铜簠铭文“黄孙须颈子伯亚臣”。1984年，在光山宝相寺黄君孟夫妇合葬墓中出土春秋早期的43件青铜器，其中大部分器物上均有“黄”字的铭文。G1随葬器物中有青铜器14件，其中一件青铜器上有一行十四字铭

黄国故城西城墙

文"黄君孟自作行器，子孙则永宝宝用"，玉器共54件，石器1件，竹器1件。G2随葬器物中有铜器22件，其中铜鼎口沿下有一周十四字铭文。出土玉器128件、竹器2件、漆木器6件、麻鞋底2件、丝织品6件。G1出土的青铜器中有11件铸有"黄君孟"铭文。因此，可以确定死者为黄君孟。G2出土的青铜器中，有14件铸有"黄子作黄夫人孟姬"铭文，棺内人骨保存完好，经鉴定为40岁左右女性。可以确定死者为孟姬。由此可知，这是一座黄君孟及其夫人孟姬的合葬墓。黄国是周代嬴姓国，故城就在潢川县西北6公里的隆古乡，由此也可推断出当时黄国地域之广大。

黄国故城春申君墓

黄国故城及墓葬在楚文化研究中占有重要的地位，是豫东南地区保存较完整的一处故城遗址。

Located in Longgu Township, Huangchuan County, the site dates from the Spring and Autumn Period (770 ~ 475 BC) and covers about 2.80 million sq. m. Ruins of rammed-earth foundations, wells and smelteries have been discovered in the city; a number of tombs dating from the middle and late Spring and Autumn Period have been discovered outside.

共城城址

第六批全国重点文物保护单位

西周

The site of Gong City

Located in the urban area of Hui County, the site dates from the Zhou Dynasty (1046 ~ 221 BC). In a roughly square shape, it has a city wall whose circumference is about 5,000 m. Moats have been discovered around the north, east and south walls.

共城城址位于辉县市区内。始建于西周初年，因是西周晚期共国国君共伯和的封地，故称“共城”。

共城自西周末创建之后，秦、汉、唐、宋时期多有修补增建。经调查得知，共城有大小两城。大城即共城，近正方形，南北长1300米，东西宽1200米，为西周时期所筑。另发现有汉、唐时期修补的平夯痕迹。小城为新城，为隋代所建，今已不存。大城中的东城墙保存较好，大城外的北、东两面各有一城壕。

共城遗址最早见于《水经注》、《史记·周本纪·正义》等文献。城内多有春秋墓葬，出土了部分精美的青铜器，另有窑址发现。城外曾有战国铸铁遗址、商周墓葬。共城遗址文化内涵非常丰富，该城延续时间长，对研究东周青铜制造和铸铁工艺都有重要价值。

共城城址不仅是目前国内为数不多的西周诸侯国都城址之一，最重要的是共城城址凝聚了“共和行政”、“共和元年”等历史事件的发生，使其成为中国历史纪年上的分水岭。

共城城址规模宏大，气势雄伟，是研究我国古代建筑技术和早期都城建制的重要实物佐证。

共城城址东城墙

滑国故城

东周

The site of the Hua-state capital

滑国故城位于偃师市东南府店镇滑城河与府店北河之间的台地上。偃（师）登（封）公路在城址南部穿过。城垣因地势而折转，城址呈南窄北宽不规则状，南北长2500米，东西宽500～1500米。

经考古勘探得知，四周城墙多被夷为平地，除西北部以外，大部分城墙埋于地下，地上地下的城垣基本上还能连成一整体，东城垣几乎全部湮埋于地下。在滑城河村北有道光十七年所修的“古滑城”城门，上有“古滑城”三字匾额，现存基本完整。城门南侧有一段城墙保存于地面上，夯层清晰可见，质地坚硬，呈红褐色或灰褐色。西城垣南自今府店村偃登公路北侧开始，北到桑家沟村西南断绝。北城垣东自滑城河村东北河沟转弯处起，西到桑家沟村北。该城址东北部有较丰富的仰韶、龙山文化遗存，城墙建于仰韶、龙山文化层之上，底部夯土为春秋时期所筑，应是春秋滑国故城城墙，与文献记载较为吻合。从现存的上部城墙中夹杂有大量的汉代、晋代绳纹瓦片等现象可以看出，该城址在汉至西晋时期曾多次修葺沿用。

滑国故城的发现，对于研究春秋战国时期的历史，特别是研究滑国的历史具有重要的价值。

清代城门题记

清代城门

Located north of Fudian Village, Yanshi City, the site dates back to the period from the Spring and Autumn Period to the Han Dynasty (770 BC ~ 220 AD), extending about 2.5 km from north to south and 0.5 ~ 1.5 km from east to west. Part of the rammed-earth city wall remains.

滑国故城南城墙

滑国故城全貌

叶邑故城

第六批全国重点文物保护单位

东周

The site of the ancient city of Yeyi

叶邑故城位于叶县旧县乡旧县村。城方18里，北依澧水，东邻烧车河。春秋时期曾为许、应国都。城内街道、城门、城墙、寺庙等遗址大部分尚得保存。

叶邑春秋时曾为楚国政治家、军事家叶公沈诸梁的封地，叶公尹叶期间修水利、劝农桑。使叶邑地丰民强，成为楚国北方重城之一。今叶县尚存东、西二坡遗址及叶公陵墓。叶邑故城地上、地下文化遗存十分丰富，古城址周围10公里以内，墓冢累累，地下墓葬数以百计，距城址较近处已发掘的常庄村3座墓均为楚国墓，出土器物包括青铜器、木器、陶器、玉器、铅器、车马等，其中不乏国内精品。通过对常庄村4号墓发掘，从出土器物看，该墓为春秋时期许国国君许宁公（许灵公）之墓。出土的编钟是目前我国发现的由纽钟、甬钟、镈钟三组成套的唯一的一套，这套编钟一反古乐的五音规范，包含了七个音阶，这对研究我国古代音乐发展史有着重要价值。常庄4号墓的发掘填补了我国东周时期考古学的空白，证明叶邑城在历史中的重要地位。

叶邑故城

叶邑古围堰

叶邑古石桥

Located west of the old town street of Ye County, the site dates from the Zhou Dynasty (1046 ~ 221 BC). In a rectangular shape, it extends about 1,160 meters from north to south and about 850 meters from east to west, covering about 990,000 sq. m. There are a number of congregated sepulchers dating from the Spring and Autumn Period and the Warring States Period outside the city.

轵国故城

第六批全国重点文物保护单位

东周

The site of the Zhi-state capital

轵国故城位于济源市轵城镇。今轵城镇政府、东西轵城村皆在故城城垣内。

该城始筑于春秋时期，为东周畿内地。据《左传》载：周襄王十七年（公元前635年），晋文公助周平叛有功，襄王将周之阳樊、温、原、赞茅四邑予晋。阳民不服，阳樊（今济源曲阳村）城守仓葛遂率阳民退聚轵村，始以战车列卫，继而筑城，故曰“轵”。故城经春秋战国、秦、汉、三国、两晋、南北朝、隋唐，历时1260余年，曾四度封国。至唐贞观元年（627年）省入县治，渐沦为村落。

故城平面略呈方形，面积为326.36万平方米，城内文化堆积丰富，发现有灰坑、窖藏、墓葬等，陶器、建筑构件等遗物也较多。现存的遗迹有夯土城墙、制陶作坊、护城河、大明寺（西汉时为轵王祖庙）、关帝庙等，城垣外有泗涧贵族墓地、聂政墓、钟公四冢、西留养遗址等。

轵国故城的发现对研究古代城池布防、建制等方面均具有很重要的学术价值。

轵国故城南城墙

汉代彩绘神兽多枝灯

Located at Zhicheng Village, Jiyuan City, the site dates from the Eastern Zhou Dynasty (7700 ~ 221 BC). In a roughly square shape, it covers a total area of about 3.28 sq. km. The ruins of two city gates, two watergates, rammed-earth foundations and a number of pottery kilns have been discovered.

下河湾冶铁遗址

第六批全国重点文物保护单位

战国至汉

Iron smelting site at Xiahewan

下河湾冶铁遗址位于泌阳县东南40公里的马谷田镇南岗村委下河湾村东30米处。南面、东面临小河，北面是上武高速公路。遗址南北长400米、东西宽300米，总面积12万平方米。

该遗址未遭受大的破坏。遗址内随处可见大量的炉壁残块、炼渣、铁块、铁矿石、陶豆、陶釜、盆、罐、板瓦、筒瓦等残片和大量红烧土块。另外还发现一石范块和鼓风管残片。在遗址东部和北部的断壁上，还残留着6座冶铁炉，保存基本完好。从地表面堆积最大的一处炉壁残块及地层堆积分析，遗址的冶铁炉至少应有100座以上。由于长期从事冶铁活动，遗址表面的颜色已呈现深灰褐色，烧土堆积也特别集中，文化内涵非常丰富。

该遗址冶铁作坊从战国中晚期一直延续到汉代，使用时间至少在一百年以上，是一处规格较高的官营手工业作坊。下河湾冶铁遗址的发现，在中国冶金史上具有重要的学术价值。

下河湾冶铁遗址炉壁遗迹

下河湾冶铁遗址全景

Located at Xiahewan Village, Miyang County, the site dates back to the period from the Warring States period to the Han Dynasty (475 BC ~ 220 AD) and covers about 120,000 sq. m. The ruins of 100 furnaces have been discovered.

望城岗冶铁遗址

第六批全国重点文物保护单位

汉

Iron smelting site at Wangchenggang

望城岗冶铁遗址位于鲁山县城南与张店乡望城岗村北之间。现地表为耕地，遗址保存完好。该遗址自西汉至东汉时期，历时300余年，面积达36万平方米，文化层堆积厚2～5米，是河南省目前已发现的最大的汉代冶铁遗址。

该遗址经考古发掘，出土有炉渣、炉壁、鼓风残块、泥模范块、矿石块、矿石粉、铁块、煤渣、木炭渣、残砖、陶范及陶器，五铢钱等汉代遗物。另有汉代墓葬、陶窑、水井、水渠、贮水池等遗迹。并发现刻有篆文“阳一”、“河口”、“六年”等陶范。另外，还发掘出一巨型冶铁炉，炉缸内径东西长4米，南北宽3米，有出铁、排渣、鼓风、填料、供水、冷却等系统。冶铁炉可连续冶炼，同时出铁、出渣，需150人连续轮换作业。此炉是我国迄今为止所发现规模最大的汉代冶铁炉，它代表了汉代冶铁技术的最高水平。

Located north of Wangchenggang Village, Chengnanguan, Lushan County, the site dates from the Han Dynasty (206 BC ~ 220 AD) and covers 480,000 sq. m. Feeding tables have been unearthed.

望城岗冶铁遗址1号炉（由东向西）

瓦房庄冶铁遗址

第六批全国重点文物保护单位

汉

Iron smelting site at Wafangzhuang

瓦房庄冶铁遗址

瓦房庄冶铁遗址位于南阳市城北瓦房庄村的西北边。这是一处集冶铁、冶铜、制陶为一体的汉代手工业作坊，是汉代南阳郡“阳一”铁工场所在地。遗址分布范围东西长300米，南北宽400米，总面积为12万平方米。遗址距今约2000多年。

1959～1960年河南省文物工作队曾对该遗址进行了发掘，发掘面积4864平方米。主要发掘出熔炉基址9座，锻炉基址8座，炒钢炉1座，烘范窑和退火脱碳窑4座，勺形鼓风机械坑1座，两汉水井11眼，以及数以百计的铸范和铁器。

通过对该遗址出土器物研究，发现冶炼技术在当时是非常先进的。如它的热鼓风熔炉的使用缩短了熔炼时间，提高了铁水质量，是中国最早的热鼓风熔炉装置；人力传动鼓风机械的发明与应用，双堆叠铸技术及用整套翻砂模具制造铁范及铁范的广泛使用，使南阳郡成为汉代向外郡供输铁器最多的郡，产品远销西南、南部、东南部和西部广大地区，并涌现出孔仅等一批冶铁家。

瓦房庄冶铁遗址在我国汉代钢铁冶铸业中居于领先地位，对于研究我国汉代社会在钢铁冶铸方面具有重要意义，也是宛城作为汉代国家设置“铁官”和“工官”的重要证据。

Located at Wafangzhuang outside the North Gate of the old city of Nanyang, the site dates from the Han Dynasty (206 BC ~ 220 AD) and covers 180,000 sq. m. It was the No.1 smeltery administered by the Iron Office of Nanyang Prefecture in the Han Dynasty.

三杨庄遗址

第六批全国重点文物保护单位

汉

Sanyangzhuang Site

三杨庄遗址位于内黄县城南30公里梁庄镇三杨庄村北。2003年6月，因开挖硝河引黄工程，于地表下4.5米处先后发现7处古代建筑遗存。

在遗址范围内相距不到500米的距离，已初步清理出了四组保存较为完整的汉代建筑群落。第一处建筑遗存清理面积400余平方米，清理出的建筑遗迹有院落基址、房基、瓦屋顶、夯土墙、拌泥池、灶、灰坑及未使用的瓦、建筑废弃物等。第二处建筑遗存清理面积1700平方米，可初步确定为两进院落，布局清晰可辨，房顶保存完好，并出土了大量的石臼、石磨、石滚等工具。2005年又清理了第三处和第四处建筑遗存，其周围的农田田垄和树桩遗迹保存完好。从清理出的“货泉”铜钱和“益寿万岁”瓦当及筒瓦、板瓦判断，其年代为西汉

三杨庄遗址第三处宅院清理现场（由北向南）

三杨庄遗址第二处宅院内出土陶水槽

三杨庄遗址第二处宅院二进院西厢房内出土陶豆

晚期。如此完整的汉代建筑聚落遗址，在目前的考古发掘中属首次发现，为研究中国古代建筑工程技术提供了新的佐证。另外，该遗址地层文化堆积单纯，未被后人扰乱，这实为目前在全国汉代建筑遗址中所仅见。为完整地揭示汉代某一特定建筑群（比如一个城镇或一个庄园）的规模、布局以及对各类单体房屋建筑结构与建筑技术方面的研究提供了珍贵的实物资料。

Located north of Sanyangzhuang Village, Neihuang County, the site dates from the Han Dynasty (206 BC ~ 220 AD). The excavated area is 9,000 sq. m. The ruins of four south-facing courtyards have been discovered, all integral in layout.

三杨庄遗址第一处宅院主房瓦顶原状（由北向南）

三杨庄遗址第二处宅院（由南向北）

三杨庄遗址第三处宅院主房瓦顶原状（由西向东）

山阳故城

第六批全国重点文物保护单位

汉

The site of the ancient city of Shanyang

山阳故城位于焦作市东郊。故城面积约300万平方米。

山阳故城始建于战国时期，从汉代到东魏一直为山阳县治所。东汉是山阳城鼎盛时期，至魏王曹丕废汉献帝封其为山阳公，山阳城为其食邑而闻名。

山阳故城平面呈不规则长方形，周长约5000米，四周有护城河。城墙大部分高出地面，北城墙长1850米，东城墙长1350米，西城墙长1000米，南城墙仅剩两端约200米。四边城墙各有一城门。墙基宽30～46米，上部宽14～16米，系夯土筑成，夯层清晰，每层厚10～15厘米，夯窝明显。城址的东面为白庄汉墓群，西面为马作汉墓群，北部为李河汉墓群，出土有汉代“山阳”铭文罐、陶仓楼等珍贵文物。山阳

山阳故城北城墙

山阳故城东城墙

故城的发现，对研究豫北地区汉代政治、经济的发展和城市布局具有重要的历史、科学价值。陶仓楼的出土，是汉代单体、组群、高层建筑的再现，其斗栱的演变也是古建筑发展、完善的缩影。

Located north of Ma Village, Qiangnan, Jiaozuo City, the site dates from the Han Dynasty (206 BC ~ 220 AD). In an irregular rectangular shape, it has a circumference of 5 km. Grounds paved with green slab-stone have been discovered in the city.

段店窑址

唐至元

Porcelain Kiln site at Duandian

段店窑址

段店窑址位于平顶山市鲁山县梁洼镇段店村。窑址南北长1100米，东西宽700米，现存面积77万平方米，文化层厚2～5米，文化堆积十分丰富。

该窑址是我国北方地区一处重要古代窑址，上起唐代，下至元代，唐宋时期非常兴盛，是汝窑和钧窑的前身民窑瓷器的烧制地。古有“清凉寺到段店，日进万贯”之美誉。

1990年经河南省文物考古研究所考古发掘，发现窑炉、澄泥池等重要遗迹，出土瓷器有唐代花瓷、宋汝民窑瓷、宋三彩、白釉珍珠地划花、元代钧瓷和白地黑花瓷等，品种多样。鲁山花瓷腰鼓在唐人南卓《羯鼓录》中即有记载，被认为是当时的名品之一。北京故宫博物院现存的唐代花瓷拍鼓，就是段店瓷窑所产，显示出高超的工艺技术水准。

段店窑址的发现，从其历史、科学研究、艺术诸方面，均有极为重要的价值。

Located northeast of Duandian Village, Lushan County, the site dates back the period from the Tang Dynasty to the Yuan Dynasty (618 ~ 907 AD) and covers 20 sq. m. It was famous for producing ‘flower china’. Glaze colors were mainly white/blue/motley spots on a black background; products were most typically shaped like yaogu, or waist drums.

大周封祀坛遗址

第六批全国重点文物保护单位

唐

The ruins of Great Zhou Sacrifice Altar

大周封祀坛遗址位于登封市中岳大街西端万羊岗，是唐代武则天封禅的遗迹。坛上现存封祀坛碑一通，唐万岁登封元年（696年）刻立。碑早已倒伏并被土掩压，外露部分高2.90米，宽1.05米，厚0.60米。圆首，方形碑趺弃置在距碑身西约2米处。碑额题刻篆书“大周封祀坛碑”6字。碑文楷书，共37行，行71字，首行题曰：“大周封祀坛碑并序”，因碑身下部剥蚀，每行碑文仅存40字左右，文中有武则天新制文字。武三思撰文，薛曜书丹，但薛之姓名已毁无存。天册万岁元年（695年），武则天命人在登封市嵩山上下建有登封、封祀二坛，同年腊月她带领百官来此举行封禅大典。她先到太室山中峰上的登封坛行祭天之礼，礼毕亲自撰文立《大周升中述志碑》于峰顶（坛、碑早毁）。然后于初三日来到少室山下的封祀坛行祭地之礼，礼毕命武三思和薛曜撰写了此碑，立于坛上。此坛上圆下方，以象征天地。至今仍可看出其大致轮廓。其碑存留至今，实属可贵。碑文剥落较多，从现存部分看，其内容首论天地的重要和历代国君对封禅大典的重视。描绘了封禅典礼的盛大规模和庄重肃穆的气氛以及颂扬武则天的功德，执政时期的升平景象，诸如说武则天临朝以后“皇威远举”、“万方翘首”、“烟尘息，九区静，文轨同而万方泰”等等。该碑书法与薛曜所书《夏日游石淙诗并序》和《秋日宴石淙序》两碑的字体相比，其结构更为遒密，堪称薛书之上品。

大周封祀坛遗址

大周封祀坛碑

大周封祀坛碑座

Located at Wanyanggang, west suburb of the Dengfeng City, the alter dates from the Tang Dynasty (618 ~ 907 AD). With a round top and a square base, it was used by Empress Wu Zetian to offer sacrifices to Taishi Mountain. There is a tablet recording the event on top of the altar.

扒村窑址

宋、金

Porcelain kiln site at Pa Village

扒村窑址堆积

扒村窑址位于禹州市浅井乡扒村。是一处分布在下宋河两岸规模宏大的窑址，面积达170余万平方米。该窑址属宋、金时期磁州窑系的一个重要部分，以烧制白地黑花瓷器为主，同时也生产三彩、加彩和钧瓷。

扒村窑所烧造的品种丰富多彩，从高温的黑、白瓷，到低温的釉彩，几乎无所不有。产品主要有白釉、白地绘黑花、白地划花、黑釉、翠青地绘黑花、翠青地印花、红褐地绘黑花、绿釉、黄釉、宋三彩、宋加彩、黑白釉及加彩玩具、钧釉、青釉等。器形有碗、盘、盆、罐、瓶、枕、壶、玩具等。其生产的生活用品极为丰富，白地黑花枕的形状有八角形、长方形、如意形、伏虎形，人物图案枕面，是宋代民间的小品画。白地黑花的盆、罐等生活用品，曾长期为北方农村所喜用，至今在许多地方的窑场中还保留着这种烧造工艺。白地黑花碗内绘花草纹，碗心中有“张”、“花”、“秦”、“记”等字，而盆内绘有莲瓣、荷花、水纹、鱼藻、花草或书“盆”字。三彩器多为刻花，纹饰有花草、莲瓣、飞鸟等，有的则使用红、黄、绿、白、黑多种颜色，红色尤其鲜艳。扒村窑址较好地保存了历史原貌，是宋、金、元时期北方烧制瓷器的一处重要遗存，具有较高的历史、科学和艺术价值。

扒村窑址近景

Located at Pa Village, Yuzhou City, the site dates from the Song Dynasty (960 ~ 1279 AD) and covers about 1.2 sq. km. It is a large site of privately run kilns that belonged to the Cizhou Kiln System.

当阳峪窑址

宋

Porcelain kiln site at Dangyangyu

当阳峪窑址位于修武县西北部的当阳峪村。遗址南北长2000米，东西宽1000米，总面积达200万平方米。

2003年，河南省文物考古研究所对该窑址进行了考古发掘，发现窑炉6座，窑洞式作坊5孔，出土了一大批珍贵文物。器物种类十分丰富，有碗、钵、唾盂、灯、盘、罐、盏、枕、盒、瓶等，工艺有剔花、刻花、划花、绘花等。以白釉瓷为主，酱釉瓷次之，另有绿釉、褐绿釉三彩、绞胎瓷器等，其釉色光润明亮。特别是酱釉瓷器，胎质细白，器体轻薄，釉色润亮，堪称精品，可与定窑同类器相媲美。绞胎瓷器，纹理变化万千，尤其闻名于世。

当阳峪窑址始于唐，盛于宋，终于元。遗址现存有北宋崇宁四年（1105年）《德应侯百灵翁之庙记》碑一通，记录当年窑业之盛况，是目前所知全国仅存的两通北宋神庙碑之一，具有珍贵的价值。

当阳峪窑址

当阳峪窑址出土绞胎罐

当阳峪窑址出土白釉褐彩刻花枕

当阳峪窑址出土绿釉花卉纹枕

当阳峪窑址出土白釉黑褐彩花卉纹罐

Located northeast of Dangyangyu Village, Xiuwu County, the site dates from the Song Dynasty (960 ~ 1279 AD) and covers about 2 sq. km. It is one of the most important sites of privately run porcelain kilns in the north of Henan.

张公巷窑址

第六批全国重点文物保护单位

宋

Kiln site at Zhanggong Lane

张公巷窑址位于汝州市区中大街与张公巷交汇处。遗址面积约120000平方米，重点保护区域面积20000平方米。

该遗址是一处北宋时期重要的制瓷场所，专为宫廷烧制御用瓷器的官窑遗址，为北宋晚期宋徽宗年间指定烧制的御用官窑。2000～2004年经过三次发掘，已发现有作坊、澄泥池、灰坑等，文化内涵十分丰富，出土器物有碗、盘、碟、器盖、细颈盘口瓶等生活用品及工艺品，种类繁多，且多为天青、粉青、月白色釉，绝大部分为裹足支烧，为宋代官窑常见器物。同时出土的还有制瓷工具骨刀、窑具、垫饼、支钉等。

张公巷窑址是一处瓷艺精良，艺术卓绝的制瓷场所，它的发现为我国陶瓷界探寻了半个多世纪的北宋官窑之谜提供了重要线索，而且对于进一步研究中国陶瓷史有着极为重要的学术价值。

张公巷窑址出土青釉碗

Located at the juncture between Zhanggong Lane and Zhongda Street, the site dates from the Song and Yuan dynasties (960 ~ 1368 AD). Its central area covers about 3,600 sq. m. It was mainly used to produce celadon.

张公巷窑址出土盘口折肩瓶

张公巷窑址灰坑

荥阳故城

第六批全国重点文物保护单位

唐至元

The site of Xingyang City

荥阳故城位于郑州市西北24公里的惠济区古荥镇及其东部和南部。战国以前，是当时的北方重镇，交通要塞，春秋时期晋楚争霸多次在此征战，秦末楚汉相争，曾以鸿沟为界，中分天下。

城址呈南北长、东西宽的不规则形，现存南、北、西三面城墙和东北城角、东南城角，东墙因黄河泛滥冲毁，面积约144万平方米。城墙高11.6、宽30米，黄土夯筑而成。城中部偏北有夯土基址，东北部有仓廪，南部有青砖砌筑的房基，城西墙外有冶铁作坊遗址。城内出土有大量板瓦、筒瓦、铺地花纹砖、陶水管等建筑材料，铁器有镬、凹形臿、铲、犁铧、锄、凿和双齿镢等，陶器有瓮、罐、壶、豆、盆等，陶器上有戳记铭文，出土马蹄金4件，另外还发现有中小型墓葬。

2006年国务院公布第六批全国重点文物保护单位时，将荥阳故城与第五批全国重点文物保护单位古荥冶铁遗址合并，称为荥阳故城。

荥阳故城城墙

Located in east and south of Guying town in Huiji District, 24 kilometers away from northwest of Zhengzhou city, the city site is in irregular shape, covering south and north, extending east and west. It is approximately 1.44 million square meters. The city walls were 116 meters high and 30 meters wide. There were some storehouses in the north-east and foundations built of blue bricks in the south. Out of the east city wall were the ruins of smelttery.

荥阳故城城墙西北角

荥阳故城南墙、西墙

荥阳故城城墙夯层

神垕钧窑遗址

第六批全国重点文物保护单位

唐至元

The Jun kiln site at Shenhou

神垕钧窑遗址位于禹州市神垕镇西南。遗址沿白峪河分布在刘家门、下白峪等村周围的数平方公里内，面积约7万平方米。

2001年9月至2002年元月对该遗址进行了发掘，发现不同时代的窑炉遗迹8座，石砌澄泥池3座以及窑前工作场所5处，出土了大批瓷器残件、窑具，总数达十余万片。出土唐代器物主要是黑釉、茶叶末釉及褐黄釉，有的饰以月白釉斑点，器形以碗为主，另有钵、罐等，胎较厚重，内部满釉，外部只施半釉。刘家门窑址为北宋晚期至元代，烧造水平极高，部分器物仿当时的金银器造型，之后又出现了白釉和黑釉，并有三彩、红绿彩和绞胎等产品。出土器物主要有碗、盘、瓶、罐、香炉、盆、枕等。其中完整或复原器物有数千件。另外首次发现一座北宋晚期至金代的土洞式长方形分室式窑炉，窑室中间以一道矮墙隔为前、后室，形制独特。神垕钧窑遗址因其地处偏僻，人为破坏较轻，较好地保存了历史原貌。

2006年国务院公布第六批全国重点文物保护单位时，将神垕钧窑遗址与第三批全国重点文物保护单位钧台钧窑遗址合并，称禹县钧窑址。

神垕钧窑遗址堆积情况

神垕钧窑遗址全景

Located in southwest of Shenhou town in Yuzhou city, the site lies around some villages such as Liujiamen and Xiabaiyu along Baiyu River, covering an area of approximately 70,000 sq.m. There were 8 kiln stoves remains of different times, 3 pools built of stone for depositting mud, and 5 workplaces where prepared for kilning. They unearthed large number of incomplete china and kiln utensil, amounting to more than 100,000 pieces.

巩义窑址

第六批全国重点文物保护单位

隋至唐

The Gongyi kiln site

巩义窑址位于巩义市北山口镇水地河、白河、铁匠炉村附近白河两岸台地上。南北长5公里，东西长1公里，面积约500万平方米。根据出土器物看，窑址始于北朝，发展于隋，盛于唐，衰于宋金。早期生产青瓷，隋代开始生产白瓷，唐代主要生产白瓷、黑釉瓷。白瓷胎质坚细，洁白莹润。

出土器物有：隋代的碗、青

白河窑发掘现场

瓷高足盘等，唐代的白瓷碗、盘、罐、壶、枕、碗等。

巩义窑址的发现为研究中国白瓷的起源与发展提供了实物资料，同时也为我国青花瓷的发展奠定了基础，在中国陶瓷史上占有重要地位。

2006年国务院公布第六批全国重点文物保护单位时，将巩义窑址与第五批全国重点文物保护单位黄冶三彩窑址合并，称巩义窑址。

The Gongyi kiln site (From Sui dynasty to Tang dynasty)
Located in the tableland of the Bai river of Beishankou town in Gongyi city , the site covers 500 sq.m. According the articles unearthed, the Gongyi kiln dated from Bei dynasty, developing in Sui dynasty, flourishing in Tang dynasty, falling in Song dynasty and Jin dynasty.

上蔡楚国贵族墓地

第六批全国重点文物保护单位

周至战国

The cemetery of Chu-state nobles in Shangcai

上蔡楚国贵族墓地位于驻马店市上蔡县境内的岗地。墓地位于岗地中部，平面近长方形，南北长约7公里，宽约4公里，面积约28平方公里。

墓地以大中型楚墓居多，其中不乏“甲”字形楚国贵族大墓。由于历代破坏，许多大墓的封土已无，仅残存肖里王楚冢、郭庄楚冢、湾李楚冢等。墓葬密集，排列有序。经多次发掘证实，墓葬形式为大中型土坑墓，时代多为战国时期。2005年5月至12月发掘的郭庄楚冢M1是一座战国早期积沙积石的大墓，结构奇特，规模宏大，出土了一批青铜礼乐重器，墓葬规格说明墓主人级别很高。

另外，墓地中还有郭庄周代遗址、郭马陈战国铸铁遗址等。

2006年国务院公布第六批全国重点文物保护单位时，将上蔡楚国贵族墓地归入第四批全国重点文物保护单位蔡国故城。

上蔡楚国贵族墓葬区弯李1号墓

上蔡郭庄楚墓 M1 椁室全景

上蔡郭庄楚墓 M1 俯瞰

Located on the mound of Shangcai county in Zhu Madian city, the cemetery was in the middle of the mound covering 28 million sq. m.

Most of the tombs were large or middle size tombs of Chu-state. The tombs arranged densely and orderly, most of them were built in Warring States Period.

In addition ,there were Guozhuang ruins in Zhou dynasty and Guo Machen ruins of iron casting in Warring States Period.

韩王陵

战国

The king' s mausoleums of Han state

韩王陵位于新郑市。11个墓区28座陵墓分布在郑韩故城周围，计有辛店镇许岗村东墓冢4座，观音寺镇王行庄村北墓冢4座，城关乡庙庄村南墓冢2座，辛店镇冢岗村南墓冢1座，城关乡暴庄村西墓冢5座，城关乡胡庄村北墓冢1座，梨河镇宋庄村东墓冢2座，梨河镇冯庄村南新郑监狱院内墓冢2座，观音寺镇柳庄村北墓冢3座，新村镇七里井村西北部墓冢3座，西亚斯商业学院内墓冢2座。自韩国迁都（前375年）新郑至秦灭韩（前230年），先后有九世侯、王及宗室分别葬在韩国都城周围。墓均为南北向，除宋庄一处南北向排列，其余均为东西向排列。每座墓均有陪葬的车马坑和贵族墓，形成规模很大的陵墓群。

出土和征集的器物有铜鼎、编钟、石编磬、玉圭、玉璧、玉人、车马饰件、银卧牛、陶鼎、陶豆、陶壶等200余件。

冢岗韩王陵

西亚斯商业学院韩王陵

陪葬的车马坑规格不一，随葬车马数量不等。其中一王陵的陪葬马56匹，分14排排列，所葬马均为杀死后埋葬的，56匹马正好是14辆车的架数，由此可推断出韩国国君的用车、用牲的数量。

韩王陵规模大、数量多，基本保存完整，在我国现存战国时期王陵中十分罕见，是研究战国时期六国陵墓的重要实物资料。

2006年国务院公布第六批全国重点文物保护单位时，将韩王陵归入第一批全国重点文物保护单位郑韩故城。

宋庄韩王陵

Located in Xinzheng city, the mausoleums ranged around the city site of Zhen and Han states, including 11 tomb regions and 28 mausoleums. Every tomb had horse-and-chariot burial pits and Aristocratic tombs as accessory burial, forming a great group of mausoleum. It is the important materials to research the mausoleums of Six States in Warring States Period.

胡庄韩王陵

古 墓 葬

Ancient Lemetery

古墓葬

Ancient Cemetery

河南文化遗产

全国重点文物保护单位

Brief Information on Major Historic Sites under National Protection in Henan Province

古墓葬

Ancient Lemetery

宋陵

第二批全国重点文物保护单位

北宋

Song Mausoleum

宋陵，是北宋的皇家陵寝，位于巩义市西村、芝田、孝义、回廓镇一带，北临黄河，南依嵩山。陵区面积约156平方公里。

宋陵自北宋乾德元年（963年）开始营建，陆续营造了一百六十多年。北宋共有九个皇帝，除徽、钦二帝被金人掳去死于漠北，其余七帝均葬于此。另外，宋太祖赵匡胤于乾德元年将其父赵弘殷迁葬于此，称永安陵。先后兴建了太祖（赵匡胤）永昌陵，太宗（赵光义）永熙陵、真宗（赵恒）永定陵、仁宗（赵祯）永昭陵、英宗（赵曙）永厚陵、神宗（赵顼）永裕陵、哲宗（赵煦）永泰陵，总称七帝八陵。另有皇后陵二十一座，亲王、公主、皇子、皇孙、诸王夫人墓一百四十四座，名将勋臣墓七座，各帝系子孙墓二百余座。

宋陵陵园的建制基本相同，均坐北朝南，周围筑有行宫、寺院。每陵皆筑高大的陵台，陵台之下即是安放灵柩的地宫，规模宏大。陵台四周筑有围墙，称神墙，四角各有角楼。四面神墙中间各设神门，南神门外为神道。神道两侧对称排列着雄伟壮观的石雕仪仗。

宋陵神道石雕是我国现存唯一一组宋代大型石雕群，现存石

永定陵全貌

永定陵石人、石马

永定陵石刻

永定陵石刻

雕像皇帝陵四百零七件，皇后陵三百三十六件，陪葬墓六十九件，共八百一十二件。

宋陵依所在方位和建造先后可分为四个陵区。西村陵区，东北距市区15公里，在锦屏山、白云山、黑砚山脚下，四周地势较高，形成盆地。该陵区葬有宋宣祖赵弘殷，宋太祖赵匡胤和宋太宗赵光义，还祔葬皇后陵十座、子孙墓一百四十多座。蔡庄陵区，北距市区5公里，陵区西北紧临伊洛河。真宗（赵恒）永定陵就在此区。祔葬李后陵、刘后陵和杨后陵三座后陵。陪葬的名臣墓有高怀德墓、蔡齐墓、寇准墓、包拯墓。孝义陵区，位于市区孝义镇南部。有宋仁宗（赵祯）永昭陵、英宗（赵曙）永厚陵，二陵东西并列，相距200米左右。祔葬有仁宗曹后陵，陪葬曹后陵的有濮安懿王三个夫人王氏、韩氏、仙游县君任氏之墓。祔葬英宗的高后陵，陪葬名臣墓有赵普墓、曹彬墓、狄青墓和杨延昭墓等。八陵陵区，在市区西南15公里的八陵村。村东是神宗（赵顼）永裕陵，村西南为哲宗（赵煦）永泰陵。祔葬有神宗向后陵、朱后陵、陈后陵，徽宗王后陵，哲宗刘后陵；陪葬有徽宗第七女惠庆公主墓、哲宗第四女杨国公主墓。

永昭陵神道石刻

永定陵石刻像与象奴

永定陵石狮

永昭陵石刻

Located in Gongyi City, the mausoleum dates from the Northern Song Dynasty (960 ~ 1126 AD). It contains the tombs of seven emperors, over 20 empresses, and over a hundred members of the imperial clan and high-ranking ministers.

永昭陵全貌

张衡墓

第三批全国重点文物保护单位

东汉

Zhang Heng's Tomb

张衡（78～139年），字平子，南阳人。东汉元初二年（115年）任太史令，主持全国天象观测。四年（117年）制造出世界上第一台天文仪器——浑天仪。著有《地形图》、《浑仪图注》、《灵宪》等天文学理论著作，书中已使用赤道、黄道、南北极等概念，画出了我国第一张完备的星图，共有二千五百颗恒星，并认识到宇宙的无限性。阳嘉元年（132年）他创造了世界上第一架测定地震方向的仪器——地动仪。永和三年（138年），这架安放在洛阳灵台上的地动装置，测出了发生在千里之外的甘肃东南部的地震。张衡还制造了指南车、计里鼓车、候风仪。此外，他在史学、哲学、地理、绘画方面的成就也很突出，曾被后人列为东汉六大名画家之一。

张衡墓位于南阳市卧龙区石桥镇小石桥村。墓为土冢，高8米、周长79米。墓冢周围栽植苍柏，墓前立有“汉征尚书张公平子墓”碑。现张衡墓园为张衡博物馆，建有双阙、大门、小拱桥、石象生、祭台、石享堂、张衡塑像等。大门两侧有门房、廊房，四隅有角楼，整体为仿汉建筑。

张衡墓

Located at Xiaoshiqiao, Shiqiao Town, the City of Nanyang, this is the tomb of Zhang Heng (78 ~ 139 AD), a famous scientist and writter in the Eastern Han Dynasty. It is 8 meters high, with a circumference of 79 meters, and surrounded by decorated walls. In front of it are two tablet-housing pavilions, and to the north of it is the site of a platform where Zhang Heng used to study.

打虎亭汉墓

第三批全国重点文物保护单位

东汉

Han-dynasty tombs at Dahuting

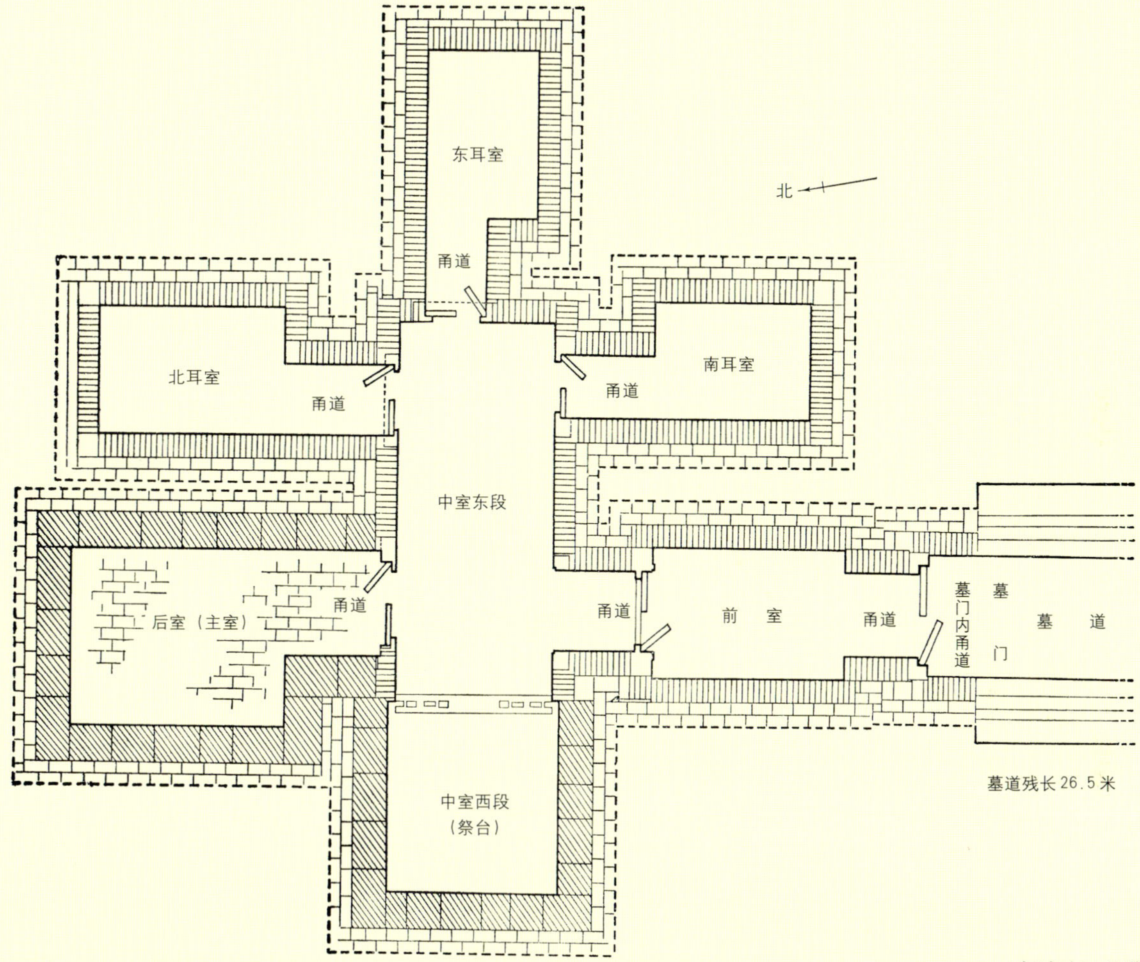

打虎亭2号墓平面图

打虎亭汉墓坐落在新密市城西约6公里的绥水南岸，为东西并列的两个夯筑土冢。西冢（M1）高15米、周长约228米，东冢（M2）高7.5米、周长约113米。1960年对这两座汉墓进行了发掘。

两座墓室都采用砖石混合结构，M1为画像石墓，M2为壁画墓，两座墓都遭受多次盗掘，墓内已无随葬品，但墓内的石刻和壁画大部保存完好，是汉代弥足珍贵的艺术史资料。两座汉墓门前皆有斜坡墓道。墓室的形制结构也基本相同，都由墓道、墓门、甬道、前室、中室、后室、南耳室、东耳室和北耳室组成。M1墓室外扩长26.46米、最宽处20.68米，券顶最高处为6.32米。M2外

打虎亭汉墓墓室壁画

圹长19.8米、最宽处18.4米、券顶最高处6.72米。

M1第一道石门门扉的背面中部刻铺首衔环浮雕，圆环中部刻一虎，环之表面刻四龙。石门的四边刻青龙、白虎、朱雀、玄武和云气纹组成的花边，门上的其他空间用云纹界成不规则的小格，在小格内分别刻有鹿、獐、熊、虎、牛、驼、力士驯牛等，构图精细，布局匀称。南耳室的南壁刻一幅地主收租图，东西两壁分别雕刻侍者、车辆以及马、牛、鸡、鸭、鹿、羊、猴、飞鸟、树木等。东耳室的墙壁上雕刻有杀鸡、宰牛、挂肉、烹调、酿酒等画面，北耳室墙壁上雕刻着封建贵族的庭院，院内陈设有垂幔、几、案、箱、柜等杂物，并刻有捧物、抬壶、执灯的奴仆画像。以上三耳室的雕刻多是现实生活场景的刻画。

M2各室多有彩色或墨绘壁画，在中室东段的券顶和东、南、北三面墙壁上绘制有彩色壁画，内容有各种人物、车马、厨事、烹饪、宴饮、乐舞百戏、迎宾出行及神仙等。壁画题材多是反映汉代封建贵族奢侈生活和充满幻想的神仙世界。这些壁画以中室藻井、南壁的迎宾图和北壁的宴乐百戏图最为精彩。此外，中室南壁的贵族车骑出行图、中室顶部的藻井彩绘，都是汉代壁画中的精品。

打虎亭汉墓壁画相扑图

Located west of Dahuting Village, the City of Xinmi, these are two stone tombs dating from the Eastern Han Dynasty (25 ~ 220 AD). Standing side by side, they contain large murals and stone relieves. Tomb No. 1, measuring 26.50 meters long, mainly contains stone relieves; Tomb No. 2, measuring 19.80 meters, mainly contains murals.

打虎亭汉墓画像酿造图

打虎亭汉墓画像庖厨图

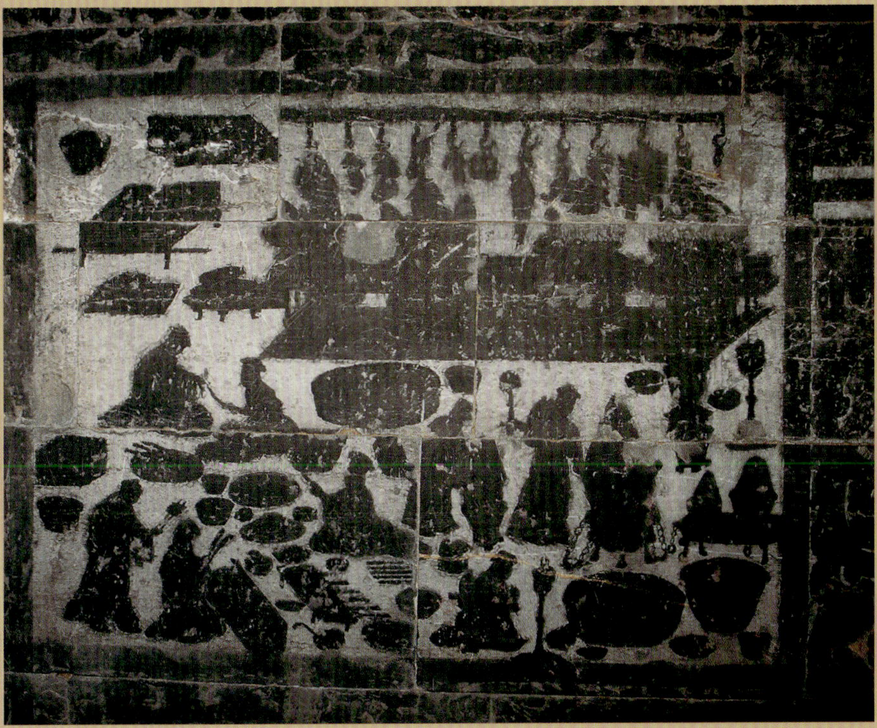

张仲景墓及祠

第三批全国重点文物保护单位

东汉

Zhang Zhongjing's tomb and shrine

张仲景墓及祠位于南阳市东关温凉河畔。

张仲景，名机，东汉时南阳郡涅阳（今邓州市穰东镇）人。弃官从医，著《伤寒杂病论》、《金匮要略》等医学经典之作，熔理法方药为一炉，开辨证论治之先河，为中医学发展奠定了基础，被后人尊称为医圣。其祠名为医圣祠，其墓在祠内。

医圣祠建于明嘉靖二十年（1541年），由前、中、后三院及西苑、后花园组成。中轴线上有仲景塑像、碑亭、山门、拜殿、墓冢、过殿、正殿；两侧有双廊、春台亭、秋风阁、仁术馆、仲景堂、智图斋、寿膳堂等，总占地面积11429平方米。医圣祠是历代医学研究者祭拜的地方，历史上曾多次修葺，1982年以来又进行了大规模的修整。这座纪念性建筑，自古至今起着促进仲景医学思想和传统文化交流与发展的积极作用。

张仲景墓

张仲景祠

Located on Zhongjing Road, Dongguan, Nanyang City, they date from the Eastern Han Dynasty (25~ 220 AD). The tomb, about 2 meters high, with a bottom diameter of 3.50 meters, is housed in Medical Sage Shrine, built in the reign of Jiajing in the Ming Dynasty and covering about 10,000 sq. m.

虢国墓地

第四批全国重点文物保护单位

周

Guo-state cemetery

虢国墓地位于三门峡市湖滨区北部上村岭。

1956年冬，在上村岭发现了著名的1052号太子墓，确认了虢国墓地的所在。1957年后，在对墓地开展普遍钻探的同时，进行了第一次大规模发掘。共发掘了二百三十四座墓葬、三座车马坑、一座马坑。在这批墓葬中，有三十八座出土青铜器皿，共计一百八十一件，其中十四件为有铭铜器；有一百二十座墓葬共出土陶器五百二十二件。此外，还出土礼器、乐器、工具、兵器、车马器、装饰品等一万四千余件，木车遗迹二十辆和马数十匹。

20世纪90年代的第二次发掘共清理了包括M2001虢季墓、M2009虢仲墓、M2011太子墓、M2012国君夫人梁姬墓与M2013丑姜墓在内的十八座墓葬、四座车马坑和两座马坑，出土了铜、铁、金、铅、玉、石、陶、骨、角、蚌、牙、木等各类珍贵文物近两万件。M2001虢季墓出土的玉柄铁剑，经鉴定为目前我国发现的最早的人工冶铁制品；两座国君墓、国君夫人墓及贵族夫人墓出土的大量精美玉器令人叹为观止。

虢国墓地南北长590米、东西宽550米，占地范围32.45万平方米。墓葬是长方形竖穴土坑墓，有的墓葬底部设有腰坑。葬具有木质棺椁，有单椁双棺、单椁单棺、单棺等多种情况。随葬铜器可分为礼器、工具、车马器、

M2012梁姬墓出土青铜盖罐

M2001 虢季墓出土铜簋和列鼎

兵器等，玉器可分为礼玉、佩玉、敛玉等，陶器大都是生活用器皿和少量装饰品。贵族墓主要随葬铜器、玉器，铜礼器组合形式为鼎、簋、壶、盘、匜（或盉）等，间或有盨、簠，国君墓与太子墓还随葬有铜编钟、铜钲、石编磬等乐器；一般平民墓葬则基本上都随葬陶器，以鬲、盂、豆、罐为主要组合。

虢国是西周时期的姬姓封国，河南省三门峡市的虢称为“南虢”。三门峡虢国墓地的发现与发掘，不仅证实了古文献对南虢国的记载，而且从墓地的使用年代也可推知此虢国自宝鸡东迁而来的大致时间。同时由于该墓地发现了可能为周王卿士的虢国国君墓，在周天子墓面世之前，两座卿士墓可算是迄今发现两周时期最高级别的墓葬，因而显得尤为重要。

M2001 虢季墓随葬器物出土情况

M2001 虢季墓出土玉鹿

M2001 虢季墓出土金腰带饰

Located in and around Shangcunling, northeast of the urban area of Sanmenxia City, the cemetery dates from the Western Zhou Dynasty and the Spring and Autumn Period (1046 ~ 476 BC) and covers about 324,500 sq. m. 252 tombs, 7 chariot and horse pits and 3 horse pits have been excavated, and over 14,000 pieces of relics have been unearthed.

虢国墓地玉面罩

虢国墓地玉鸟

汉梁王墓群

第四批全国重点文物保护单位

西汉

Han-dynasty Prince Liang's cemetery

汉梁王墓群，是西汉梁孝王刘武及后代各王的陵墓。墓葬分布在永城县芒砀山周围近10平方公里的范围内，目前能够确定的已有八处十四座大型陵墓。

1992年对保安山二号墓及发现的梁孝王寝园进行了考古发掘，探明了陵园、寝园的建筑布局和自梁孝王以下所有梁国王陵的布局。

梁孝王及王后陵园位于保安山周围，陵园平面近方形，四周设陵墙。梁孝王寝园位于陵墓东侧偏北，寝园平面呈长方形，南北长110米、东西宽60米，由围墙、回廊、寝殿、庭院、房屋等几部分组成，最南端为寝园外的庭院，即文献所载的“外朝”。寝园大门内有一长方形大院落，院落四周有回廊，北侧有近方形高台建筑——寝殿。寝殿是寝园的主体建筑，是一夯土台基，四周回廊环绕，夯土

汉梁王墓王后墓2号甬道

汉梁王墓四神壁画

梁孝王墓“孝园”铭筒瓦

台四周有排列整齐的柱础，为寝殿周围的壁柱。寝殿后为成排的房屋，反映了前朝后寝的建筑格局。寝园东门两侧的护墙上，有垒砌墙体的方石块，石块上发现五处刻字，有“二月己未”、“三月己未”、“五月壬申”、“正月己丑”等，据此可以推断出梁孝王寝园始建年代为公元前150年。梁孝王寝园属西汉前期，其建筑特点是保留战国以来的礼制建筑风格，但又有变化，在中国建筑史上起到承前启后的作用。

梁孝王王后墓位于梁孝王墓北200米，是一处大型崖洞墓，墓室将保安山北峰打通，形成东西两个墓门。墓全长210米，墓内面积达1600平方米，由两个墓道、三个通道、三十四个墓室组成。整个墓葬犹如一座地下宫殿，是目前发现规模最大、结构最复杂的大型墓葬。墓内有几千块一吨左右的塞石，大部分塞石都有刻字，对于研究墓葬结构和时代提供了重要资料。在王后墓南发现一陪葬坑，出土鎏金铜车马器、玉器、兵器等各类文物近两千件，车马器为实用器，形体大，制造精美，代表了汉代的最高水平。出土一铜印，印文“梁后园”，为确定墓主人身份提供了直接证据。

僖山墓位于梁孝王墓东北的僖山山顶，是一座凿山竖穴土坑墓。该墓门向东，墓道前段出土有鎏金铜车马器、兵器等，墓室内出土有大量精美的玉器，有玉璧七十多块，玉质刀剑装饰品二十四件及玉戈、玉钺、玉圭、玉猪、玉鸽、玉鸠和玉质男女舞蹈俑等。墓内出土的一千余枚玉片，已复原成金缕玉衣。

柿园墓因位于柿园村后而得名。从墓葬形制看，应是一代梁王。主室顶部及两侧绘有一幅大型壁画，色彩鲜艳，线条流畅，是我国目前发现时代较早、保存较好的大型墓室壁画。

Located on the hills surrounding Mangdang Mountain in Yongcheng City, the cemetery dates from the Han Dynasty (206 BC ~ 219 AD) and covers over 20 sq. km. It contains 18 tombs, which fall into three categories: large double-passage, multi-chamber tomb caves in cliffs, large single-passage, multi-chamber tomb caves in cliffs, and large single-passage vertical tombs with stone chambers.

汉梁王墓厕间

永城保安山二号墓前庭发掘现场

潞简王墓

明

Prince Lujian's Cemetery

潞简王墓位于新乡市北郊13公里的凤凰山南麓。

潞简王墓与次妃赵氏墓东西并列，两座墓园建筑布局大致相同。潞简王名朱翊镠，明穆宗第四子，神宗皇帝的胞弟。生于明隆庆二年（1568年），封为潞王，万历十七年（1589年）藩卫辉；卒于万历四十二年（1614年），谥曰简；葬于卫辉西五龙岗，即今地。次妃赵氏墓在潞简王墓西侧。两墓均坐北向南，总占地面积15万平方米。

墓区南北长500米，神道两旁列置石华表一对，石象生十六对（石兽十四对，石人两对），这在数量和种类上都超过了皇陵，其雕造工艺也不亚于明皇陵，在明代陵寝石刻中具有典型的代表性。过仪仗越水池即是墓园门楼，门楼与高峻的城墙相连，门楼为歇山式，绿琉璃瓦顶，下辟三道拱券门，砖石结构。墓园内，中门、拜台、享殿、明楼、宝城（墓冢）依次建在中轴线上，宝城用青石砌成，高9.35米、直径40米。宝城下即为地宫，也是仿照明十三陵修建的，墓室结构类似定陵，总面积185平方米，高大而宽敞。

潞简王墓与次妃赵氏墓营造逾制，其地面建筑物之完整、规模之宏大，在全国现存明代藩王墓葬中少见。次妃赵氏墓冢两侧还建有两个直壁覆斗的丫环墓，这在明代藩王墓园也是绝无仅有。

潞简王墓神道石刻

潞简王墓地宫

潞简王墓五供

潞简王墓享殿基址

Located at the foot of Phoenix Hill, Beizhan District, the City of Xinxiang, the cemetery dates from the Ming Dynasty (1368 ~ 1644 AD). Facing south, it covers 150,000 sq. m. It contains the mausoleum of Prince Lu, brother of Emperor Shenzong and the tomb of Zhao, his concubine in the Ming Dynasty.

邙山陵墓群

第五批全国重点文物保护单位

汉至北魏

Cemetery cluster on Mang Mountain

邙山陵墓群位于洛阳市与孟津县一带的邙山上。墓群东西长近50公里、南北宽约20公里，分布有东汉、曹魏、西晋、北魏四个朝代百余座帝王的陵寝和皇后、大臣的墓葬；还有大批唐宋时期的墓葬，总数在千座以上。

据《后汉书》载，光武帝葬原陵、明帝葬显节陵、章帝葬显节敬陵、和帝葬顺陵、殇帝葬康陵、安帝葬恭陵、顺帝葬显陵、仲帝葬怀陵、质帝葬静陵、桓帝葬宣陵、灵帝葬文陵。

陵墓自南向北依次为，第一

汉安帝陵

邙山陵墓群鸟瞰

个大冢“大汉冢”，高55米，占地十余亩；第二个大冢称“二汉冢”，高40米，占地八亩；第三个大冢是“三汉冢”，高35米，占地八亩余。光武帝陵位于孟津县白合乡铁谢村西南的黄河之滨，南倚邙山，北临黄河。陵园呈长方形，由陵园、祠院两部分组成，面积6.6万平方米。墓冢位居陵园正中，夯土筑起，高17.83米，周长近500米，周围广植古柏近一千五百株，整个陵园为古柏所笼罩，郁郁葱葱，肃穆庄严。陵园右侧有光武帝祠。其左前方竖立宋代开宝六年（973年）“新修后汉光武帝庙碑”一通。由宋大夫苏德祥奉敕撰文，翰林侯诏中散大夫孙崇望奉敕书丹。碑文记述了光武帝由南阳起事、决昆阳之战、扳邯郸之垒、定都洛阳等功业。

东汉帝陵区出土黄肠石百余块，其上刻有永初、永建、阳嘉、建宁、熹平年号，以及制作的月日、职官、姓名等内容。石人一尊，作跪状，高1.25米。还有大型石象、辟邪等，堪称汉代石刻精品。

东部曹魏（文帝、明帝、废帝、元帝陵等）、西晋（武帝、惠帝、宣帝、景帝、文帝等）帝陵因山而建，无封土；北魏陵区（文帝长陵、宣武帝景陵、孝明帝定陵、孝庄帝静陵等）现存地面封土冢三百余座，土冢呈覆斗形或圆锥形，高低大小不一，最大的直径100米、高50余米。已发掘的墓葬中有形制巨大、地宫用大砖或黄肠石垒砌的，也有规模较小的土穴墓。出土的大量历代墓志，内容涉及当时社会的政治、经济、军事、文化、中外交往、民族关系等诸多方面。

汉光武帝刘秀陵全景

The cluster is located on Mang Mountain, which, extending nearly 50 km from east to west and about 20 km from north to south, covers parts of the Luoyang City, Mengjin County and Yanshi City. It contains the mausoleums of more than ten emperors of four dynasties-Eastern Han, Wei (in the Three Kingdoms Period), Western Jin and Northern Wei, and tombs of imperial kinsmen and ministers. There are altogether over 1,000 tombs.

恭陵

第五批全国重点文物保护单位

唐

Gong Mausoleum

恭陵位于偃师市缑氏镇东北2.5公里的滹沱岭上。是唐高宗李治第五子、武则天长子李弘的陵墓，是中原地区保存较完整的帝陵之一。

陵园坐北朝南，平面正方形，建筑规划工整，长宽各约440米。四周原有神墙围护，今地面已无存。现已探明墙基大部分保存完好，基槽宽2.8米，神墙四角有角阙，阙台之上应有角楼建筑，现仅存阙台夯土台基，地面之下尚存砖砌墙基，地面之上保留着夯土土丘，高3～4米、长宽各约20米。四面神墙中部各置神门，南神门外设神道，宽54米、长300米，神道两侧分列有石象生。在神道南50米处设有对称的阙台，基址尚存。陵园内有灵台和哀皇后墓，灵台呈长方形覆斗状，东西长164米、南北宽146米、残高24米。

哀皇后墓位于灵台东北40米处，呈方锥形，长、宽各约50米、残高13米。1998年以来，在该墓的墓道壁龛内出土有黄釉带盖三足罐、蓝釉彩灯、蓝釉净瓶、彩绘骑马男乐俑、彩绘骑马胡服女俑等文物百余件，具有较高的学术和艺术价值，是研究初唐文化不可多得的实物资料。

陵园地面现存石刻十九件。

恭陵全景

恭陵唐代石人

恭陵唐代石狮

恭陵唐代石华表

东、西、北三神门外各置一对坐狮，南神门外为一对立狮。神道两侧石象生分别为望柱一对、天马一对、石翁仲三对，东列第二、三翁仲之间立唐高宗李治撰书"孝敬皇帝睿德之纪"碑一通。恭陵石刻造型生动、雕造细腻，堪称唐代石刻艺术的瑰宝。

Located south of Hutuo Village, Yanshi City, dating from the Tang Dynasty (960 ~ 1126 AD), this is the mausoleum of Li Hong, the fifth son of Li Zhi, or Emperor Gaozu. It is in the shape of a square, each side measuring 440 meters. Remaining relics are 19 carved stones and the foundations of towers, altars and walls. It also contains the tomb of Empress Ai.

后周皇陵

第五批全国重点文物保护单位

五代

Later Zhou-dynasty imperial mausoleums

后周皇陵位于新郑市区北18公里的郭店村附近。现存嵩陵、庆陵、顺陵和懿陵四座陵墓。

嵩陵为太祖郭威陵，郭威（904～954年）字文仲，邢州尧山（河北隆尧）人，后汉时为邺都留守，乾祐四年（951年）代后汉称帝，建都汴京。在位三年，显德元年（954年）以疾崩，四月葬此。现在冢高约12米、周长110米。

庆陵为世宗柴荣陵，柴荣（921～959年），邢州龙岗（今河北邢台西南）人，太祖郭威养子，954年太祖崩，柴荣即位。他奖励生产，励精图治，力图统一中国，显德六年（959年）进军幽燕途中病逝。现存冢高10米、周长105米。明初建有正方形陵园，四周建砖墙，边长200米。大门向南，院内有甬道，宽3米、长80米，直达墓前。陵墓四周植柏树，墓前置有方形祭坛，祭坛附近碑石林立。

顺陵为恭帝柴宗训陵，位于庆陵东北500米处。柴宗训为世宗

庆陵碑刻

第四子，显德六年（959年）嗣位，立八月，因殿前都检点赵匡胤发动陈桥兵变逊位入宋，封为郑王，开宝六年（973年）卒，同年葬此。现存冢高4米，周长40米。

懿陵为世宗皇后符氏陵，位于庆陵东侧100米处陵上村内，冢高3米、周长30米。

五代十国为中国历史上割据纷争时期，后周世宗时，进行经济和政治改革，国力增强，为北宋统一事业打下了基础，因此在中国历史上占有一定地位。后周皇陵薄葬且形制较小，无石象生等石刻，但陵园和祭碑有较高的历史和科学价值。

Located nearby Guodian Village, the City of Xinzheng, the mausoleums date from the Later Zhou Dynasty (951 ~ 960 AD), one of the dynasties in the Five Dynasties period. The mausoleums are respectively named Song, Qing, Shun and Yi.

庆陵全景

嵩陵土冢

庆陵碑刻

朱载堉墓

第五批全国重点文物保护单位

明

Zhu Zaiyu's tomb

朱载堉墓位于河南省沁阳市东北山王庄镇张坡村东。

朱载堉（536～1611年）字伯勤，号句曲山人，明怀庆府河内县（今沁阳市）人，明太祖朱元璋九世孙，郑藩之六代王子郑恭王朱厚烷之子。近代音乐理论的先驱，也是近代科学的开拓者之一。精研历数之学，著有《乐律全书》、《律吕正论》等书，在音乐史上最早确立了十二平均律理论。

朱载堉殁后，明神宗追谥为“端靖”，赐葬于九峰山下。该墓坐落于山前三级台地上，面向南，墓前竖立“朱载堉之墓”碑，墓区砌筑围墙，神道宽10米、长120米。郑藩乐府旧址位于市区北寺大街中段，为大四合院布局，是朱载堉研习乐律、从事科学研究的地方。现为朱载堉纪念馆。朱载堉墓及乐府对研究明代藩王生活和葬制等提供重要的实物资料。

朱载堉墓

朱载堉墓乐府旧址

The tomb is located at Zhangpo Village, Qinyang City. Zhu Zaiyu (1536 ~ 1610 AD) was the first person in the world who proposed the theory of 12-tone equal temperament, and the author of more than 10 books, such as Yuelü Quanshu (Book on Temperament). The tomb is 2.5 meters high, with the bottom diameter of 7.6 meters. In front of it is a tablet that says 'the Tomb of Zhu Zaiyu'.

应国墓地

第六批全国重点文物保护单位

西周至汉

Yingguo cemetery

应国墓地位于平顶山市新华区滍阳镇北滍村西的土岭上。是一处以西周时期应国墓和春秋时期的楚国墓为主的贵族墓地，面积达40万平方米。

应国为西周时期的姬姓诸侯国，其埋葬习俗有一定规律，具有"族坟墓"的特征，对研究西周贵族丧葬制度有重要的价值。此外，应国墓地还有春秋、战国、西汉、东汉时期的古墓群。目前共发掘墓葬近400座，出土铜、铁、铅、锡、金、陶、骨、玉石、贝蚌、木等各类文物达万余件。尤以制作精美的青铜器、玉器为大宗。其中部分青铜器上铸有铭文，明确记叙了其器是为"应公"、"应伯"、"应须"、"应姜"、"应姚"等人作，这对探讨西周的礼制及应国历史等具有重要意义。有的青铜器铭文中还透露出应国与申、邓、邢、曾等国联姻、结盟情况，还有反映西周时期教育制度的内容。

应国墓地的发现对研究西周时期的政治、经济、军事、文化等方面具有十分重要的价值。

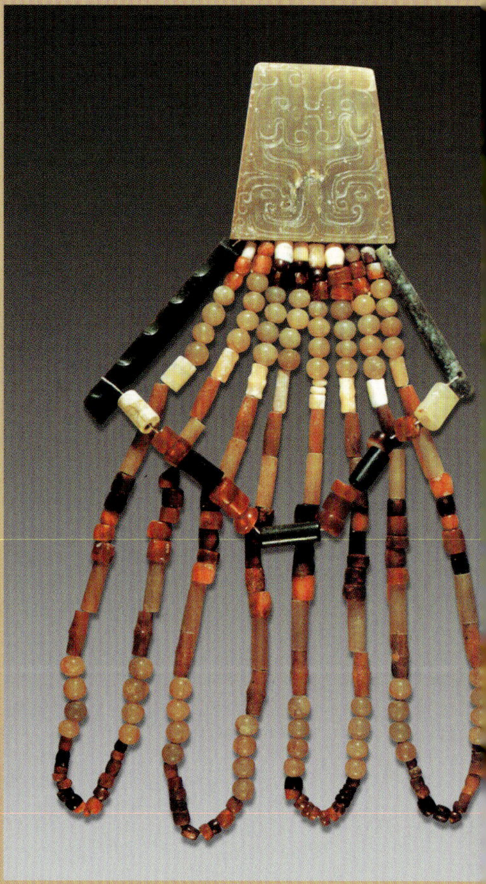

平顶山应国墓地出土组玉佩

平顶山应国墓地出土鸭形盉

Located at Zhi Village, the City of Pingdingshan, the cemetery dates back to the period between the Western Zhou Dynasty to the Han Dynasty (1046 BC ~ 220 AD) and covers about 480,000 sq. m. Over 310 tombs dating from the Zhou Dynasty, the Spring and Autumn Period, the Western Han Dynasty and the Eastern Han Dynasty have been unearthed.

许慎墓

第六批全国重点文物保护单位

汉

Xu Shen's tomb

许慎墓位于郾城县姬石乡许庄村东500米，是我国东汉时期著名的经学大师和伟大的文字学家许慎的长眠之地。

许慎（58～147年）字叔重，汝南召陵人。东汉经学大师和文学家。他呕心沥血三十载，写成《说文解字》，第一次系统地提出了“六书”说理论，首创了以部首编纂字书的方法，开创了字书编写方法之先河。《说文解字》是我国语言文字学史上出现最早、最系统、最完备的分析字形、解释字义、辨识声读的字典，也是世界上第一部字典。许慎在语言文字学上的伟大历史功绩，为历代学者所认同。

许慎墓现高5米，底径16米，周围以弧形条石围砌。墓前立有“汉孝廉许公之墓”碑、“许夫子从祀文庙碑”、“重修许慎墓碑记”碑，墓后植柏树182株。

The tomb is located east of Xuzhuang Village, the City of Luohe. Xu Shen (58 ~ 147 AD) was a scholar of Confucian classics, philologist and phonologist in the Eastern Han Dynasty. His tomb is 5 meters high and nearly 40 meters in circumference.

许慎墓

韩愈墓

第六批全国重点文物保护单位

唐

Han Yu's cemetery

韩愈墓（又称韩文公墓、韩园）位于孟州市西6公里处西虢镇韩庄村北的紫金山南麓。是我国唐代杰出的文学家、思想家、政治家，位居“唐宋八大家”之首的韩愈长眠之地。

韩愈（768～824年），字退之，河南河阳（今河南省孟州市）人。韩愈墓始建于唐宝历元年（825年），原有百亩之大，历代多次修葺。现存墓园是在清乾隆年间整修的基础上扩建而成，占地面积约50余亩。墓冢位于墓园后院，高15米，周长100米，四周砌青砖，翠柏拥簇，墓顶枣树成林。墓前有青砖碑楼两座，一座是“唐韩文公墓”碑，另一座是乾隆十五年的“谕祭碑”。

墓园内还保存有被称为“唐柏双奇”的唐代柏树两棵，宋代经幢两座，明代柏树四棵，清乾隆五十五年修建的飨堂三间，清代树立的《重修韩昌黎伯冢前碑》、《韩文公神道碑》、《韩文公墓考碑》、《重修韩文公冢前飨堂碑》、《唐柏双奇碑》等十通碑石，弥足珍贵。

韩愈墓墓园

The cemetery is located north of Hanzhuang Village, Mengzhou City. Han Yu (768 ~ 824 AD), born in Heyang (present-day Mengzhou City), was an outstanding writer, thinker, educator and poet in the Tang Dynasty; he ranked first among the 'Top Eight Tang-and-Song-dynasty Masters'. The cemetery was built in the 1st year of Baoli period (825 AD) in the Tang Dynasty and covers 3, 300 sq. m.

范仲淹墓

宋

Fan Zhongyan's cemetery

范仲淹墓全貌

范仲淹墓位于伊川县彭婆镇许营村北。

范仲淹（989～1052年），北宋著名政治家、思想家、军事家、文学家。历任兴化县令，秘阁校理，陈州、苏州、邓州等知州，右司谏，陕西经略副使，天章阁待制，参知政事等职。任职期间，他因直谏多次被贬官降职，但他以天下为己任的志向始终不改。他的《岳阳楼记》中"先天下之忧而忧，后天下之乐而乐"已成为千古名句。

范仲淹墓原形制很大，历代不断修葺。元至正七年（1347年），明成化十一年（1475年），明弘治四年（1491年），清顺治十三年（1656年）及清顺治十七年（1660年）都进行了大规模的维修。新中国成立后，各级政府对范仲淹墓的保护工作都非常重视。墓地分前后两域，前域葬范仲淹之母秦国谢太夫人及其长子监薄公纯佑；后域葬其次子忠宣公、三子中献公、四子朝散大夫侍郎公及部分家庭后裔，占地约85亩。墓地内遍植古柏947株，现存有山门、石坊、墓祠、碑刻等遗物。特别是墓地内保存的"资政殿学士户部侍郎文正公神道碑铭并

祭庙

褒贤碑

序”碑，具有很高的价值。该碑碑额、碑身为一整石所制，通体高4.1米，宽1.4米，厚0.4米。碑额由宋仁宗皇帝亲篆“褒贤之碑”四字。碑文由欧阳修撰写，王洙书丹。另有“乾隆之碑”、“万国碑记”等五块碑刻。

The cemetery is located north of Xuying Village, Yichuan County. Fan Zhongyan (989 ~ 1052 AD) was a statesman and writer in the Northern Song Dynasty. His tomb is about 2 meters high and about 10 meters in diameter. The cemetery contains a shrine and a xiangtang (sanctuary for worship).

欧阳修墓

第六批全国重点文物保护单位

宋

Ouyang Xiu's tomb

欧阳修墓位于新郑市辛店镇欧阳寺村。

欧阳修，字永叔，号醉翁，晚年更号六一居士，北宋著名文学家、史学家和金石学家，唐宋八大家之一。欧阳修于北宋熙宁五年（1072年）闰七月二十日卒于颍州（今安徽阜阳市）私邸。熙宁八年（1075年）九月二十六日，赐葬在开封府新郑县旌贤乡刘村之源（今新郑市辛店镇欧阳寺村）。曾赐田千亩建立墓园及祠堂。宋代王安石、曾巩、苏轼、苏辙等先后致祭。宋熙宁以来各处祠宇或修或补，后明、清时期又多次修葺、增建。

欧阳修墓及祠分前后两部分。墓位于祠堂以北，大殿后，地面为封土冢，周长15米，高5米。墓前立有石碑，刻"宋太师欧阳文忠公之墓"，墓前甬道立有石人、石马、石羊、石狁等，今仅残存石人。

欧阳修墓大门

欧阳修祠堂位于墓南，坐北朝南，宋代曾赐田千亩修建欧阳修祠堂。原中轴线有外照壁、大门、内照壁、东西两庑、大殿等建筑，四周建有围墙，规模宏大。现沿中轴线依次为大门、中殿、大殿、东西配殿。大门为单间硬山式建筑，灰瓦顶，琉璃花脊，两侧建歇山式配房。中殿为三间单檐歇山式过厅建筑，檐下施彩绘五踩单昂斗栱，隔扇门，槛窗，灰瓦顶，琉璃花脊。大殿为五间，单檐歇山式前出廊建筑，檐下施彩绘五踩单昂斗栱，隔扇门，槛窗，灰瓦顶，琉璃花脊。东西配殿均为五间悬山式建筑，前出廊。各殿之间由步廊连接。祠堂内有王安石、曾巩、苏轼、苏辙等祭欧阳文忠公石碑及明清时期重修欧阳文忠公墓记等石碑七十余通。

欧阳修墓碑与祠堂组成欧阳修陵园，南北长113米，东西宽97米，占地16.5亩，四周建有围墙。陵园内祠堂前东西两侧各建六角亭一座，陵园前后广植花草及松柏百余株。

欧阳修墓及祠是一处较为完整的陵园式建筑群，其中的碑刻墓铭集中颂赞了欧阳修的事迹及贡献。

欧阳修墓墓冢

欧阳修墓中殿

欧阳修墓大殿

The tomb is located north of Ouyangsi Village, Xinzheng City. Ouyang Xiu (1007 ~ 1072 AD) was a writer and historian in the Northern Song Dynasty. His tomb is about 6 meters high and over 40 meters in circumference.

李诚墓

第六批全国重点文物保护单位

宋

Li Jie's tomb

李诚墓位于新郑市龙湖镇梅山脚下于寨村西。

李诚，字明仲，郑州管城人，出生于北宋官吏家庭，曾任曹州县尉、虢州知州，元祐七年在将作监供职达13年之久，历任将作监主簿、监承、少监和将作监，主持营建了许多规模巨大的建筑工程。北宋大观四年二月（1110年）卒，葬于新郑梅山。

经过调查，李诚墓原有墓园达十余亩。现李诚墓地夯筑封土高3米，周长10米。墓冢坐北朝南，冢下有墓室，为砖室墓，近圆形，南北长5.3米，东西宽4.7米，高5.7米，墓顶已塌。墓道位于墓南面，其甬道长3.2、宽2米，墓道长21米，宽1.2米，斜坡。墓室内填五花土，经过夯打。墓冢前建有四角碑亭，亭内立有石碑。另外，在李诚墓右侧有四座砖室墓，为其家族墓。

李诚一生最大的成就是编写了《营造法式》巨著，这是建筑史上的一次重大革新，对中国建筑史的发展产生了深远的影响。

The tomb is located southwest of Zhai Village, Xinzheng City. Li Jie (? ~ 1110 AD) was an outstanding architect in the Song Dynasty, and the author of A Treatise on Architectural Methods. His tomb is 2 meters high and 40 meters in circumference.

李诚墓

近现代重要史迹及代表性建筑

Ancient Architecture Ancient Architecture

河 南 文 化 遗 产

全 国 重 点 文 物 保 护 单 位

Brief Information on Major Historic Sites under National Protection in Henan Province

近现代重要史迹及代表性建筑

Ancient Architecture Ancient Architecture

鄂豫皖革命根据地旧址

1931 年

The site of the Hubei- Henan-Anhui Revolutionary Base

鄂豫皖革命根据地旧址位于新县县城。包括中共中央鄂豫皖分局和省委、省苏维埃、鄂豫皖军委航空局、鄂豫皖革命军事委员会等革命旧址。

1928年春，中国共产党领导的黄（安）麻（城）起义部队转战到柴山堡一带山区（今新县陈店乡），开创了鄂豫皖边区第一块革命根据地，并建立了中国工农红军第十一军三十一师。1930年4月，根据中共中央指示，在箭河成立了中国共产党鄂豫皖特委，将红十一军三十一师、三十二师、三十三师合编为红一军，鄂豫边、豫东南、皖西三块革命根据地实行统一领导。至10月发展成为中共中央确认的全国六大革命根据地之一。1931年2月，红军攻克新集（今新县县城），将其改为新集市，鄂豫皖苏区党、政、军的首脑机关相继迁至新集。5月12日在这里成立了中共鄂豫皖中央分局，并成立了新的鄂豫皖革命军事委员会。1932年1月，根据中共中央指示，又成立了鄂豫皖省委。新集成为鄂豫皖革命根据地的首府和政治、经济、军事、文化的中心。

中共中央鄂豫皖分局和省委旧址坐落在新县县城中原路62号，为一座五进、七栋旧式楼房的大宅院，占地面积1980平方米。门楼顶部为花砖挑脊，两端有封火墙，下部有白色石鼓形门枕石一对，门额上方悬挂着1980年徐向前同志题写的“中共中央鄂豫皖分局旧址”匾额。

Located at Chengguan in the town of Xin County and the Dabie Mountain region, the base include the Hubei-Henan-Anhui branch of the Central Committee of the Communist Party of China (CPC), the CPC Revolutionary Military Committee of Hubei, Henan and Anhui, the Provincial Party Committee of Hubei, Henan and Anhui, the provincial Soviet capital and the Air Force Bureau of the CPC Military Committee. CPC led revolutionary activities here from 1928 to 1931.

鄂豫皖革命根据地旧址

中共中央中原局旧址

第三批全国重点文物保护单位

1938至1939年

Site of Central Plains Bureau of the CPC Central Committee

中共中央中原局旧址位于确山县城西32公里的竹沟镇。在土地革命战争和抗日战争时期，中共中央中原局和中共河南省委曾先后设在竹沟镇。它地处确山、桐柏、泌阳三县交界处，是桐柏山的心腹地，三面环山，东面平坦开阔。镇东大沙河自北向南流过，东临南北交通干线平汉铁路，地理位置十分优越。1938年9月30日至11月6日，中共中央六届六中全会决定建立中原局，驻地设在竹沟镇，领导长江以北，陇海铁路以南的河南、湖北、安徽、江苏地区党的工作。刘少奇、李先念、彭雪枫、朱理治、陈少敏等曾在这里高举抗日民族统一战线的旗帜，组织和开展游击战争，开创华中地区抗战新局面。竹沟镇成为新四军成长壮大的一个重要基地，缔造了新四军第二、四、五师，为中国共产党

中共中央中原局组织部办公室旧址

中共中央中原局刘少奇办公室旧址

中共中央中原局张震办公室旧址

中共中央中原局北窑军事会议旧址

培养了三千多名军政骨干。因此竹沟镇有中原抗日圣地“小延安”之称。

1939年11月11日拂晓，国民党顽固派纠集地方反动武装围攻竹沟镇，未及撤退的新四军伤病员、家属及当地群众二百余人被杀，制造了震惊中外的“竹沟惨案”。激起了全国抗日军民的极大愤慨，毛泽东、朱德、刘少奇、彭德怀、朱理治、彭雪枫等分别发表演讲和通电，谴责国民党顽固派破坏抗日、制造摩擦的罪恶行径。

中共中央中原局旧址由四所民居建筑组成，坐北面南，有房屋三十二间。其中有中原局办公室、刘少奇工作室和住室、接待室、警卫人员住室，有刘少奇亲手种植的石榴树、郭述申住室等。房屋均为青砖灰瓦硬山式建筑。在竹沟镇还有新四军八团留守处、教导队和镇北会议砖窑旧址等。

Located north of Laojie Road, Zhugou Town, Queshan County, the site consists of four adjacent quadrangles containing brick-and-tile houses, which were built as shops by merchants from Shanxi in the late Qing Dynasty, extending 60 m from east to west and 24 m from north to south. They were used as offices of the Central Plains Bureau of the Central Committee of CPC from 1938 to 1939. Some were used by Liu Shaoqi and other high-ranking leaders.

红二十五军长征出发地

第四批全国重点文物保护单位

1934 年

The starting point of the 25th Red Army's Long March

红二十五军长征出发地位于罗山县铁铺乡何家冲。

何家冲是鄂豫皖革命根据地组成部分之一。1934 年 11 月 16 日，中国工农红军第二十五军由此地出发，经豫西南、鄂北、陕南、甘肃等省区，长驱数千里，在各支长征队伍中先期到达陕北。

红二十五军长征出发地由三部分组成，一是何家祠堂，即红二十五军军部旧址，现存房屋十余间，具有南方宗祠建筑特点。当年吴焕先、程子华、徐海东等人都曾在此居住，并召开过多次重要军事会议。二是红军医院旧址，由四所院子组成，现存房屋八十余间，豫南民宅建筑。三是一棵高大的银杏树，高约 20 多米，是当年红二十五军集合誓师出发的地方。

1932 年原红二十五军合编成立红四方面军，10 月，红四方面军主力撤出鄂豫皖苏区后，敌人又以三十万大军"清剿"苏区。中共鄂豫皖省委于 11 月 30 日在槽树岗重建红二十五军，继续坚持根据地的武装斗争并取得了一系列重大胜利。1934 年 11 月红二十五军收到程子华从瑞金带来的中共中央《关于组织抗日先遣队的通知》和《致鄂豫皖省委训令》等文件以及中央军委副主席周恩来的有关指示，决定立即实行战略转移。13 日，红二十五军在何家冲进行战略转移前的准备工作，整编部队、政治动员、安置伤病员、准备粮食和草鞋，轻装待命。16 日，红二十五军在省委的带领下，高举"中国工农红军北上抗日第二先遣队"的旗帜，在何家冲银杏树下，发布了《中国工农红军北上抗日第二先遣队宣言》，宣告红二十五军开始长征。1935 年 9 月红二十五军到达陕北，10 月与毛泽东率领的中央红军会合。

Located at Hejiachong, Luoshan County, it consists of the site of the headquarters, the site of the Red Army hospital and a gingko tree. The former two were used by the 25th Red Army before it began the Long March, and the tree was where they rallied to pledge resolution before setting off.

红二十五军长征出发地

焦裕禄烈士墓

第五批全国重点文物保护单位

1967 年

The cemetery of Martyr Jiao Yulu

焦裕禄烈士墓位于兰考县城北。

焦裕禄，山东淄博人，生于1922年，1946年参加革命工作，1962年调兰考县任县委第二书记、书记。他在兰考期间访贫问苦、带病工作，率领全县人民治理内涝、沙荒和盐碱，取得了很大成效，使兰考的面貌有了巨大的改变。因积劳成疾，他不幸于1964年5月14日病故于郑州。

为了纪念焦裕禄同志，1966年2月1日河南省人民政府追认他为革命烈士，2月26日兰考县委根据焦裕禄同志生前的遗愿和群众的要求，将焦裕禄同志的遗体安葬在兰考县城北黄河故堤的沙丘上，1967年兰考县民政部门在此修建了烈士墓区，面积为210平方米。

墓冢为汉白玉砌成，高0.55米、长4.95米、宽2.3米，长方形底座。墓后屏风式纪念壁上镌刻着毛泽东的题词“为人民而死，虽死犹荣”。墓前两侧竖立两座高6.5米、宽4.2米的诗词碑，分别刻有董必武、郭沫若撰写的歌颂焦裕禄烈士的长诗。

焦裕禄烈士墓

焦裕禄烈士纪念碑

Located at Beiguan in the town of Lankao County, the cemetery was built in 1966, when Jiao Yulu (1922 ~ 1964), secretary of the county Party committee, died of illness caused by overwork. He was cited as 'a good cadre of the Party and a good role model for the secretaries of county Party committee'. The cemetery covers 120,000 sq. m.

邓颖超祖居

第六批全国重点文物保护单位

清

Ancestral Home of Deng Yingchao

邓颖超祖居位于信阳市光山县城关镇解放街白云巷（原贡院街筷子巷）。邓颖超（1904～1992年），原名邓文淑，祖籍河南光山，伟大的无产阶级革命家、政治家、著名的社会活动家，坚定的马克思主义者，党和国家的卓越领导人，中国妇女运动的先驱，曾任全国政协主席。

清咸丰年间（1851～1861年）邓颖超祖父邓功显来此居住。邓功显于1891年病逝，所住房宅改为县衙贡院，现祖居保存完好。祖居坐北朝南，前后两进，东西两院，占地近2000平方米。中置一厅，属砖木建筑，七架梁木结构，是一座典型的具有南方特点的清代建筑。祖居现藏有邓颖超遗物70余件，革命文物60件，邓家遗物215件。

邓颖超祖居外景

邓颖超祖居正厅

邓颖超祖居庭院

Located at Baiyun Lane, Jiefang Street, Chengguan Town, Guangshan County, the house dates from the Qing Dynasty (1644 ~ 1911 AD). Facing south, it consists of two rows of courtyards and covers nearly 2,000 sq. m. It was inhabited by Deng Gongxian, Deng Yingchao's grandfather, in the reign of Emperor Xianfeng in the Qing Dynasty. It is well preserved.

刘青霞故居

第六批全国重点文物保护单位

清末民初

Former Residence of Liu Qingxia

刘青霞故居包括两处，一处位于开封市顺河回族区北土街刘家胡同；一处位于尉氏县城关镇人民路。故居由开封市刘家宅院和尉氏县师古堂（东院）及西院组成。刘青霞（1877～1922年），原姓马，名马青霞，安阳县蒋村人。是我国近代著名的资产阶级民主革命家、教育家、社会活动家，辛亥女志士。辛亥革命前后，她被选为北平女子法政学校校长、北平女子学务维持会会长、北平女子参政同盟会会长和河南国民捐总理。其一生致力于办义学、兴善举和妇女解放及教育事业，积极参加并出巨资支持革命事业，与当时的“鉴湖女侠”秋瑾齐名，被誉为“南秋北刘”。

开封市刘青霞故居后院正房及两厢房

尉氏县刘青霞故居全景

开封市刘青霞故居前院东厢房

开封市刘家宅院，建于清光绪六年（1880年），为刘青霞当时在河南省城内的居所。故居坐北朝南，系三进四合院建筑。尉氏县城的师古堂（东院）及西院，为当时尉氏县大地主刘耀德庄园的一部分，建于清末，师古堂现存后院及中院部分建筑，坐北朝南，为二层硬山式楼房三面围合而成，建筑面积640平方米。西

尉氏县刘青霞故居师古堂背面、西厢房及正房

院与师古堂毗邻，坐西朝东，现存建筑十二座共八十八间，建筑面积1600平方米。

刘青霞故居规模较大，布局层次分明、错落有序，建筑装饰精美，建筑形式多样，现保存基本完好，是清末民初中原地区四合院民居建筑的活标本，具有研究及观赏价值。

Dating from the Qing Dynasty, these include the house of the Liu family in Kaifeng and Shigu Hall in Weishi County. The former, located at Liujia Hutong, Beitu Street, is a typical quadrangle-style house. Divided into an east part and a west part, it covers a floor space of 689 sq. m. Shigu Hall is located on Renmin Road, Chengguan Town, Weishi County. Its eastern courtyard is surrounded on three sides by two-story flush-gable-roof buildings, which consist of 38 rooms and cover a floor space of 640 sq. m. The adjacent west courtyard contains 12 houses, which consist of 88 rooms and cover a floor space of 1,600 sq. m.

河南留学欧美预备学校旧址

第六批全国重点文物保护单位

民国

The Site of Henan Preparatory School for Studying in Europe and America

河南留学欧美预备学校旧址位于开封市顺河回族自治区明伦街。1912年，河南留学欧美预备学校是在清代河南贡院的旧址上创办的。当时是国家派遣留学生、培养高级专门人才的重要基地。旧址现仅存复建的大门，1923年改建为“中州大学”，1930年改名“河南大学”，建国后几易其名，1984年恢复为河南大学至今。河南留学欧美预备学校建于1915～1936年，主体建筑从学校大门向北至大礼堂构成一条南北向的中轴线，中轴线东内侧有“六号楼”，东外侧有十座分布整齐的斋房（俗称为“东十斋”），中轴线西内侧有“七号楼”，西外侧有两座斋房（俗称为“西二斋”）。

河南留学欧美预备学校旧址基本保持了民族建筑的坡屋顶形式，檐下采用传统木雕装饰，又融合了西方建筑手法，美观实用，浑厚典雅，是20世纪初期大型民族建筑设计与工程的代表作，是近代中国公共建筑中具有组群特色的建筑类型。

六号楼全景

七号楼全景

大礼堂全景

斋房垂花木雕

河南留学欧美预备学校旧址

河南贡院执事楼

东斋房

Located in the compound of Henan University, No. 85 Minglun Street, Hui Nationality District, Shunhe, Kaifeng City, the preparatory school was built from 1915 to 1936. Main buildings along the south-north central axis are: a main gate, an auditorium, Buildings No. 6 and 7, and a 'fasting house'. It covers an area of nearly 400, 000 sq. m., and a floor space of 17,579 sq. m.

吕潭学校旧址

第六批全国重点文物保护单位

民国 The site of Lütan School

吕潭学校旧址位于周口市扶沟县吕潭镇。由吕潭学校旧址和吉鸿昌将军故居组成。吕潭学校是吉鸿昌将军于1928～1930年间修建，现为吉鸿昌学校。因吉鸿昌将军一心革命从不置产业，当学校建成之后，校董会于1931年便在学校东墙外，为其修建宅院一处，供吉鸿昌将军回来小憩。

吉鸿昌（1895～1934年），字世五，河南省扶沟县吕潭镇人，家极贫，1913年十八岁的吉鸿昌参加了冯玉祥部队，曾任军长、宁夏主席等职；1932年在上海加入中国共产党，1933年5月就任抗日同盟军北路前敌总指挥兼第二军军长，多伦大捷威震中外。1933年10月因叛徒出卖在天津被捕，1934年11月24日在北平英勇就义。

吕潭学校旧址现有大门、东西厢房、中山殿等建筑。吉鸿昌故居由大门、东西厢房、正房等建筑

吕潭学校旧址大门

吕潭学校旧址校园

吕潭学校旧址中山殿

吉鸿昌旧居

组成。故居为传统四合院中轴线对称布局，均为砖木结构硬山式灰板瓦顶建筑，抬梁式木构架。

吕潭学校从创办至今，为中国革命和社会主义建设培育了大批有用人才，被誉为“英才的摇篮”。建筑群布局简约规整，体现了中国近现代建筑的传统特色。

Located at Lütan Town, Fugou County, the school, founded by General Ji Hongchang, was built from 1928 to 1930. It contains such buildings as a main gate, east and west houses and Zhongshan Hall, covering a floor space of 300 sq. m. It consisted of a primary school, a junior middle school and a senior middle school at that time.

中国工农红军第二十五军司令部旧址

第六批全国重点文物保护单位

1933 年

The site of the headquarters of the 25th Red Army

中国工农红军第二十五军司令部旧址庭院

中国工农红军第二十五军司令部旧址位于信阳市新县箭厂河乡方湾村，原为闵氏宗祠。1932年秋，红四方面军主力西征后，鄂豫皖省委于11月底在檀树岗重建红二十五军，由吴焕先任军长，下辖七十四、七十五两个师，全军约7000人，坚持根据地的武装斗争。不久，红二十五军司令部迁驻闵氏宗祠，旧址西山墙现仍保留有当年红军标语，字迹清晰，字体流畅。1933年7月至11月，红二十五军军部驻在这里。此旧址是红二十五军英勇斗争的历史见证。

闵氏宗祠，建于清咸丰六年（1856年）。倒座与正房面阔五间，与东西各两间厢房围合构成“四水归池”封闭的天井四合院。院中条石砌铜池，承接四檐之雨水。占地面积316平方米。建筑为带封火山墙的硬山式灰板瓦顶，花瓦调脊，穿逗式梁架。

中国工农红军第二十五军军部旧址是对广大人民群众特别是年轻一代进行爱国主义和革命传统教育的生动教材。其建筑具有豫南地方特色，是河南穿逗式建筑的实物例证。

中国工农红军第二十五军司令部旧址外景

中国工农红军第二十五军司令部旧址全景

Located at Fangwan Village, Jianchanghe Township, Xin County, the headquarters used to be the ancestral shrine of the Min clan. It consists of two rows of houses, each having 5 rooms, with two wing rooms on both sides, covering an area of 316 sq. m. It was used by the 25th Red Army from July 1933 to November 1933.

八路军洛阳办事处旧址

第六批全国重点文物保护单位

1938～1942 年

The site of the Eight Route Army's office in Luoyang

八路军洛阳办事处旧址位于洛阳市老城区贴廓巷。旧址建于清道光十一年（1831年），至抗日战争前夕，一直由庄氏家族使用，抗战爆发后庄氏家族举家迁徙。1938年10月，八路军洛阳办事处机关进驻此院，至1942年2月撤离，一直是我党我军在国统区洛阳设立的一个公开办事机构，承担了与国民党第一战区的联络，掩护、帮助地方党组织开展工作，统战与情报等多项重要工作，为抗日战争的胜利做出了贡献。刘少奇、朱德、彭德怀、徐海东、彭雪枫等领导同志多次到八路军洛阳办事处指导、部署工作。据不完全统计，途经八路军洛阳办事处的我党、我军人员约70批，1400余人。

院落坐南朝北，由三路三进四合院组成，采用中国传统的建筑风格，中轴线对称布局；三座院落各开有偏门互通往来。占地面积4388余平方米。建筑均为二层硬山式灰板瓦屋面、花瓦调脊，砖木结构，抬梁式木构架。

八路军洛阳办事处旧址不仅是重要的革命传统、爱国主义、国防教育基地，还是一处保存完好的、具有一定规模的、带有浓重豫西特色的、较完整的清代民居建筑群。

八路军洛阳办事处旧址前院

八路军洛阳办事处旧址刘少奇住室

八路军洛阳办事处旧址会议室

Located at No. 35, Tiekuo Lane in the old city of Luoyang, the site dates from the Qing Dynasty (1644 ~ 1911 AD). Facing south, it consists of three courtyards and 129 houses, covering a floor space of over 3,300 sq. m. It was used as the Eighth Route Army' s office in Luoyang from Oct. 1938 to Feb. 1942.

八路军洛阳办事处旧址全景

冀鲁豫边区革命根据地旧址

第六批全国重点文物保护单位

1941～1946 年

The sites of the revolutionary base of Hebei-Shandong-Henan Border Region

冀鲁豫边区革命根据地旧址位于清丰县双庙乡单拐村和范县颜村铺乡颜村铺。冀鲁豫边区地处华北的门户，冀鲁豫三省结合部，联结中原地区向四周拓展的战略枢纽，是中国共产党在抗日战争时期创立较早的革命根据地之一，见证了抗日战争时期和解放战争初期冀鲁豫革命根据地从创立到巩固，并由“小冀鲁豫”发展为“大冀鲁豫”，从而奠定了解放战争胜利基础的过程。

颜村铺革命旧址是抗日战争时期冀鲁豫边区“濮、范、观”中心区，边区党委、行署、军区机关常驻地之一。段君毅、杨得志、曾思玉等在这里领导八路军和广大人民群众同日伪、国民党、土匪进行了殊死斗争，创立和巩固了以濮县、范县、观城为中心的冀鲁豫边区敌后抗日根据地。现保存有领导人及机关住址房屋二十一间。

单拐革命旧址是1944年9月至1946年秋，中共中央北方局、

清丰县冀鲁豫军区第一兵工厂旧址外景

范县杨德志、万里住处

范县朱德、段君毅住处

范县冀鲁豫边区革命根据地颜村铺旧址

平原局（也称冀鲁豫分局）、冀鲁豫军区司令部和军区第一兵工厂所在地，平原分局、北方局在这里领导边区军民开展整风运动、民主民生运动和大生产运动，指挥对日伪军的攻势作战和战略大反攻。兵工厂则制造出我军历史上生产的第一门大炮——“盖亮号”九二式七十毫米步兵炮，为中国革命做出了杰出贡献。现保存有冀鲁豫军区司令部及旧址，以及邓小平、宋任穷、王宏坤、杨勇、曹里怀等同志旧居二十余处建筑。

冀鲁豫边区革命根据地旧址建筑群建于清末民初，为硬山式灰瓦顶、抬梁式结构建筑，具有鲜明的中原民居建筑特点，建筑装饰做工精细，可以反映出豫北地区这一时期建筑风格。

清丰县冀鲁豫军区第一兵工厂旧址庭院

清丰县冀鲁豫军区司令部旧址

They include one site at Yancunpu and the other one at Danguai. The former, located at Yancunpu Village, Yancunpu Township, Fan County, consists of one quadrangle with 21 houses. It was one of the permanent seats of the Party committee, administrative office and military organs of the border region.

The other site is located at Danguai Village, Shuangmiao Township, Qingfeng County, including the offices of North Bureau, Branch Bureau of the Plain, the military headquarters of the Hebei-Shandong-Henan Military Area Command, No. 1 Munitions Factory of the military area command, and the former residences of Deng Xiaoping and other leaders.

嵖岈山卫星人民公社旧址

第六批全国重点文物保护单位

1958～1983年

The site of Weixing People's Commune at Chaya Mountain

嵖岈山卫星人民公社旧址位于驻马店市遂平县嵖岈山乡。成立于1958年4月20日，是我国建立的第一个人民公社，由遂平县西部的杨店、土山、鲍庄三个乡和张台乡的友谊第八农业合作社等二十个高级农业合作社合并而成。公社成立之初模仿苏联的“卫星集体农庄”，5月更名为“卫星公社”，6月定名为“嵖岈山卫星人民公社”。1958年7月《红旗》副主编李友久会同信阳地委、遂平县委和公社领导起草了《嵖岈山卫星人民公社试行简章》（草案），8月经中央政治局会议审定后，《人民日报》、《红旗》杂志相继发表，全国各地报刊纷纷转载，成为全国人民公社化运动的指导性文献，毛泽东主席曾于1958年11月13日实地考察了解嵖岈山卫星人民公社的情况。1983年12月公社体制撤销，嵖岈山人

嵖岈山卫星人民公社全景

嵖岈山卫星人民公社会议室

嵖岈山卫星人民公社
大食堂旧址

民公社改为嵖岈山乡。

旧址东西长172米，南北宽162米，建筑面积3051平方米。现存办公楼始建于1958年10月，为二层砖木结构筒子楼。墙上保留有1958年标语“人民公社万岁”、毛主席语录及画像。20世纪70年代，新建大礼堂一座和用于公社招待所的两层砖混楼房三座。在公社旧址西侧的山坡上有当年栽植的松柏，构成“人民公社万岁”几个大字。

人民公社在中国现代史上有独特的地位，嵖岈山卫星人民公社是中国社会经济发展特定阶段的产物，具有重要的历史意义。

Located at Chayashan Township, Suiping County, the site contains an office building that was built in Oct. 1958. It is of two-storey brick-and-wood structure, covering an area of 27,864 sq. m. and a floor space of 3,051 sq. m. Founded on April 20, 1958, it was the first people's commune in China.

红旗渠

第六批全国重点文物保护单位

1969 年

Red Flag Canal

红旗渠位于林州市的任村镇、姚村镇、石板岩乡、陵阳镇、合涧镇、原康镇沿太行山东麓南北一线。被誉为人工天河，全长1525公里，林州境内1505公里，流经全市14个乡镇，410个行政村。红旗渠工程开始于1960年，1969年7月竣工。总干渠长70.6公里；第一干渠长39.7公里；第二干渠长47.6公里；第三干渠长10.9公里；分干渠10条，长304.1公里；支渠51条，长524.2公里；斗渠290条，长527.9公里。沿渠一、二类水库48座，塘堰346座，提水站45座，小型水力发电站45座，渡槽152个，隧洞211个。红旗渠年引水量2.8亿立方米，有效灌溉面积54万平方米，解决了全市67万人口和3.7万头家畜的吃水问题。红旗渠被林州

红旗渠

青年洞

人民称为“生命渠”、“幸福渠”。

红旗渠科学地利用地形、地貌，采用自然落差，使引水、蓄水、排水、灌溉的综合效益得到全面发挥，实现了吃水、灌溉、发电一水三用目的，是我国水利工程史上的一个典范。同时又是当地人民自力更生、团结协作、艰苦创业、改造自然奋斗精神的体现，也是我们国家和民族的精神财富。

Extending from north to south along the eastern foot of Taihang Mountain, Linzhou City, the canal was dug from 1960 to 1969. With a total length of 1,525 km, it consists of 3 trunk canals. Capable of channeling 280 million cubic meters of water per year for an effective irrigation area of 540,000 mu (1 mu = 1/15 hectare), it makes full use of channeling, storage, drainage and irrigation to achieve comprehensive benefits.

郑州二七罢工纪念塔和纪念堂

第六批全国重点文物保护单位

1971年、1952年

The memorial tower and hall in memory of the Feb. 7 Strike at Zhengzhou

郑州二七罢工纪念塔位于郑州市二七广场中央。1951年在二七罢工领袖汪胜友、司文德牺牲地的长春桥旧址，建纪念木塔；现在的纪念塔是1971年在原址重建，建筑面积1923平方米。塔为钢筋混凝土结构，平面呈两个并联五角形，仿古联体双塔，塔高63米，共十四层，其中塔基座为三层石栏环绕阅台，塔身为十一层，每层塔檐为挑角飞檐，绿色琉璃瓦覆顶，塔顶建有钟楼，大钟为六面，直径2.7米，整点报时。

二七纪念堂位于郑州市二七区钱塘路82号。1952年11月落成，坐西向东，建筑面积3917平方米。纪念堂分主楼和两侧配楼；主楼为礼堂，正中镌刻“二七纪念堂”五个金字，两侧配楼为俱乐部，均为二层楼，内设“二七”史迹陈列馆。青砖垒砌，硬山式红瓦屋面，是砖木结构的现代纪念建筑。

二七大罢工是中国共产党领

郑州二七罢工纪念堂

郑州二七罢工纪念塔

导的第一次有组织的反帝反封建政治斗争。郑州是二七大罢工的策源地，二七罢工纪念塔和纪念堂具有特殊的政治意义，它已成为二七大罢工和郑州革命城市的象征。

Located in the middle of Feb. 7 Square in Zhengzhou City, the memorial tower was built in 1951 and rebuilt in 1971 at the original site. It has 14 stories and a height of 63 meters. The memorial hall, located at No. 82, Qiantang Road, Feb. 7 District, was built in Nov. 1952. It covers an area of 6,440 sq. m. and a floor space of 3,917 sq. m. It consists of a main building and two side buildings, all of which, built of grey bricks, have two stories and pointed roofs covered by red tiles.

后　记

为弘扬民族优秀文化，宣传河南文化遗产，充分发挥全国重点文物保护单位在构建社会主义和谐社会中的作用，实现河南由文化资源大省向文化强省的跨越，河南省文物局编写了《河南文化遗产——全国重点文物保护单位》。

为编好这本书，省文物局成立了以陈爱兰局长为主任，孙英民、李玉东副局长为副主任的编委会，组织领导、安排协调了各项有关工作。国家文物局局长单霁翔和中共河南省委常委、宣传部长、副省长孔玉芳在百忙中写了序言，河南省文化厅厅长郭俊民撰写了前言，并均对本书给予了高度评价。首先，我们向有关领导致以谢忱。

在策划、编辑《河南文化遗产——全国重点文物保护单位》的过程中，由各省辖市文物部门提供了基础资料。常俭传、郭振勇、孙红梅、孙新民、秦文生、张志清、杨育彬、郝本性、曹桂岑、蔡全法、袁广阔、陈彦堂、魏兴涛、潘伟斌等同志撰写了有关文稿；王蔚波、祝贺、郭民卿、蔡全法、周立、张宁、荣德顺、高虎、蔡强、陈巍、钟山、齐军、申明卿、刘群、路伟、高俊海、李自省等同志摄影或提供图片。杨育彬同志撰写了概述和提要。秦文生、王瑞琴同志负责全书的编辑和校对工作。黄纪苏先生承担了单霁翔局长撰写序言的翻译和全部英文的审校；其余英文稿均由中国对外翻译出版公司翻译。文物出版社的李莉和姚敏苏同志为本书的编辑、出版付出了艰辛的劳动。在此，我们向上述单位和同志一并表示衷心的感谢！

编者

2007年5月